PLOTS AND PROPOSALS

D1521199

PLOTS AND PROPOSALS

American Women's Fiction, 1850–90

Karen Tracey

UNIVERSITY OF ILLINOIS PRESS

URBANA AND CHICAGO

Publication of this book was supported by grants from the Department of English Language and Literature and the Graduate College of the University of Northern Iowa.

♾ This book is printed on acid-free paper.

Library of Congress Cataloging-in-Publication Data
Tracey, Karen, 1961–
Plots and proposals : American women's fiction, 1850–90 / Karen Tracey.
p. cm.
Includes bibliographical references (p.   ) and index.
ISBN 0-252-02523-7 (alk. paper)
ISBN 0-252-06839-4 (pbk. : alk. paper)
1. American fiction—Women authors—History and criticism.
2. Feminism and literature—United States—History—19th century.
3. Women and literature—United States—History—19th century.
4. American fiction—19th century—History and criticism.
5. Southern States—In literature.
6. Women's rights in literature.
7. Courtship in literature.
8. Marriage in literature.
9. Sex role in literature.
I. Title.
PS374.F45T73   2000
813'.4099287—dc21   99-6380
CIP

1 2 3 4 5 C P 5 4 3 2 1

For Grant

Contents

$\mathcal{A}$CKNOWLEDGMENTS

AT every stage of this book's development, I have enjoyed the support and encouragement of talented mentors and colleagues. In particular, I would like to thank Nina Baym, Carol Farley Kessler, Jerry Klinkowitz, and Robert Dale Parker, all of whom provided tremendously valuable advice. I also thank Robert Baird, David Ericksen, and Joel Super, who patiently read the most primitive drafts of the following chapters and discussed them with me.

My gratitude to the University of Northern Iowa, in particular to Jeffrey S. Copeland, head of the Department of English Language and Literature, who supported this project with enthusiasm and helped protect my time so that I could revise the manuscript, and to David Walker and the Graduate College, who made the final phase of research much easier with summer fellowship and project grant support.

Earlier versions of two chapters in this book have been previously published, and I am grateful to the journals for permission to reprint them. Chapter 2 appeared in *Journal of Narrative Technique* 28 (Winter 1998) as "'Little Counterplots' in the Old South: Narrative Subterfuge in Caroline Hentz's Domestic Fiction," and chapter 5 appeared in *Southern Quarterly* 37 (Winter 1999) as "Recasting Women's Roles: Southworth's *Britomarte, the Man-Hater* as Civil War Fiction."

A special thanks to Emily Rogers of the University of Illinois Press for her marvelous work at every step of the review and publication process.

And finally, my thanks and love to the other members of Team Tracey: Grant, Caitlin, Elizabeth, and Devin. I trust you know that your contributions of encouragement, conversation, time, love, and delight are inscribed on every page of this book.

The Renegotiation of Marriage

IN 1857 the British novelist Wilkie Collins, disingenuously posing as a family man who avidly reads novels, protested the tendency of contemporary women novelists to create aggressive heroines and to place those heroines in peculiar proposal plots. In an unsigned column entitled "Petition to Novel-Writers," which was printed in both Britain and the United States, Collins celebrates the conventional heroine of the popular novel, characterizing her as the "old-fashioned Heroine, who has lived and loved and wept for centuries. I have taken her to my bosom thousands of times already, and ask nothing better than to indulge in that tender luxury thousands of times again. I love her blushing cheek, her gracefully-rounded form, her chiselled nose, her slender waist, her luxuriant tresses which always escape from the fillet that binds them" (183). He then complains about a new heroine who appears to be replacing the yielding and responsive traditional one: "[We] now protest positively, even indignantly, against a new kind of heroine—a bouncing, ill-conditioned, impudent young woman, who has been introduced among us of late years. I venture to call this wretched and futile substitute for our dear, tender, gentle, loving old heroine, the Man-Hater; because, in every book in which she appears, it is her mission from first to last to behave as badly as possible to every man with whom she comes in contact" (183).

What makes this "Man-Hater" so different from the old-fashioned heroine? Her bad behavior primarily consists in taking control of her own courtship plot by denying the initial advances of the hero she is in love with, by directing her life course by some star other than "being in love": "When her lover makes her an offer of marriage, she receives it in the light of a personal insult, goes up to her room immediately afterwards, and flies into a passion with herself, because she is really in love with the man all the time—comes down again, and snubs him before company instead of making a decent apology—pouts and flouts at him on all after-occasions, until the end of the book is at hand—then, suddenly, turns round and marries him!" (183).

What new plot is this? Heroines have always turned down unsuitable suitors, so that cannot be Collins's complaint. These new heroines are aggressively turning down the very heroes they are eventually to wed; they are presumably finding something better to do (for a while, at least) than marry their destined mate, the (un)fortunate suitor they humble for chapter after chapter before relenting and accepting a proposal after all:

> If we feel inclined to ask why she could not, under the circumstances, receive his advances with decent civility at first, we are informed that her "maidenly consciousness" prevented it. . . . Every individual in the novel who wears trousers and gets within range of her maidenly consciousness, becomes her natural enemy from that moment. If he makes a remark on the weather, her lip curls; if he asks leave to give her a potato at dinner-time . . . , her neck curves in scorn; if he offers a compliment, finding she won't have a potato, her nostril dilates. Whatever she does, even in her least aggressive moments, she always gets the better of all the men. (184–85)

What is wrong with this new plot?—not merely the heroine's bad manners, but the disturbing fact that she "always gets the better of all the men." In this reading of popular fiction, plots are not just stories to while away the time. They may represent reality, perhaps may even wield the cultural power to change reality. In the case of this new heroine and this new plot, Collins attempts to laugh the significance away, to mock the writers and their heroines in an attempt to disempower both and to force them to retreat into the more comfortable old-fashioned courtship mode.[1]

Collins shifts his concern to the relationship between novel conventions and real life, between fictional characters and real people. He objects to the "new-fashioned heroine" because, he insists, she "is a libel on her sex. As a husband and a father, I solemnly deny that she is in any single respect a natural woman" (184). And yet he fears she may reflect or inspire a change in actual female behavior, because the opposition heroine is set up "by lady-novelists, who ought surely to be authorities when female characters are concerned. Is the Man-Hater a true representative of young women, now-a-days?" (184). If she is, then as a father he fears for his sons. In his assumed persona, Collins considers the horrors his son may face when he becomes of marriageable age, if he is confronted with a woman who dares to assert her dignity by controlling her own courtship:

> My unhappy offspring, what a prospect awaits you! One forbidding phalanx of Man-Haters, bristling with woman's dignity, and armed to the teeth with maidenly consciousness, occupies the wide matrimonial field, look where you will! Ill-fated youth, yet a few years, and the female neck will curve, the female nostril dilate, at the sight of you. You see that stately form, those rustling skirts, that ample brow, and fall on your knees before it, and cry "Marry me, marry me, for Heaven's sake!" My deluded boy, that is not a woman—it is a Man-Hater—a whited sepulchre full of violent expostulations and injurious epithets. She will lead you the life of a costermonger's ass, until she has exhausted her whole stock of maidenly consciousness; and she will then say (in effect, if not in words): "Inferior animal, I loved you from the first— I have asserted my womanly dignity by making an abject fool of you in public and private—now you may marry me!" Marry her not, my son! Go rather to the slave-market at Constantinople—buy a Circassian wife, who has heard nothing and read nothing about Man-Haters, bring her home . . . and trust to your father to welcome an Asiatic daughter-in-law, who will not despise him for the unavoidable misfortune of being—a Man! (184)

However ironically the passage is cast (the comic mask slips from the diatribe with the phrase *whited sepulchre*), the article betrays a fear that women who "hear and read" about the fictional Man-Haters might become more like them: "Ever since I read the first novel with a Man-Hater in it, I have had my eye on [my daughters'] nostrils, and I can make affidavit that I have never yet seen them dilate, under any circumstances or in any society. . . . In men's society, their manners (like those of all other girls whom I meet with) are natural and modest; and—in the cases of certain privileged men—winning, into the bargain" (184). Despite such reassuring observations, Collins's persona finds this new paradigm of marriage so horrifying that he falls back on imperialism and racism to invoke a preferred model of silence and submission. His son should take the drastic measure of buying himself a slave of another race rather than encourage displays of womanly dignity. By drawing, however facetiously, an analogy between wife and slave, Collins sets up the very comparison used by feminist crusaders in their efforts at marriage reform.[2] The passive, clinging feminine nature represented in the "old-fashioned heroine" permits the husband's dominance; the assertive new heroine challenges that dominance at a vulnerable point: the proposal scene that should ensure the transference of woman from father to husband.

In this study I will excavate and reconstruct the American wing of the countertradition in popular nineteenth-century women's novels identified and critiqued by Wilkie Collins. Double-proposal novels, as I call them, can be identified by the heroine's rejection and acceptance of proposals from the same suitor, and they can be analyzed according to how their authors deploy two specific opportunities created by the double-proposal device: the opened space between rejected and accepted proposals and the inherent contrast between rejected and accepted marriage conditions. The unique grammar of the double-proposal plot offers unusual opportunities for a study of literary history. Because of the force of regional sociopolitical identities and the major historical epochs marked off by the Civil War, American double-proposal novels published between 1850 and 1890 render a particularly compelling story of how popular fiction can generate a longitudinal and lateral dialogic relationship with the particular literary, social, and political conditions within which it is produced and read. Each writer considered in this study writes double-proposal narratives that manifest both how she is determined by her historical circumstances and how she is determined to change those circumstances. The novels in this tradition are not ready to shun marriage as the heroine's best long-term option, but through their double-proposal plots they argue for more egalitarian concepts of marriage and for greater autonomy for women both without and within marriage. When American writers deployed the British-born double-proposal plot, they demonstrated how literary adaptations may become, perhaps inevitably, cultural negotiations.

Several double-proposal novels have already been given readings as potentially powerful feminist texts, though the function of the double-proposal plot as central to that power has not been specifically identified. But they all share the strong heroine, countertraditional courtship plot, and interest in marriage reform that Wilkie Collins discerned with such apparent dread. The most recognizable double-proposal stories are from the British side of the Atlantic: Jane Austen's *Pride and Prejudice,* Charlotte Brontë's *Jane Eyre,* and Elizabeth Barrett Browning's *Aurora Leigh.* The American version best-known today is probably Elizabeth Stuart Phelps's *The Story of Avis,* which specifically invokes *Aurora Leigh* as its inspiration, but several of the most successful nineteenth-century writers also used the plot, among them Augusta Evans and Caroline Hentz, who attempt in their novels to negotiate a balance between loyalty to the antebellum southern polity and desire for increased freedom for privileged white women. Some double-proposal novels, including *Jane Eyre* and Evans's *St. Elmo,* were phenomenal popular successes, while others, such as Laura J. Curtis Bullard's overtly feminist *Christine,* received little notice and no reprintings.[3] As I reconstruct this plot and its cultural history, I look at particular authors, texts, and contexts, examining the books themselves and any records I could uncover of how they were read, reviewed, or critiqued. At times the intertextual dialogue is clear and specific, at other times it is more oblique. At times readers and reviewers specifically noted their reaction to the courtship plots, at other times they were silent.

Because this study tells the story of a plot, my arguments are rooted in close readings of the novels, readings that then open out into questions of reader response, literary traditions, and social history. Judith Fetterley has expressed concern that studies of nineteenth-century writers that are not grounded in such close reading may be functioning to re-exclude women writers from scholarly consideration rather than to forward the work of recovery and reevaluation. She suggests that the negating slant of much criticism and the scarcity of large-scale studies of nineteenth-century women's writing may be attributed in part to "the dismantling of the interpretive strategies developed during the 1950s and '60s to establish the current canon of American literature, the strategies of close reading and thematic study":

> While a variety of new interpretive strategies less interested in textual analysis may be performed on works already canonized without affecting their canonical status, it is not clear that such strategies can substantially affect the literary status of noncanonical works. . . . Those of us interested in nineteenth-century American women writers may need to find ways to revitalize modes of criticism no longer fashionable because these modes may represent stages in the process of literary evaluation that we cannot do without. (605)

By drawing on theories of the intertextual and dialogic workings of texts, my study of these novels is a venture toward this revitalization. Throughout the formal analyses of particular novels, I work to retain a continuous sense of the texts as dynamically interacting with readers and critics, both contemporary and historical, and with various regional, cultural, and political realities. The result poses one response to the contradiction Fetterley has noticed between her students' enthusiastic response to reading the work of nineteenth-century American women writers and critics' persistent tendency to dismiss the same work as irrelevant: "I puzzle over the juxtaposition of, on the one hand, a powerful connection between the contemporary reader and the texts of nineteenth-century American women, a connection that offers one strategy for making these texts central to the discourse on nineteenth-century American literature, and on the other, a critical climate that

seems, whether by design or not, to undermine that connection and interpretive strategy" (606). One rich site where we can investigate the connection between these texts and the readers who are enthusiastic about them
(then and now) is provided through the dialogue produced by double-proposal fiction. This dialogue is generated at the level of plot but, because the
inherent structural elements of the double-proposal plot themselves open up
literary and cultural debates about women's work, courtship, and marriage,
the conversation also incorporates extratextual literary and cultural voices;
as a result, these courtship narratives provoke discussion at multiple levels:
the intratextual, the intertextual, and the contextual.

Within each text, the debates generated by the double proposal are sometimes left implicit between the bifurcated plot lines, but at other times they
are articulated by narrators and characters, producing a multivocal dialogue
that lends itself to analysis in terms of Bakhtin's heteroglossia: "Each character's speech possesses its own belief system. . . . Thus it may also refract
authorial intentions and consequently may to a certain degree constitute a
second language for the author" (315). Double-proposal authors apparently
have many such "second languages," which makes it difficult to fix on a single message in their texts. That difficulty becomes a power rather than a fault
because the novels are then more compelling as cultural artifacts of American history in a time of rapid change. As Diane Price Herndl has suggested, the critic, like the text, can establish a dialogic stance by looking "for points
where disagreeing discourses do not cohere and examin[ing] what those
points of contradiction can tell about the boundaries themselves"; the goal
is to "emphasize the plural meanings—even contradictory meanings—in the
text" rather than to privilege a single reading ("Dilemmas of a Feminine
Dialogic" 18). Double-proposal novels frequently lead readers toward contradictory conclusions because the impetus of the development plot is de-
railed or muffled by the apparently incompatible movement of the courtship
plot. This derailing and muffling, I believe, becomes a crucial part of the story
of women's lives as told by the novels.

The conversations that I identify between double-proposal texts and their
cultural milieux take place both through explicit allusion and through more
subtle intertextual means. The grammar of the double-proposal plot provides the intertextual poetics that relate these novels to one another and to
other narratives to which they are both similar and dissimilar. To borrow the
terminology of Jonathan Culler, the "rhetorical or literary presupposition"
(116) inherent in these novels helps us articulate ways in which texts engage

one another and the discursive space of their historical moment without requiring evidence of direct influence. Double-proposal novels address each
other, and they also presuppose the existence of other versions of courtship
plots: the single-proposal plot, the double-suitor plot, and the seduction plot
(or, the courtship plot gone awry). They also, typically, anticipate a reader's
familiarity with certain recurring character types, in particular the Byronic
hero and the domestic heroine. But even more intriguing than the literary
intertextuality is the historical contextuality of double-proposal novels because, taken as a group, they generate an ongoing dialogue that replicates
within a defined body of texts what Hans Robert Jauss argues is the general
story of literary history: "The historicity of literature as well as its commu-
nicative character presupposes a dialogical and at once processlike relationship between work, audience, and new work that can be conceived in the
relations between message and receiver as well as between question and answer, problem and solution" (19). Double-proposal novels pose questions and
problems about courtship and marriage in the rejected proposal(s) and then
partially answer those questions or solve those problems with the accepted
proposal. The marriage endings of these novels always contain within themselves the seeds of new questions, present renewed problems (sometimes
identified as "tensions"), which subsequent double-proposal novels then take
up. When a double-proposal protagonist accepts the very suitor she rejected earlier, the novels draw attention to the contrasted potential marriages
and suggest a view of love as a relative rather than an all-subsuming value
for women and of marriage conditions as negotiable. Doubling proposals
allowed authors to explore competing ideologies about women's roles while
containing some of the potential disruption through marriage conclusions.

As Collins's review of the double-proposal form demonstrates, the double-proposal plot could profoundly challenge a reader's expectations; in the
conventional courtship story, heroines do not turn down heroes unless a
misunderstanding or insuperable barrier interferes. When a double-proposal
heroine refuses the hero not because of misunderstanding but because she
prefers to remain unmarried or because she disapproves of the hero, readers
are frustrated and puzzled, and the cognitive dissonance they experience may
lead to a change in their thinking. Terry Eagleton suggests that criticism
should "seek to explain the literary work in terms of the ideological structure of which it is a part, yet which it transforms by its art: it would search
out the principle which both ties the work to ideology and distances it from
it" (19). For the novels I study, the double-proposal plot is itself the "princi-

ple" that ties the novels to marriage ideology and distances them from it, that creates dissonance within the reader that is not entirely resolved by apparently harmonious happy endings.

Literary theorists speculate that both writers and readers are aware of changing ideologies at unconscious levels and that such awareness may call out questions or resistances within writers and readers that can be expressed and responded to through literature; if this is true, then popular literature must be both voice and instrument of social change. Jauss argues that when a reader confronts texts which break his or her literary or cultural horizon of expectations, that reader undergoes a "'change of horizons' through negation of familiar experiences or through raising newly articulated experiences to the level of consciousness" (25). We may think of Jauss's "newly articulated experiences" as existing within author and reader as Raymond Williams's "structures of feeling," an unarticulated set of "meanings and values as they are actively lived and felt, and the relations between these and formal or systematic beliefs" (132). Because the double-proposal plot enabled writers and readers to have their independent heroine and marry her off as well, and therefore to deny or turn back or ignore the very challenges that give life to the protagonists' plots, I would guess that the ideological negotiations apparent in the dialogue generated by double proposals may have often worked at unconscious levels. The double-proposal novels provide an example of how a literature that appears in its surface structure to offer no challenge to literary or cultural expectations, to be what Jauss would dismiss as merely "'culinary' or entertainment art" because it fulfills expectations and "confirms familiar sentiments," may, for a reader more carefully engaged with characters and plots, in fact be challenging and altering the very conventions it appears to blandly reproduce (25).

To make informed guesses about how double-proposal novels may have influenced or spoken for or challenged or pleased readers, I attempt in this study to historicize readers as much as limited information permits. Some scholars have provided compelling social histories of women in the nineteenth century that enable me to reconstruct some of the cultural circumstances that would have influenced the writing, publishing, and reading of these novels. In addition, adapting James Machor's approach to reader-response criticism allows me to consider how nineteenth-century discourses construct groups of readers and then to examine how specific novels invoke and respond to such groups. Machor argues that criticism should identify and analyze "assumptions about the way reading should proceed and the types of readers that existed, as well as assumptions about the way fiction engaged its audience and the roles it implied for its readers" ("Fiction and Informed Reading" 326). This approach partially brackets the question of whether the posited audiences are "real," but yet, Machor argues, "Examined in light of interpretive strategies of the time . . . the relation between antebellum fiction and its audience can be seen as a process of reconciliation and disruption that depended on the conventions readers were expected to bring to fiction" (342). Grounded in public discourses and literary conventions, Machor's "process of reconciliation and disruption" correlates with Jauss's more general pattern of "question and answer." When I speculate about how authors may have anticipated and addressed certain groups of readers—for example, the reviewers as self-styled cultural arbiters, the avid consumers of fiction (widely presumed to be young and female), the moral guardians (parents or clergy of those avid consumers)—I adapt Machor's strategy while keeping in mind the cultural and literary horizon of expectations I have defined through historical and literary research.

To pause for an example of how a text may confirm one reader's set of expectations while challenging another's, consider the case of *Ruth Hall* (1855) by Sara Payson Willis Parton (Fanny Fern). Nina Baym identifies Parton's work as angry, containing "the fiercest repudiation of kin and blood ties in women's writing of the time," and the most cursory review of *Ruth Hall*'s plot bears out that statement (*Woman's Fiction* 251). Parton's heroine, widowed and impoverished early in the novel and neglected by in-laws and blood relations, forges an independent career, rejecting marriage. One of *Ruth Hall*'s first reviewers managed, however, to read it as a conventional domestic novel, in fact as the quintessential domestic novel, a paradigmatic example of "the miracle of *inspired mediocrity*," which is described as follows:

> It is rather everybody's experience; it is pious, pathetic, funny, and dramatic—it is equal from first to last—never rising above the key note, never sinking below it; always intelligible; always correct and proper; not one new thought is introduced from first to last; the heroine is within the scope and reach of every honest woman, the hero is within the grasp of every honest man. The villains, are every day villains, to be met with in every square and on every wharf; there is nothing astounding, nothing incredible, and to crown all, virtue is seen to bring its own reward. (Rev. of *Ruth Hall* 443)

This *Southern Quarterly Review* critic claims that this list includes "all the conditions demanded by the middle class" (443) from whence comes the mass of readers with their "small intelligences" (449), identified as four-fifths female and only moderately educated (440). This group is contrasted to "an audience of taste, more appreciative, more rewarding, than even the massed enthusiasts of inspired mediocrity . . . the audience that turn abashed and insulted from the presumptuous littleness of 'Ruth Hall'" (450). The writer appears not to notice the obvious contradiction implied by the claim that the audience of taste contrasted to the "small intelligences" once "thrilled to Jane Eyre" (450). A huge popular success, *Jane Eyre* must have been enjoyed by many of the readers who this reviewer wishes to believe could not have responded to it: "What has Nancy [a hypothetical reader of inspired mediocrity] to do with the storm-gusts of passion that heave and vex the pale governess of Miss Brontë?" (441–42).

Working with these assumptions about readers, and operating within an interpretive strategy that allowed for only those readings of women's novels that affirmed the domestic sphere and the imperatives of marriage, this same reviewer denies that a person like Ruth Hall could be both an engaging character and a public success: "From the commencement of her literary career to the publication of 'Life and Sketches,' Ruth Hall ceases to be an interesting woman" (449). Thus negating the possibility that a reader might identify with a career woman, the reviewer concludes that the author makes Ruth Hall a heroine by "marrying her to literature and making her the mother of a book" (450); Ruth Hall is accorded heroine status only insofar as her career plot can be read as a conventional domestic story celebrating marriage and motherhood.

Other reviewers were either less obtuse or not as clever in relegating *Ruth Hall* to a safe spot on the sentimental bookshelf because the book attracted controversy as well as readers. When the novel was read as autobiography, reviewers interpreted the anger in it as distinctly unfeminine and unconventional. An editor at *Putnam's Monthly* explained that "most of its readers" had discovered that the work was largely autobiographical, and on these terms it is interpreted: "Very seldom has so angry a book been published. It is full and overflowing with an unfemininely bitter wrath and spite" ("Editorial Notes" 216). A critic for the *Knickerbocker* reacted similarly: "If 'Ruth Hall' be really an autobiography, as seems to be inferred by many of our contemporaries, it is without exception the most 'out-spoken' production of its kind we ever encountered" ("Literary Notices" 84). When understood to be portraying real people, "Fanny Fern" came under attack for breaking with conventional gender codes: "[*Ruth Hall*] appears to have been exploded in a fit of desperation, to revive the writer's sinking fame, and to revenge herself on her relatives, and everybody she imagines ever injured her" (Moulton 61). The editor for *Harper's* seemed befuddled: "The whole book is embittered. It is not easy to say why, nor to what good result." This reviewer explains that "private experience" is valued by readers only if "it becomes historical and of universal meaning," and *Ruth Hall* is not such a story: "If it be such an autobiography, . . . are we instructed, or helped in any way? are we even entertained by the stories?" ("Editor's Easy Chair" 551). And as if to complete the dismissal of the book from critical notice, the *National Era* announced: "We do not happen to ride in the troop of admirers of Fanny Fern. Her Ruth Hall . . . is a book not to be commended or justified" ("Literary Notices" 55). *Godey's Lady's Book and Magazine* refused to discuss the novel at all: "As we never interfere in family affairs, we must leave readers to judge for themselves" ("Literary Notices" 176). Nathaniel Hawthorne, operating on a different interpretive tack from the didactic reviewers, professed to admire Fern for the anger that drives her writing: he excepts her from his general condemnation of women authors, complimenting her for writing "as if the devil was in her . . . the only condition under which a woman ever writes anything worth reading" (78).

Here then are at least six possible nineteenth-century reading groups: the reviewer who sees even a patently angry and rebellious book in conventional, placid terms; the conventional, placid mass reader as constructed by such a reviewer; the other reviewer-constructed audience (presumably including the reviewer) who appreciates genius but rejects *Ruth Hall;* reviewers who treat the work as autobiography and condemn it accordingly for breaking with gender and genre conventions; the male literary artist who recognizes the feminist impulse behind the rebellion but who is not part of the reviewing or consuming reading groups; and, unrepresented in print but strongly represented in book sales and subscriptions, the target reader who does ride "in the troop of admirers," who eagerly identifies with the heroine and enjoys the book immensely.

We may venture a few possible conclusions concerning these disparate groups of midnineteenth-century readers, "real" and "posited." Hawthorne's example shows that subversive elements in the text could be appreciated by nineteenth-century readers as well as by later critics. The reviewers themselves, however, whether treating the novel as conventional fiction or as autobiographical satire, are using different interpretive strategies from Hawthorne and certainly from the target readers. The self-styled gatekeepers of appropriate literature are imagined by the critic for the *Southern Quarterly Review* to be "gigantic porters keeping watch and ward at the castle gates against all comers of ordinary size" (450). Women novelists were usually categorized as "comers of ordinary size" and given only cursory reviews. One such reader is John Reuben Thompson, a *Southern Literary Messenger* reviewer who often claims to have only glanced at the novels casually recommended to young readers: "We have not yet heard the opinion of the little lady to whom, after a cursory examination, our own copy was presented, but feel quite justified in commending the tale to all" ("Notices of New Works" [1854] 772). The author of a *North American Review* article entitled "Female Authors" explains that most reviewers treat women writers with a "half contemptuous leniency," and if they "have the good fortune to be brought under notice at all, they are the theme of neatly turned compliments and ingenious congratulations" (Abbot 163).

When reviewers either refused to employ or lacked the interpretive strategies necessary to process the disruptive elements of texts they assumed would fit a predetermined and harmless genre, women writers could produce subversive works that would predictably be relegated to standard, nonthreatening categories. The mass of readers of popular fiction are strikingly different from the reviewing audience. Operating within assumptions that trivialized women as readers and women as writers, reviewers in effect could be neutralized by a book that, in its broad outlines, fit the expected schema for women's novels. If we may assume that writers and consumers of popular fiction identified with the heroines and took them seriously, and if we may infer from the popularity of *Ruth Hall* that such readers reveled in the story of a heroine who married a career and gave birth to a book, we may also be justified in assuming that these readers indeed were employing different heuristic strategies from those of gatekeepers who professed not to enjoy women's novels and different heuristic strategies yet again from those that the gatekeepers, who professed strong faith in the "good and pure imaginations" of the middle classes (Rev. of *Ruth Hall* 442), thought they were using. We have to infer those strategies rather than demonstrate them because the mass of readers were not running the periodical presses or otherwise leaving much record of how they read novels. Part of my project in the following chapters is to do some of that inferring, although here and there I have located evidence of excited and engaged readers who may be identified as belonging to the target reading group. I work such evidence into the dialogic history of the double-proposal novel whenever possible.

Ruth Hall is the story of a woman's life plot fulfilled outside of marriage; as such, it did not escape criticism from establishment readers even though one entrenched reviewer was able to domesticate it. The many, many disguised women's plots, under which broad definition I would include the double-proposal novels, were approved by the gatekeeper audience under one interpretive strategy but very likely read eagerly by the target audience within quite different strategies.

The common justification for reinvestigation of women's nineteenth-century novels is their historical significance; thousands of people whose lives we would now like to understand better read them eagerly.[4] Working with historical and reader-response strategies of increasing sophistication, critics have established that women writers were preoccupied with the competing ideologies of their times and that their work contributed to contemporary debates.[5] But very little work has been done on interrelated groups of texts and their connections to the culture in which they were written and read. As both Susan K. Harris and Joanne Dobson have noted, there is much still to be done if we are not only to recover interesting texts but also to understand the cultural work in which they participated. Harris argues that American women's literature should be studied on contextual, rhetorical, and retrospective levels as we search for "traces of changing consciousness, building blocks for an ideologically self-conscious literary history" ("'But Is It Any Good?'" 59). Dobson similarly advocates criticism that focuses "on the interconnections of literature and culture" and so helps us "to consider imaginative engagement with pressing social and political issues" ("American Renaissance" 167). Fetterley has deplored how little has been done to write the history of midnineteenth-century women writers, arguing that "we need to find ways to solve the problems of doing literary history because we cannot do without it; it represents an essential stage in the process of integrating women writers into the field of nineteenth-century American literature" (605).

This study is offered as a contribution to this crucial process. American double-proposal novels written between 1850 and 1890 constitute a tradition that can be connected with cultural shifts of profound relevance to women and with literary forms that gave imaginative shape to women's lives: the courtship novel, domestic fiction, and the bildungsroman or *Künstlerroman*. Because marriage and divorce laws and the threat of social ostracism provided daunting obstacles to dissolving marriages until quite late in the century, the grave importance of the state of marriage and the choice of mate for women is hard to exaggerate. Thanks to the work of social historians, I am able to reconstruct with some detail and consistency the evolution of societal factors my particular authors were concerned with: the shifting understanding of what "love" meant, the congruent shift in middle-class expectations for "companionate" marriage, and the parallel movement of women toward independent thought, then independent action. Double-proposal novels reveal complex "imaginative engagement" with changing nineteenth-century perceptions of courtship, marriage, and women's work.

In short, the double-proposal tradition participated in the cultural work of change, much as the persona created by Wilkie Collins feared it would. When double-proposal novels are read closely, with conscientious attention to cultural factors, a persuasive story of the intersection and interaction of popular fiction and middle-class culture emerges. Once the traditional courtship plot is opened up, once the conventional, clinging, vulnerable heroine has had both backbone and brain instilled in her, these novels begin a vital dialogue about societal issues fundamental to middle-class life, a dialogue that is carried on textually, intertextually, and contextually. A range of authors working with this particular plot over a period of at least forty years involved their literary traditions and their social milieux in dialogue about what female characteristics are most apt to contribute to the happiness of the individual, to the solidity of the middle-class family, and to the strength of a nation, about what path a woman could and should take when she chooses to delay or forego marriage, and about how romance, love, and marriage should be conceived and reconceived.

The boundaries between the British and American literary worlds were quite permeable in the nineteenth century, and books, articles, and periodicals were freely reprinted and distributed on both sides of the Atlantic. While many commentators were preoccupied with identifying and reinforcing distinctions between British and American culture and literature, most readers consumed whatever came their way, and so an understanding of the popularity and power of British writers profoundly informs any understanding of nineteenth-century U.S. readers. The literate American world was saturated with British work, both imaginative and critical, a saturation that is evident when we examine the pervasive presence of British double-proposal models in the United States. The British double-proposal texts that provided models for American writers, and that were very well-known works in the literary-historical context in which the American double-proposal tradition developed, generated a dialogue with each other, a dialogue to which American authors, writing out of their distinctive social milieux, added their voices.

The earliest of the British double-proposal novels are Jane Austen's *Pride and Prejudice* (1813) and *Persuasion* (1818). In *Pride and Prejudice,* Elizabeth Bennett refuses Darcy's first unflattering offer of marriage (which he presumes she will accept with alacrity) and accepts his second proposal (which he humbly offers with some doubt of her response). In *Persuasion,* Anne Elliot refuses Frederick Wentworth at the behest of a trusted family advisor, and only after eleven years, when Wentworth has proven himself in the navy while she endured life with her uncongenial family, does he overcome his wounded pride and renew the offer.

Not coincidentally, critics see Elizabeth and Anne as more self-determining than most courtship heroines. For example, Joseph Boone comments that Elizabeth is an "unconventionally active shaper of the plot of her self-awakening" (93). Tony Tanner finds Elizabeth's refusal of Darcy's "first lordly proposal," when "she refuses to respond in the role of passive grateful female, as he obviously expects she will" one of the most pleasurable scenes in the novel: "The assertion of the free-choosing self and its resistance to the would-be tyranny of roles imposed on it from socially superior powers is a spectacle which delights us now quite as much as it can have done Jane Austen's contemporaries" (Introduction 29).

It is not when Elizabeth, or Anne Elliot, refuses the wrong suitor that we get this particular delight; refusal of Mr. Wrong is an expected part of a heroine's progress toward Mr. Right, as Jean E. Kennard has argued. When Elizabeth rejects Darcy because he has not yet earned her respect and love, and when Anne breaks her engagement with Wentworth because of a higher sense of duty, each prolongs control of her life beyond scenes that might have ended her self-determination—the first proposal from the hero. Elizabeth and Anne exercise their right of refusal to their own eventual advantage, for they maintain their self-respect while increasing the respect the hero has for them. The hero matures in ways calculated to make him a better mate; the marriages that end *Pride and Prejudice* and *Persuasion* are more egalitarian than the earlier marriages promised to be. This plot dynamic may explain why one critic comments that Austen's heroines "thrive" in the limitations placed on them by "the conventions of plot and society which move them inexorably toward the *telos* of marriage. . . . There is power to be read in their experience of limits: Anne Elliot after Elizabeth Bennett chooses with a certain freedom the man and the manner of the happy end" (Miller 155–56).

Although *Pride and Prejudice* and *Persuasion* demonstrate the power in the double-proposal plot device, they differ from *Jane Eyre* and the American double-proposal novels because Austen's heroines, while self-determining in how they handle courtship, never venture beyond their family units and so do not develop the skills of independence Jane Eyre needs once her wedding is interrupted and she refuses Rochester's proffered protection. An

Austen heroine never faces the world on her own, deprived of family, money, and even identity. Elizabeth and Anne struggle for independence within the stifling restrictions of their families, but are never pushed outside those family circles. Boone puts it another way: "As the subject of a female bildungsroman, therefore, Elizabeth remains inscribed within the one arena, the one destiny, permitted by the mechanics of love-plotting" (93). In contrast, Jane Eyre, Aurora Leigh, and a host of other double-proposal heroines do strike out toward other destinies, although they return to the love plot at the end.

In the United States, *Jane Eyre* and *Aurora Leigh* quickly became integral to discourse about literature, particularly women's literature. Brontë's novel was a popular success before British or American critics had noticed it. One of the first reviews, printed in Britain and reprinted in the United States, exclaims, "Indeed, the public taste seems to have outstripped its guides in appreciating the remarkable power which this book displays. For no leading review has yet noticed it, and here we have before us the second edition" ("Jane Eyre" 481). E. P. Whipple, writing for the *North American Review,* also testifies to the instant popularity of the novel, described unsympathetically as "a distressing mental epidemic, passing under the name of the 'Jane Eyre fever,' which defied all the usual nostrums of the established doctors of criticism" (355).

Letters, journals, and reviews of other novels further document *Jane Eyre's* impact; their off-hand references to Brontë's work reveal how much Currer Bell (only later revealed to be Charlotte Brontë), Jane Eyre, and Rochester were part of the current literary vocabulary. Reviewers in America took reader familiarity with *Jane Eyre* for granted, using Currer Bell as a measure for native writers. John Greenleaf Whittier, writing in the *National Era* just two years after the publication of *Jane Eyre,* noted that E. D. E. N. Southworth's *Retribution* "reminds us of Jane Eyre, and the later productions of that school. It has their strength and sustained intensity, while it embodies, as they can scarcely be said to do, an important moral lesson" (150), and the *New York Literary World* similarly judged Southworth's *The Curse of Clifton* (1852) worthy of Currer Bell (qtd. in Boyle 57). The extraordinary influence of *Jane Eyre* upon American novelists continued to be acknowledged throughout the succeeding decades. Augusta Evans's *Beulah* was once termed a "very humble and feeble and intellectually unremunerative" imitation of *Jane Eyre (Baltimore Daily Exchange* 27 [1859], qtd. in Fidler 80). An 1855 essay entitled "Modern Novelists—Great and Small," printed in Britain and in the United States, attests in sweeping terms to Brontë's influence, to which the following quote refers: "The effect of a great literary success, especially in fiction, is a strange thing to observe,—the direct influence it has on some one or two similar minds, and the indirect bias which it gives to a great many others" (646); the article's conclusion, a reaction to the sudden news of Brontë's death, adds an even more telling remark: "Perhaps no other writer of her time has impressed her mark so clearly on contemporary literature, or drawn so many followers into her own peculiar path; and she leaves no one behind worthy to take the pre-eminent and leading place of the author of *Jane Eyre*" (654). In 1856 another reviewer declared that "Charlotte Brontë initiated the new mode in fiction, in those wonderful narratives wherein she exposed to view the inward workings of a restless and fiery nature. . . . Since Miss Brontë, many other writers have essayed the same psychological style of fictitious composition" ("Notices of New Works" 478). Robert Henry Newell, writing in 1863 under the pen name Orpheus C. Kerr, bewailed the pervasive and persistent influence of *Jane Eyre:* The "unnatural and unmitigated ruffian for a hero" typical of "gushing fiction," he wrote, is modeled on "that old humbug, Rochester, the beloved of 'Jane Eyre.' The character has been done-over scores of times since poor Charlotte Brontë gave her famous novel to the world, and is still 'much used in respectable families'" (63–64). The compliment offered in an 1864 essay entitled "Female Novelists" echoes many others: Jennie June names Brontë the "most intense female writer of modern times" and adds that American "female aspirants to literary honors" who might "develop the fervor of 'Jane Eyre'" would be welcomed by the world (121–22).

Letters and journals bear out critical assumptions about *Jane Eyre*'s popularity and testify to how powerfully Charlotte Brontë and Elizabeth Barrett Browning influenced their American literary sisters. Susan K. Harris reports that many women responded warmly to Elizabeth Barrett Browning's *Aurora Leigh* as well as to Charlotte Brontë's works: "Women's responses to *Aurora Leigh* were universally positive," and "responses to Charlotte Brontë reveal nearly the same level of adulation" (*Nineteenth-Century American Women's Novels* 26). Mary Virginia Terhune wrote in an 1889 letter, "Since my early girlhood, Brontë has been more to me than any other writer, living or dead" (qtd. in Kelley 121), and the novelist Elizabeth Drew Stoddard frequently expressed her admiration of Brontë and Browning, once commenting that Brontë possessed "more moral strength than the government and gunpowder heroes of the day" (317). Julia Newberry's 1871 list of books that she considers "particular friends & books that I read all the time & over & over again" is headed by "Jane Eyre. And all that Charlotte Brontë ever wrote" (153–54), and Celia Thaxter, a poet, wrote to a friend, "To think of your asking such a question as 'Do I care about Charlotte Brontë'! As if I did not care everything I am capable of caring for anything!" (8).[6]

Drawing on American periodicals, Dorothy Mermin concludes that "Barrett Browning had a strong following among women . . . especially in America, where 'many of the most cultivated of her sex' regarded her with an 'ardor of admiration'" (222). One such admirer was Lydia Maria Child, who wrote after reading *Aurora Leigh* upon its publication late in 1856, "It is full of strong things, and brilliant things, and beautiful things" (301), an opinion she still held shortly after Barrett Browning's death in 1861: "Aurora Leigh is a great book; intellectually very great, morally still greater. It kindled in me a glowing enthusiasm while I read it" (389). One reviewer, who claimed "no stronger, wiser poem [than *Aurora Leigh*] has ever been written by a woman's hand," expressed doubt that "Mrs. Browning will ever be popular with school girls or sentimental young ladies," but evidence suggests this reviewer was incorrect ("Elizabeth Barrett Browning" 152–53). A poem by Adelaide Anne Proctor that details a list of things she loved culminates with "The poets that you used to read to me / While summer twilights faded in the sky; / But most of all I think Aurora Leigh" ("A Woman's Answer" 143). A humorous article entitled "A One-Sided Correspondence" includes this comment: "I don't know why, but immature femininity generally dotes on 'Aurora Leigh'" (404). The young Mary Willard, writing in 1861, might have been an example: "I've been reading Aurora Leigh. The divine of Mrs. Browning's nature shines out in every line" (qtd. in Willard 179). Ada Parker's letters include several lavish tributes to Barrett Browning, of whom she writes, "I do love her, and every little verse of hers which I find in the newspapers is made precious property" (152), and "I long to possess her poems,—to have them by my pillow with the most precious of my books, as a personal inspiration to faith and courage" (155). Like *Jane Eyre*, *Aurora Leigh* appealed widely to women readers, both "cultivated" and "immature."

Jane Austen's two novels are the earliest of the nineteenth-century British double-proposal texts and were certainly still widely read at midcentury, but Charlotte Brontë and Elizabeth Barrett Browning developed the double-proposal stories that most profoundly influenced American writers and readers. Austen restricts her heroines' movement within their family circles instead of allowing them a divergent journey; thus, her double-proposal novels appear more unified than *Jane Eyre*. The double-proposal plot as deployed by Charlotte Brontë and improvised on by others *dis*unifies the novel's structure—it makes the part of the novel after the rejected proposal a doubled trajectory, responding to two questions: What would happen if the heroine remains unwed? What would happen if, after all, she marries the reformed hero? The double proposal allows readers to project two possible plots, one a story of character development and one a second courtship, either of which could typically resolve with the heroine's well-being.

The character development of the heroine is elaborated in *Jane Eyre* and provides a prototype for the double-proposal plot that many authors, including Barrett Browning, borrowed, adapted, or challenged. The first part of the novel follows Jane from her education through her gothic adventures to her first proposed union with Rochester.[7] Jane accepts Rochester's proposal against her better judgment, but after her wedding is interrupted by the revelation of his living wife, Bertha Mason, she refuses to become his mistress. Her plot is thus deflected from its courtship trajectory. Although Jane Eyre accepts Rochester when she believes he is offering her legitimate marriage (in which respect she is different from the double-proposal heroines who follow her), a double-proposal structure is implicit in the novel. As Rachel M. Brownstein puts it, "A white wedding, the conventional novel's and heroine's end, begins to take place in this novel's middle, but it fails to come off, and effects the heroine's separation from her lover, not her joining with him" (156). Once Jane's plot is deflected from union with Rochester, her character development comes to the forefront until the courtship is renegotiated.

Prior to the disruption, Jane and Rochester's relationship is clearly flawed. Jane's struggles during her first engagement reveal the potential dangers of marrying even the hero, even the "right man" before achieving independence and establishing a more equal bond. Jane must exercise all her strength during her engagement to resist Rochester's efforts to possess her. She does not wish to be seen "glittering like a parterre," to be "dressed like a doll," to be, in short, "enslaved" (296–97). She knows she must resist Rochester's advances and combat her passionate response to him because he threatens to attach her "to a chain" once he has "seized her" (299). Jane later admits the danger of her own passion for Rochester: "I could not, in those days, see God for His creature: of whom I had made an idol" (302). Neither Jane nor Rochester is yet "right" for the other. Patricia Meyer Spacks notes that "when an external force prevents her becoming Rochester's bride, it interrupts a relationship that seems already seriously marred" (64). Maurianne Adams also notes that "marriage at this point in the novel is not a smooth developmental transition so much as a rupture, raising a host of questions which the work, to its credit, does address. . . . Jane reaches the threshold of marriage three times in the novel. She cannot cross it until she can meet her 'master' as his partner and equal, his equal by virtue of her inheritance and family solidarity, his partner by virtue of their interdependence" (152).

In the remainder and second courtship of *Jane Eyre*'s plot, Jane becomes an "independent woman." She develops her ability to support herself in the village school, she inherits money and discovers a family, and she stands up to St. John Rivers, asserting her autonomy by refusing his insistent demands for marriage. Meanwhile, Rochester does penance for his attempt to trap Jane into bigamy and then to seduce her. He becomes reconciled to God and proves his integrity when he attempts to save his wife Bertha from burning Thornfield. These character changes complete, Bertha dies along with the obstacles she represents and Jane marries Rochester. The contrasts between Jane's two proposed marriages to Rochester are clear: Jane no longer depends on Rochester's bounty, no longer stands him "in the stead of a seraglio" (297). Rochester is no longer high-handed with Jane, but depends on her. Jane declares the egalitarian and companionate nature of their union: "I am my husband's life as fully as he is mine" (474). The plot remainder and second courtship, in establishing Jane's independence, implicitly argue that a good marriage requires more than just a union between the right man and the right woman.

The ending of *Jane Eyre* has been the subject of much contemporary critical debate. For example, Nancy Armstrong argues that "too many readers have seen Jane's ascendancy in the final chapters, not as a mutually enhancing exchange, but as the symbolic castration of Rochester" (53), while Sandra Gilbert and Susan Gubar defend the ending because Rochester and Jane marry as equals (369). Ann Ronald suggests that "the readers of *Jane Eyre* get mixed messages" (184), a reading Rachel Blau DuPlessis appears to confirm: "Jane Eyre may, in an individual or particularist tactic, change the material basis of marriage; when Jane becomes financially independent, the couple is socially interdependent. But Brontë does not change the emotional basis in romantic love" (9). Adams maintains, "The 'happy' ending . . . resolves some issues but sweeps others under the carpet" (154), and Brownstein argues that "*Jane Eyre* ends in a marriage that defiantly affirms not the heroine's transformation but her remaining herself. . . . Instead of being objectified by a narrator, Jane tells her own story, an intimate confidence" (156). In my view, the critical debate about *Jane Eyre*'s ending has developed in part because we can compare two possible marriages between Jane and Rochester; we can look at what might have been (when Rochester was healthy and domineering, Jane was poor and friendless and passion characterized their relationship) with what eventually is (the interdependent marriage that concludes the novel). Critical thought about the nature of good marriage, I think, is just what the double-proposal tradition tends to generate.

Elizabeth Barrett Browning's *Aurora Leigh* (1857) incorporates and reworks the *Jane Eyre* double-proposal plot, putting the heroine in greater control of the courtship, adopting the blinded and reformed hero, and developing the bildungsroman into a *Künstlerroman* in which the protagonist openly pursues self-fulfillment, establishing herself as a recognized poet before accepting the suitor. *Aurora Leigh* quickly became an additional source for the double-proposal novel in the United States. Augusta Evans directly responds to its second proposal scene in *St. Elmo* and Elizabeth Stuart Phelps's *The Story of Avis* is in part a meditation on the *Aurora Leigh* version of a double-proposal marriage ending.

In Barrett Browning's book-length poem, Aurora Leigh refuses to marry her cousin Romney Leigh and instead follows her calling as a poet. Aurora knows she cannot be both poet and Romney's wife because of Romney's traditional expectation that she will serve his needs and help forward his projects. Romney admits his low opinion of women's genius: "We get no Christ from you,—and verily / We shall not get a poet, in my mind" (44). He wants Aurora to commit herself to his social reform schemes instead of to art. Romney is "a sort of reincarnated St. John Rivers" (Gilbert and Gubar 575), as Aurora's response to him suggests:

> *What you love,*
> *Is not a woman, Romney, but a cause:*
> *You want a helpmate, not a mistress, sir,—*
> *A wife to help your ends . . . in her no end!*
> *Your cause is noble, your ends excellent,*
> *But I, being most unworthy of these and that,*
> *Do otherwise conceive of love. Farewell.*
> (50)

Aurora believes, "I did not love him . . . nor he me . . . that's sure" (53), and that Romney has "a wife already whom you love / Your social theory" (50). Furthermore, she is committed to her own goal: "I, too, have my vocation,— work to do, . . . Most serious work, most necessary work / As any of the economists'" (52). Whereas Jane Eyre rejects an adulterous proposition to strike out on her own, Aurora chooses between a bona fide marriage offer and an uncertain future as a poet. But as first proposed, marriage with Romney would have been flawed, as Dorothy Mermin notes: "In his proposal of marriage [Aurora] reads contempt for women . . . and although she is mistaken in thinking that he does not love her, she is right about his contempt, kindly as it is" (200–201).

Aurora becomes a well-known writer while Romney, partly because his reform schemes are continually foiled, comes to appreciate her view of the world. Reading Aurora's poetry helps him recognize the usefulness of poetry, while Aurora's experiences force her to discern social injustice more clearly. Romney is blinded when his home is burned by rioting crowds although he is not, like Rochester, also disfigured. Aurora, moved by the sudden discovery of his blindness, confesses her love and agrees to marry him.

The parallels to *Jane Eyre*'s plot were of course apparent to Barrett Browning's first readers. One 1857 reviewer writes, "We are especially sorry that Mrs. Browning has added one more to the imitations of the catastrophe in 'Jane Eyre,' by smiting her hero with blindness before he is made happy in the love of Aurora. . . . We think the lavish mutilation of heroes' bodies, which has become the habit of novelists, while it happily does not represent probabilities in the present state of things, weakens instead of strengthening tragic effect" ("Belles Lettres" 306). And another reviewer found that "it is disagreeable to be so forcibly reminded of a recent and popular work [*Jane Eyre*], when a small expenditure of ingenuity would have avoided the resemblance; which is enhanced by the fact that the incident proves in each case the solution of the story's knot" ("Mrs. Browning's Aurora Leigh" 428). That Barrett Browning chose not to exercise that ingenuity may suggest she was responding to the views of love and marriage and feminine self-assertion suggested by *Jane Eyre*.[8] When Aurora accepts Romney at the end of the poem, the plan for their marriage has changed. Aurora is now an established poet, and she will continue to write after the wedding. The renegotiated proposal finds Aurora stronger and Romney less dictatorial. Critics of *Aurora Leigh* debate the virtues of the marriage outcome, drawing its double-proposal precursor into the conversation. Helen Cooper notes that Aurora marries "a man with whom she can live as a sexual and intellectual equal," a conclusion she yet terms a "conventional happy ending" (185). Mermin sees the ending as Aurora's triumph and not such a conventional one since it transcends the norms of Victorian literature: "She gets much more than the nineteenth-century marriage plot usually allows its heroines: love *and* work *and* fame *and* independence *and* power. . . . Even *Jane Eyre* had no real independence and no vocation comparable to Brontë's or Barrett Browning's" (215). Gilbert and Gubar note that Aurora's rejection of Romney is set "into precisely the tradition of rebellious self-affirmation" pioneered when Jane Eyre rejected St. John Rivers; thus, "*Aurora Leigh* begins where *Jane Eyre* leaves off" (576). Cora Kaplan argues that the poem as a whole "should be read as an overlapping sequence of dialogues with other texts, other writers" (16), including, of course, *Jane Eyre*. Such intertextual and intercritical links demonstrate the literary and cultural dialogue motivated by double-proposal novels.

The double-proposal plot as presented in *Jane Eyre* and *Aurora Leigh* and adapted in other novels announces midway through a story (sometimes later) that the heroine has something to strive for other than marriage with the right man, and the novel shifts to a post-courtship bildungsroman or sometimes *Künstlerroman*. Usually, both the heroine and the hero mature, although the novel almost always focuses on the heroine's development. After refusing the hero's proposal, she might strive for more education, for achievements as a teacher, writer, or artist. She may develop other friendships that an early marriage would preclude, or, alternatively, she may prove that solitude is acceptable and perhaps even enjoyable or productive for a woman. The double-proposal plot also demands that the hero change. Typically, the first proposal does not result in marriage at least in part because something is wrong with the hero-to-be. If the heroine were to marry him the first time, she would sacrifice herself to a marriage that would inhibit her individual growth and subject her to a dominating husband. It is not enough that the suitor "loves" the heroine passionately; he needs to be reformed, humbled, or otherwise transformed so that when the heroine does accept him the marriage will be more egalitarian.

Because of its focus on reforming the hero and on the "peculiar terms" necessary for a more egalitarian relationship, the double-proposal plot destabilizes the myth of "Mr. Right," a myth that the traditional courtship plot tends to reinscribe. Boone describes the "Mr. Right" myth this way: "Each desiring subject is destined to meet the one perfect love-object 'made' for him or her; the perfect end of love is everlasting union with that individual; love will strike at first sight; sexual love transcends all material concerns; emotions are more valuable than reason in matters of the heart" (6–7). The double proposal challenges such notions by suggesting that the hero may have to undergo changes to become "Mr. Right," that the heroine might not fall in love at first sight, that the heroine may resist her sexual desires in deference to other, higher, or more reliable indexes to personal fulfillment and happiness, and that the heroine may rely on her reason to combat the desires of her body when her own welfare is at stake.

The interproposal space and the second version of the courtship create dialogue within the double-proposal plot and are often intertextual points of contact across double-proposal texts. In the plot remainder, the heroine pursues new goals and confronts new obstacles while the hero is on the side, usually improving himself for the second courtship. The second version of the courtship projects a comparison between two possible marriages between the same pair of characters. The doubled courtship suggests that marriage is a negotiable option that does not automatically grow out of the heroine's encounter with the right man. Instead, a good marriage is contingent on the maturity of the partners and on the fairness of the emotional contract between them. During the first engagement, Rochester contrasts conventional marriage with Jane's demands: "I fear you will compel me to go through a private marriage ceremony, besides that performed at the altar. You will stipulate, I see, for peculiar terms—what will they be?" (298). The second engagement and ensuing marriage articulate these "peculiar terms."

Reader response to double proposals suggests how the plot could generate dialogue about both its literary qualities and its relation to contemporary social reality. Consider the form-altering work of the double proposal in Jauss's terms:

> A literary work . . . predisposes its audience to a very specific kind of reception by announcements, overt and covert signals, familiar characteristics, or implicit allusions. It awakens memories of that which was already read, brings the reader to a specific emotional attitude, and with its beginning arouses expectations for the "middle and end," which can then be maintained intact or altered, reoriented, or even fulfilled ironically in the course of the reading according to specific rules of the genre or type of text. (23)

A double-proposal novel awakens expectations for a happy ending when the character marked out by the text as "hero" (even if he is not yet as admirable as most heroes of single-proposal fiction) proposes to the heroine. When the heroine, not because of misunderstanding or accident, but through her own choice, decides not to marry the hero, readers must adjust their "specific emotional attitude" and somehow process the altered plot. Readers may be frustrated by the schismatic nature of the double-proposal plot or puzzled because the weakening of the suitor typical of double-proposal conclusions makes him less like the conventional strong hero. Critics tend to process the rejected proposal as an aspect of the heroine's development. Adams's observation of "the neglect of the Moor House episodes in the interpretive and critical literature" (158) on *Jane Eyre* might, however, suggest that even aca-

demic readers have trouble working with episodes outside the normal narrative trajectory. Why do many readers and critics ignore the Moor House
section or find it boring? I have heard colleagues complain that the Moor
House part "goes on forever." Students also report being frustrated during
the latter portions of the novel and are not easily persuaded (in spite of considerable textual evidence) that Jane made a good decision when she struck
out on her own. Possibly Brontë did not write the Moor House chapters as
well as the earlier ones, but then again, perhaps even in a literary world pop-
ulated with alternative plots, late twentieth-century readers are still not prepared to read an alternate plot for a heroine once she is directed toward
marriage with the hero. Hollywood, not surprisingly, exaggerates our tendency to crowd out the alternate plot and push ahead to the marriage ending we have been trained to anticipate. Some film versions of *Jane Eyre* and
Pride and Prejudice cut short the post-refusal elements of the plots. The Moor
House episode disappears entirely in the 1944 film *Jane Eyre,* and in the 1940
version of *Pride and Prejudice* Lady Catherine's character is completely altered, so that instead of blocking the marriage (one of her functions in the
novel) she promotes it, helping to rush Elizabeth and Darcy back together
as soon as possible. It is difficult, of course, to judge how readers (or viewers) confront plot twists, but anecdotal and textual evidence suggests that they
may find it uncomfortable to process the double-proposal plot as a typical
delay of courtship consummation.

    The earliest readers of double-proposal novels at times gave evidence that
they, too, found double proposals distracting or puzzling. Reviewers' responses to a British double-proposal novel illustrate such discomfort. The
title character of *Grace Lee* (1855), a novel by the popular writer Julia Kavanagh, repeatedly turns away her suitor, John Owen, a surly and intensely passionate young man struggling to establish himself as a physician.[9] In one
review, written for *Blackwood's Edinburgh Magazine* and reprinted in *Littell's
Living Age,* a critic ascribes the faults of *Grace Lee* to Kavanagh's habit of re-
telling the story of *Jane Eyre,* "this conflict and combat of love or war"; *Grace
Lee* "exaggerates the repetition beyond all toleration" ("Modern Novelists—
Great and Small" 647). The reviewer ascribes the delays in the courtship to
Grace's capriciousness and John's ill-humor: "The lady first persecuted the
gentleman with attentions, kindnesses, scorn, and love; and the gentleman
afterwards persecutes the lady in the self-same way" (647). For this reviewer,
the double proposal is an annoying repetition of the *Jane Eyre* plot. All the
same, this writer seems to expect a courting couple to unite as soon as possible, sneering that "it is not till after a separation of many years, and when

they are at least middle-aged people, that this perverse couple are fairly settled at last" (647).

Writing for the *Westminster Review* in 1855, another reviewer briefly
praises the "animated, eloquent, and impassioned style" of *Grace Lee* as well
as the "power, pathos, grandeur, and imagery, which is both startling and fascinating," but spends most of the review puzzling over the prolonged courtship of the two main characters, both of whom "comport themselves in the
most extraordinary manner" by taking turns treating each other badly. This
reviewer's sympathies are with John Owen, for "who can forgive a woman,
who, because 'she is proud—very proud,' goes and hides herself away for seven
years from a man whom she knows is devoted to her, and whom she loves?"
Perhaps Owen should have left Grace in "her self-chosen obscurity" and wed
the other woman: "Marriage at thirty-three, with a winning and mobile
young beauty, would, we imagine, with most men, be preferred to marriage
at forty with a plain and middle-aged woman, however high-minded"
("Belles Lettres" 591–92). In offering this contribution to the double-proposal dialogue, this reader identifies with the "torture, neglect, and despair"
suffered by the suitor, rather than with that hero's reformation or with the
pride of the middle-aged heroine.

A writer for the *North American Review,* admiring the novel and its heroine overall, is frankly puzzled by the double-proposal plot. Admitting that
Grace is "proud, very proud" and that John did not always treat her well, this
reviewer has trouble understanding why, when "she afterwards loves him, as
he does her, with an intense and devoted love," Grace still refuses to marry
John: "We dare not call her a coquette, and she is not capricious; but she
knows, and in truth she values, the intensity of his love; she can measure it
by her own:—has she a *right* to refuse his hand without any reason which
can convince him of her firmness of purpose?" ("Grace Lee" 264). A *right* to
refuse! The reviewer is astonished that the heroine should exercise her power
of choice to reject a man who loves her and whom she loves in return. Romantic love is so powerful to this reviewer that Grace's knowledge of John's
faults, which include his obvious desire to possess and control her, are not
"reason enough" for the refusal. When Grace at length agrees to marry, she
offers to wed "to-morrow if you like, or in another seven years. I do not
care. . . . Love is immortal; yet love knows youth and age. When love is young
love knows no bliss beyond union and human happiness, because love is weak.
When love has lived and suffered, love grows strong and can bear solitude"
(293–94). Through the heroine's dialogue, *Grace Lee* contributes to cultural
and literary discussion about the definition of love and its place in a wom-

an's life, but as the reviewers testify, readers are not readily persuaded to give up their ideals of love. Kavanagh further explains her understanding of "love" in its different manifestations when she tells us that John's "very love, though passionate and mighty, was like himself, full of faults, full of errors" although it was also "perhaps his only virtue,—if virtue it could be called,—that he could love long and ardently a noble woman" (296, 299).

Neither Kavanagh's celebration of tested love nor her criticisms of the hero convinces the *North American Review* writer that Grace was justified in delaying the marriage so long. The reviewer admits that "much of the story would have been lost, but for these very misunderstandings," and that "we never tried to write a novel, and if we had, we should probably know no better." Still, a good writer such as Kavanagh should be able to "write a novel in which the story shall not depend upon a forced incident, or a want of consistent action on the part of her heroine" (266–67).

These reviews give us an unusually clear window into how readers may attempt to process a text that breaks literary and historical expectations. Consider such readers in Jauss's terms as "addressees" of the double-proposal text whose "active participation" makes possible the cultural work of novels such as *Grace Lee:* "The historical life of a literary work is unthinkable without the active participation of its addressees. For it is only through the process of its mediation that the work enters into the changing horizon-of-experience of a continuity in which the perpetual inversion occurs from simple reception to critical understanding, from passive to active reception, from recognized aesthetic norms to a new production that surpasses them" (19). The critic for the *North American Review* leaves an unusually strong record of the cognitive dissonance created when a text challenges a reader to move from "simple reception to critical understanding, from passive to active reception," while the *Westminster Review* notice shows how a reader can react to such a challenge by imagining different endings and offering judgments on the characters that defy the conclusions suggested by the text.

As demonstrated by Wilkie Collins's protest that opens this introduction, some nineteenth-century readers of double-proposal fiction recognized revolutionary tendencies in the genre, although many reviewers were too dismissive of women's novels in general and the *Jane Eyre* craze in particular to credit them with such power. Throughout this study, I will offer evidence to support the conclusion that double-proposal novels were actively engaged with the competing ideologies of their times and that writers worked with apparently inflexible plot conventions to contribute to contemporary debates on women's place at home and in the public sphere, on love and romance, on courtship and marriage. Jauss believes that "the gap between literature and history, between aesthetic and historical knowledge, can be bridged if literary history does not simply describe the process of general history in the reflection of its works one more time, but rather when it discovers in the course of 'literary evolution' that properly *socially formative* function that belongs to literature as it competes with other arts and social forces in the emancipation of mankind from its natural, religious, and social bonds" (45). Working from within the structures both of society and of that society's dominant novel form, the double-proposal tradition generates a dialogue that analyzes, critiques, and renegotiates the role of middle-class women in courtship and in public work spaces and attempts to forward the emancipation of womankind from the social bonds imposed by the dominant institution of marriage.

〜 〜

The courtship plot is perhaps the most recognized narrative in nineteenth- and twentieth-century fiction, its conventions immediately apparent to a wide range of readers. Hero and heroine meet, fall in love, encounter obstacles to their union that delay and frustrate them, and are then reconciled in the happy ending of imminent or achieved marriage. Boone describes this plot as one in which "lovers are sundered by a score of obstacles—including parents, wrong suitors, geography, personal prejudice, and class barriers—all of which must be removed to facilitate a successful alliance" (80). The courtship plot and especially the domestic novels that usually incorporate it are generally thought of as the province of the middle classes, particularly of white middle-class women, who were the primary writers and readers of popular fiction until late in the nineteenth century.[10] The utter predictability of the courtship plot and its assumed relevance to middle-class women provide a basis for understanding how the double-proposal version of that plot might have challenged readers' expectations and contributed to the ongoing reformation of both fictional and historical structures of courtship and marriage.

Courtship fiction has been read as contributing to, reflecting, promulgating, modifying, or advocating changes in middle-class perceptions of love and marriage. Even critics who subscribe to the view that the novels provide fantasy escapes from relatively mundane reality note that such fantasy is linked to "real life."[11] The happy ending typical of the courtship novel is frequently perceived as a metonym for the powerful pressure that ideology exerts on literature and on people or as a metonym for how patriarchy cir-

cumscribes women's possibilities as characters in novels or members of society.[12] While critics interpret the power of the courtship plot differently, they
agree that its relentless predictability in some way reinforces, replicates, or
registers oppressive cultural dictates, and they agree that texts that subvert,
deconstruct, or "write beyond" the conventional ending engage in the cultural work of challenging the monolithic social structure of middle-class
marriage.[13] More recently, however, critics have argued that even courtship
novelists who did not write form-breaking texts had more agency than earlier critics had given them credit for. These newer critical approaches deny
that courtship authors merely reproduce restrictive ideologies, either consciously or unconsciously.[14]

I am persuaded that courtship and marriage dominate the structure both
of middle-class novels and of middle-class lives, and I am also persuaded that
novelists used their heroines' power of choice among suitors to give those
characters some agency within the restrictive ideology of marriage. But writers of double proposals go beyond emphasizing the heroine's power of choice
between suitors to suggest that the heroine also has the power to negotiate
within given courtship contracts. In other words, a heroine might not only
accept or refuse marriage conditions set before her but also could, by exer-
cising both her right of refusal and her ability to take an alternate path, influence the marriage arrangement she eventually accepts. The double-proposal heroine is not necessarily sundered from her suitor by "a score of
obstacles," but rather by her own choice not to marry him so that she may
do something else. She is not "separated by tragic accidents" from her hero,
but might decide he is not yet the right partner for her. In other words, the
double-proposal heroine differs from the single-proposal heroine because of
how she uses her prerogative of choice. When she decides not to accept the
hero's (or hero-to-be's) offer, she creates a possibility of courtship negotiation that does not exist in the single-proposal plot. In addition, she asserts
that she might have a life goal more significant to her than marriage with
the "right" suitor.

When they doubled the proposal structure of their novels, many authors
managed to write inside and outside the courtship box in the same novel,
creating heroines who experiment with alternative plots before returning to
the courtship plot and marrying the hero after all. Double proposals allow
writers to write "beyond the ending" and to match up the couple at the end
within the same work. Double-proposal narratives stay within the letter of
the law of the courtship plot by reuniting the hero and heroine; by breaking
expectations within that plot, however, they challenge a reader's complacency

and push the boundaries of the heroine's possibilities, and by extension, of nineteenth-century woman's possibilities. The countertradition of double-proposal novels developed within the tradition before it was more radically restructured by later writers. Double-proposal novels engage in cultural dialogue over women's roles in love stories and in work stories.

The ironic distance critics frequently assume toward narratives of love and marriage might discourage us from looking closely at what definitions of "love" and what understandings of "marriage" underlie the apparently easy clichés that are operative in the "happy endings" of popular novels. But sympathetic reading of popular fiction reveals that definitions of "love" were anything but static and that authors were actively working to understand, inculcate, modify, or promote particular interpretations of "love." To understand the cultural work of the double-proposal tradition we need, as Jauss suggests, to reconstruct "the horizon of expectations, in the face of which a work was created and received in the past"; such reconstruction "enables one . . . to pose questions that the text gave an answer to, and thereby to discover how the contemporary reader could have viewed and understood the work" (28). Social histories of the nineteenth century reveal that in the culture, as in the fiction, courting couples, their parents, and social arbiters vigorously debated over "love" and over control of courtship and marriage. Throughout the period covered by this study, popular understanding continued to evolve as couples took increasing control over their courtships and, by extension, over their adult lives. Throughout this study, I use social history, tied as closely as possible to the historical moment and regional environment of a text's reception, to help interpret the work, to specify what problems it might have been attempting to solve, and to identify what new questions it may have posed. In modifying love-plot messages through the double-proposal plot, writers were responding to cultural changes in concepts of love, courtship, and marriage and in doing so attempted to influence as well as comment upon those changes. Novelists, living amid ideological shifts and conflicts, did not blandly assume that "true love" (whatever that might be) automatically guaranteed "happily ever after" marriages (however er those might be configured).

Puritans assumed that mutual affection should exist between a couple who planned to marry, so the concept that married people should love each other was hardly invented by later Americans. But Puritans believed "not so much that love ought to be the foundation or origin of marriage as that the couple could expect that time would bring love into their relationship" (Degler 14). Such early notions of love did not give sexual attraction the central place it was to attain later. Sexual impulses were suspect to the Puritan settlers because "sensual feelings were thought to disturb the emotional and moral constancy the Puritans sought . . . [and] eroticism anticipated the danger of idolatry" (Seidman 14). John D'Emilio and Estelle Freedman found that in colonial courtship a couple's choice "rested largely upon a sense of compatibility rather than on notions of romantic love. Couples hoped to develop loving relationships, and courtship gave them an opportunity to begin the process" (21).

Ideals of sex, love, romance, and marriage shifted, and the notion that romantic love should dictate who an individual chose to marry gained primacy gradually through the eighteenth and nineteenth centuries. At the turn into the nineteenth century, many Americans still distrusted romantic love, though romance was by then celebrated in fiction: "The romance of novels was not the stuff of which good marriages were made" (Rothman 103). D'Emilio and Freedman note that "parents and children who lived during this transitional period were likely to be in conflict over the relative roles of the family and the individual in choosing a marriage partner" (43). "Love" was viewed more and more as a mysterious, perhaps preordained attraction between a couple, an attraction that might include physical desire but was primarily a matter of spiritual affinities. This sort of love was the expected basis of marriage, especially among the middle classes of the Northeast. "Between the 1820s and the 1880s middle-class courtship became an intensely private affair. . . . Courtship involved a delicate ritual, a sharing of hearts that only gradually overcame middle-class reticence about sexuality [and the] language of romantic love increasingly entered the vocabulary of courting couples" (D'Emilio and Freedman 75). By midcentury, Ellen K. Rothman maintains, "with marriage so dependent on and identified with love, the ability to recognize and experience 'true love' became all important" (103). The development of this view of love is partly attributed to Romanticism, to the development of the concept of an internal self. Karen Lystra argues that the "sense of a hidden, but purer individual essence is the basis of the 'romantic self,'" and this self was used by nineteenth-century lovers "to stress that the truest portion of their personal identity was concealed by social conventions" (30). The nineteenth-century version of "falling in love" derives from the notion of this inner, true self that one could fully reveal only to a loved one; knowledge of and love for the true self of the partner established the intimacy that could lead to marriage.

The influence of these shifting ideas about love and marriage gained power rapidly. Children wrested control of their love lives from their parents because, as Lystra tells us, the "ideal of companionate marriage challenged the very ground upon which parents exercised control over the choice of a husband or wife. They could objectively measure duty and judge domestic, business, and other performance skills, but they could not evaluate the privatized experience of emotional openness and personal satisfaction" (158). The companionate marriage ideal, Seidman reports, differed from an economic exchange of domestic duties for money, security, and status or from erotic attraction, and so marrying primarily for economic or social betterment became more suspect than it had been before the ideal of romantic love became so pervasive. Furthermore, romantic love and the ideal companionate marriage that was supposed to grow from it came to have a spiritual justification, and women could claim their right to a happy marriage based not merely on personal desire for contentment but on divine sanction: "Beyond promoting female autonomy, the notion of the spirituality of love entailed a new ideal of marriage. A marriage based on spiritual love carried high expectations for personal happiness and companionship" (31). By midcentury there was widespread acceptance of the notions that love was a natural, or perhaps even preordained, attraction between people that could not be caused or prevented by an act of will. "Rather than choosing a mate whom one might come to love through marriage, middle-class youth now expected to 'fall in love' before agreeing to marry" (D'Emilio and Freedman 75). Rothman reports that falling in love became "desirable, even compulsory" (105), although the marriage that might result should be based not merely on passion but also on mutuality, companionship, and compatibility.

It is not always clear what role sexual attraction played in nineteenth-century notions of "falling in love," but certainly nineteenth-century Americans were not so prudish in their private lives as history has sometimes depicted them. To put nineteenth-century notions of "true love" into context, consider how the concept has continued to shift through the twentieth century. In his history of the "sexualizing of love" Seidman argues that the twentieth-century notion of "true love" is far more sexualized than was the nineteenth-century definition. "Love changed," Seidman tells us, "from having an essentially spiritual meaning to being conceived in a way that made it inseparable from the erotic longings and pleasures of sex" (4). For white, middle-class, Victorian America, love was "a spiritual affinity and spiritual companionship." Although Victorians did not deny sexuality, they sought "to control the place of sex in marriage" by "urging the desexualization of love and the desensualization of sex" (7). Rothman's and Lystra's research uncovered many courtship letters that include frank discussion of sexual feelings and so suggests that Seidman might be overstating the Victorian emphasis on "spiritual" love, but his overall thesis that those in the twentieth century valorized the sexual aspect of love far more than did those in the nineteenth still appears sound. From our perspective nineteenth-century depictions of love might seem to sublimate sexual attraction as a sort of spiritual love, but making sexual attraction the dominant evidence of being "in love" is a twentieth-century construct. Nineteenth-century Americans promoted a cultural ideal of marriage based on "true love," but that love was not primarily passionate, physical, sexual. Instead, love was supposed to be based on companionship and spiritual, emotional, and intellectual affinities. The ideal marriage was to be spring from spontaneous love, but was also to follow the companionate ideal: both men and women should find personal fulfillment, happiness, and contentment in marriage. In a companionate marriage, the spouses were to have similar tastes and values.

These cultural ideals of romantic love and companionate marriage contain contradictory impulses that lend themselves to exploration in novels: if "falling in love" is outside one's control, or to use a different metaphor, springs from an inner self (the heart) that is not in control of the rational self (the mind), how can one carefully choose a companion for life whose tastes and habits suit one's own? The path to true love was based on a deep knowledge of the beloved's "true self," a self that was distinguished from the public face one wore outside the realm of private relationships. But how could one both love that other self freely and passionately and rationally judge whether he or she would be a good companion? The paradox of rational choice and involuntary love provides ample material for novels in which characters struggle with contradictory forces, with passionate impulses at war with rational selves. A double-proposal heroine often faces just such an internal struggle when she rejects a suitor's first proposal. She is attracted to the hero, and she frequently labels her attraction "love," but her thinking self realizes that he would not be a good marriage companion. Double proposals attempt to resolve tensions between involuntary romantic love and voluntary choice of a life mate.

In the antebellum South, the shift toward companionate and egalitarian marriage was complicated by the hierarchical racial, social, and economic system that depended upon the supremacy of the privileged white male. Courting southern couples were inevitably influenced by the love ideals being promoted in fiction and elsewhere, but were obliged to accommodate them to distinctive southern values. Steven Stowe reports that when describing their courtships southern couples "drew upon imagery that mirrored fiction and paralleled the circumstances implied by novelists," and they "rarely analyzed particular reasons for falling in love because love was not particular to individuals. Love was destined to be" (*Intimacy and Power* 84, 86). However, southerners always had to accommodate such shifting views to their own "peculiar institution."[15] The privileged white class of the South was structured by the white male's domination of his wife and daughters as well as his slaves. Because of slavery and the economics it supported, the plantation household was an economic unit for which the North had no parallel. Parents were therefore concerned with how their children's marriages would consolidate or divide plantation wealth. New courtship and marriage ideals offered potentially dangerous economic and social repercussions. Stowe suggests how southern fathers might have attempted to circumvent such threats: "It seems that fathers were able to assert themselves in a daughter's affair by using family affection. The rise of affection as a basis for marriage, in the planter class at least, cannot therefore be seen as a simple advance in women's autonomous choice of lover or mate. Parents stood close by to influence as best they could a new family relation in the image of the old" ("Not-So-Cloistered Academy" 102). Elsewhere, Stowe contrasts southerners' attitudes toward courtship with those of northerners, who were "notably less bound by form and convention perhaps because marriage in the free states had none of the overt social display of racial authority and class continuity so important to the planter class." Therefore, "the planters continued to adhere to the older forms, however modified by romantic or sentimental idiom, which gave a formal superstructure to their desires" (*Intimacy and Power* 79, 89).

As noted above, companionate marriage ideals grew from and nurtured individualism and were therefore implicitly progressive. Southerners were conscious that companionate marriage implied some equality between husband and wife and that feminists advocated egalitarian marriages. Any change that echoed feminism, any ideal that suggested egalitarianism of course threatened the hierarchical paradigm that defenders of the South believed justified slavery and therefore planter culture as a whole. Sally G. McMillen found that "many [southern] antebellum white women embraced the ideal of a companionate relationship, an expectation that through marriage, one would find a friend, lover, and soulmate for life. Yet companionship, then as now, implies equality" (20). Privileged southern women were caught between the desire to improve their own position in marriage and the need to defend the system that accorded them status and wealth. As apologists for slavery and authors of double-proposal novels, Caroline Hentz and Augusta Evans tried to work their way around the inherent threat to the southern way of life posed by renegotiated marriage. The courtship plots they offer attempt to negotiate marriages that partake of northern ideals of companionate wedlock and offer the heroine increased power, but that also claim to strengthen the hierarchical system which demanded that women continue to defer to men. Those novels demonstrate what Stowe called the "tug of war between cultural values and individual wishes [that] was given new shape by the ascendance of romantic love as a widely shared value for personal relationships" (*Intimacy and Power* 89).

The consensus among almost all who wrote on the topic, privately or publicly, was that marriage should be based on love, but assumptions about what "love" actually was varied. Concepts of love and marriage were topics for both mainstream and reform debates. The evidence of changing love ideologies used by the social historians cited above comes from both mainstream public discourses and private correspondence. But the shifts in how people thought about being in love and getting married are revealed not only in such mainstream sources but also in the vanguard of reform. Feminists encouraged people to formulate notions of true love, courtship, and marriage emphasizing the companionate rather than the romantic or sentimental aspects of love. "The majority of nineteenth-century women may have had nothing to do with feminism or suffrage," Lystra points out, but "one of the most unappreciated effects of the first woman's movement is not measured in women's direct participation or ideological adherence to woman's rights, but rather in a growing uncertainty over female commitment to standard sex-role boundaries" (148).

William Leach's work attests to the significance of love and marriage reform in the feminist agenda. According to Leach, feminists divided cultural notions of love into three categories: romantic (based on sexual attraction), sentimental (driven by cultural objectification of women), and companionate or rational (growing from similarities between partners' values and interests). The feminists Leach surveys denigrated romantic and sentimental love and promoted rational love as the only safe basis for marriage. Sentimental love had to be demystified because it "portrayed women as idealized objects and the passive recipients of masculine affections. In their place feminists put a rational, symmetrical, and egalitarian love based on a knowledge that made no room for ideality, passion, or fantasy" (100). Romantic love had to be combatted because it "rested on fantasies of the Other (any sexual Other) that arose from needs within the self" (106). In short, embracing sentimental love could cause a woman to sacrifice self in favor of husband, while embracing romantic love could lead her to destroy herself in a passion of narcissism and self-absorption. Either mistake was bad for marriage and bad for society. "Feminists struggled," Leach tells us, "to forge a new, rational union between the sexes, a union based on what they often referred to as true love" (3). In promoting this rational love as "true" love, feminists tried to counteract what they saw as the destructive potential of both romantic and sentimental love.

Novelists, even when avowedly conservative, were often in tune with feminist reformers in the arena of love and marriage debates. The writers examined in this study tend to factor sexuality and sentimentality into their characterization in ways that suggest they agree with feminists that rational love is more likely to promote women's welfare than romantic or sentimental love. Only strong heroines can deny their physical attraction to the heroes and force themselves to wait until they know the hero better, until the hero has improved himself, or until they have achieved goals that they could not strive for in marriage. Only a thinking heroine can resist the hero's efforts to idealize her into a sentimental icon and insist that he improve himself rather than rely on her superior spiritual status to "save" him. From the perspective of the double proposal, the more spiritualized, less passionate love realized at the end of the novels is superior to its earlier, more earthy or more sentimentalized manifestation. Novelists often suggest that it is the stronger couple who marries after passion has receded or after the sentimental attraction has been tested by experience. Thus the "happy endings" that conclude double-proposal fiction are almost never blissful, unthinking endorsements of matrimony; on the contrary, they are reflective or ambiguous or awkward or visionary or tense.

The novels I will examine usually advocate the spiritual or rational definition of love as most apt to promote the welfare of women. The first proposal generally appeals to the heroine's sexual attraction to the hero, to her economic self-interest, or to her desire to fulfill a sentimental ideal for her suitor. For example, in *Pride and Prejudice,* Darcy's first proposal springs from a passion that has overcome his own rational objections, and he assumes Elizabeth will consent out of self-interest. Their eventual engagement is based on quite different premises. They know, understand, and respect each other more fully when they do marry. Jane Eyre is pressured by both her sexual attraction to Rochester and her economic self-interest to accept the first proposal. After the wedding is interrupted, Rochester appeals to the sentimental ideal, pleading with Jane to fulfill the role of angel of mercy; Jane refuses. The marriage she eventually chooses is based on their deep knowledge of each other. Mutual understanding, Jane tells us, makes their marriage ideal; Jane and Rochester achieve a companionate marriage in the place of the passionate but immoral union that would have been consummated had Jane accepted Rochester's adulterous offer.

This is not to suggest, however, that novelists subscribed to the notion—advocated by some advice writers but apparently never widely accepted—that women lacked, or even should lack, sexual feelings. American Victorians did circulate a notion that women were "passionless," but the discussion raised around women's sexual nature has to do with their control over their lives rather than over whether they experienced sexual desire. Nancy F. Cott, drawing on social prescriptions and medical and religious authorities, identified a notion of female passionlessness she described as "a cluster of ideas about the comparative weight of woman's carnal nature and her moral nature; it indicated more about drives and temperament than about actions and is to be understood more metaphorically than literally" (163). Understood in these limited terms, "passionlessness" offered advantages because it "elevated women as moral and intellectual beings and disarmed them of their sexual power" (168). Furthermore, "passionlessness" could provide women more control over the sexual aspect of their relationships both before and after marriage. Real or assumed "passionlessness," Rothman finds from examining correspondence, allowed women some control over reproduction (137). Cott also notes that "on a practical level, belief in female passionlessness could aid a woman to limit sexual intercourse within marriage and thus limit family size" (173). Feminists, Leach discovers from examining their publications, did not deny that women felt sexual desire, but did want both men and women to "develop the detached capacity to observe and study their own sexual behavior . . . to step out of their bodies. They believed that this intellectual stepping out would defuse the body's power to disrupt human relations, thereby marking the first step toward controlling sexuality" (53–54). The threat of becoming unmarriageable because of premarital sexual activity (a threat not manufactured by the seduction novel), the dangers of pregnancy and childbirth after marriage, and perhaps also the danger of becoming too subject to a husband's sexual appetite made it wise for a woman to control her own desire and thereby her mate's. Some feminists argued, for example, that a "passive, servile, dependent woman devoted only to childbearing and childrearing or an aggressive man obsessed with sexual dominance 'destroyed the best qualities of both and the best interests of Humanity'" (qtd. in Leach 32–33). The issues related to "passionlessness" all have to do with control rather than with physical desire, and when problems are caused by desire in double-proposal fiction, the issues similarly center on the heroine's control over herself and her suitor rather than on whether desire itself exists or is good or bad.

The need to control sexual activity partially explains why women were much more apt to prefer long engagements than were men. In addition, for women the choice of a marriage partner was far more momentous than it was for a man because women gave up so much more, risked so much more (legally, as well as emotionally and physically). Rothman notes that "men tended to see engagement as the time before they *could* marry, while women viewed it as the time before they *would* marry" (157). For many women, the choice of a marriage partner was the "one truly fateful choice in their lives" (163).

Because of the significance of the marriage choice for women, ascertaining the strength of her lover's emotional bond to her was crucial in assuring her future happiness. Lystra argues that new conceptions of love made marriage depend so much on the strength of emotional commitment that nineteenth-century courtship was characterized more than anything else by testing rituals, especially the woman (as the more vulnerable partner) testing the man. The tests seem designed to examine and extend the lover's emotional commitment. Women, for example, would suggest various weaknesses in themselves or other possible obstacles to a happy union and the men would have to "pass" the tests by explaining away or otherwise overcoming these obstacles. The testing ritual was "a cycle of emotional testing which required ever more convincing demonstrations of romantic love" (166). Usually courtship testing would culminate in a crisis test of sorts—often a broken engagement—and if the man (or woman, in some cases) passed this test, marriage would finally follow. Lovers felt that the process of testing and passing deepened and strengthened their knowledge of each other and therefore their love. Couples often believed that the ultimate test, the broken engagement or rejected proposal, led to a deeper commitment and a happier marriage.

Lystra's study of courtship suggests that, through their correspondence, couples in effect impressed a narrative on their lives that is similar to the double-proposal novel plot. The double-proposal plot structure, because of how it may test suitors and contrast proposed marriages with one another and with potential careers, provided a pattern that reflected many actual courtships, and writers used that plot to participate in the cultural dialogue about women's roles, courtship behaviors, and love ideology. The double-proposal structure allows novelists to test a range of possible intimate relationships, a range of possible emotional contracts. Other courtship fiction uses multiple plots as a tool for contrasting different couples, but doubling the courtship narrative of the same couple may generate more compelling multiple interpretations of love and marriage because the same couple is tested in different emotional contracts. Some novelists use the plot at once to participate in fantasies of idealized sentimental and romantic love and to critique them, a convenient strategy for writers working in generically restricted forms and writing for generically trained readers. Novelists also use the doubled plot to test the sexual component of a couple's relationship and to underscore the need for women's control of the sexual aspects of their relationships. Characters in double-proposal fiction typically struggle with the deceptions inherent in sentimental and romantic love, and they come to appreciate a rational and companionate love. When novelists portray relationships with delayed culminations, they apparently are representing how actual couples strove for the Victorian ideal of companionate, warm, spiritualized love and how courtships were directed toward choosing a marriage based on "true" knowledge of the loved one.

While reshaping concepts of love, the double proposal also holds up possibilities for heroines outside of marriage. As they deflect and defer the consummation of the love plot, authors set their heroines out on alternative paths. The heroines grow stronger and more independent after they refuse the first proposal. Relying on their own resources—typically their own intellectual resources—they develop a sense of themselves that does not rely on the hero's confirmation and approval, and in fact they often rebel directly against the hero's desires. The protagonist's increased independence aids her when finally she chooses a renegotiated marriage in which her power has been increased. Her options have been extended, not diminished, by refusing the hero the first time; she is much better off when she accepts him later.

The opportunities outside of marriage made available in the alternative plot should not be exaggerated, however. Female characters have few realistic options until late in the century. The only jobs open for genteel but needy women were teaching, dressmaking, or, for the exceptionally talented and fortunate, writing (Kessler-Harris 62–63). The novelists in this study do their best to exploit these options, but they never risk their heroines' class status by having them work in factories or go on the stage. Many protagonists, including Caroline Hentz's Eoline Glenmore and Augusta Evans's Beulah Benton and Edna Earl, follow the Jane Eyre model and achieve independence by teaching. Teaching has the advantage of demanding that heroines develop and demonstrate their intellectual capacities and may also provide a basis for beginning a writing career. For the first decade or so after *Jane Eyre* was published, genteel heroines bound by realistic expectations had no other options. Adventure heroines, such as those created by E. D. E. N. Southworth, mark out alternative plots by behaving like men, perhaps even disguising themselves as men. Drawing on opportunities made available by the Civil War, Southworth makes a case for intellectual and political equality by projecting a woman into a man's role. Later in the century, as women finally broke into the professions, heroines entered more advanced courses of study. Elizabeth Stuart Phelps creates one heroine who is a homeopathic physician and another who pursues a painting career.

After marriage, middle-class women of the midnineteenth century seldom labored for a living even in these acceptable areas; to do so might compromise their dignity, respectability, and social standing. Carl Degler argues that the "economic basis of the cult of domesticity in the 19th century was that a married woman usually did not have to work for money, that she could live on her husband's wages if he was a city dweller, or on his income if he was a farmer" (375). Single women had much more latitude for nondomestic work than married women did, and whereas middle-class women in the early and middle nineteenth century typically "counted on marriage to free them from the burdens of paid employment" (Rothman 158), the next generation was more likely to find satisfaction in a career: "Where their antebellum counterparts had looked to marriage as a release from the isolation and insecurity of school keeping, these women were more likely to see marriage as bringing an end to something they enjoyed." Because custom still made it difficult to reconcile career and marriage, "many of them chose to delay marriage or to remain single" (Rothman 249). Reform of employment and marriage laws made it more conceivable that a woman might combine marriage and career, but the visions of feminists for such dual lives for women were slow to find fruition, even in the North (Leach 167–79).[16] The social disapproval of married women who worked was strongest among the southern planter class, and southern women were slower to insist that the professions be opened to them.

As the century progressed, double-proposal heroines revealed more and more conflict when they were asked to sacrifice careers for marriages, and the novels thus track changes in women's attitudes toward work outside the home as well as their attitudes toward love and marriage. At midcentury, advanced education for women was still justified by arguments that it would better suit them for their domestic roles: "The growing acceptance of women's intellect and intellectual training was restricted to the private sphere . . . to make better wives and mothers" (Lystra 127). Although double-proposal novels may reiterate this justification for education and brief premarriage careers, generally the heroine's career influences the world beyond her childhood home or her prospective home, suggesting that the goal of women's development may be more than to fit them for the domestic sphere. Furthermore, double-proposal fiction registers women's increasing desire to enter the professions. Only one of Caroline Hentz's heroines works, and that out of temporary necessity. Augusta Evans's heroines are openly ambitious, but they justify their careers as extending womanly influence into other homes. When their marriages apparently demand they relinquish their careers, that release is painful. Elizabeth Stuart Phelps's postwar professional heroines attempt to combine marriage and career, trying to balance their longing for domestic love and security with desire for autonomy and self-development.

The double-proposal heroines are rarely openly feminist, but always ambitious for women in that their careers are more successful than a typical woman's career of the time. Even when the heroines imitate life by sacrificing their careers to marriage, the eventual marriages raise difficult questions about women's careers, autonomy, and domesticity. The renegotiated marriages that close most double-proposal novels involve some conflict, some compromise, some tension. Sometimes this is expressed by the heroine, sometimes by other characters; other times it is strongly suggested by tension or glaring silence in the text. These novels may be read as evidence that writers and readers of novels struggled with the problem of marriage and autonomy for women and advocated not necessarily radical reform, but certainly ongoing negotiation of women's roles without and within marriage.

Most critics agree that the ending of a courtship novel is of fundamental importance to the ideological bent of the work as a whole. Whether the marriage closure is critiqued as yet another repetition of the ideological prescription for marriage or valorized as a demonstration of the heroine's positive use of her power of choice, that closure is viewed as central to the cultural meaning of the novel: "Once the possibility of a straight line between the romantically attracted protagonists has been established and 'two' become 'one,' the plot in effect returns to the one-dimensionality from which it arose" (Boone 80–81). Double-proposal plots offer the potential of that "one-dimensionality" only to split the narrative again; they raise the possibility of fulfilling the "desired condition" only to deflect that fulfillment. After the first proposal, two lines may open out, and the double-proposal novel asks new questions and provokes new plots. What would happen if the heroine chose not to marry the hero? If she retained her power of self-determination beyond the moment—the proposal scene—that might have ended it? What would she do next? How would the proposal scene be different if it were replayed and the heroine chose to accept the hero after all? The double proposal can be a powerful narrative because, in the very structure of its plot, it asks such questions. It enables authors to project more than one possible plot for heroines of courtship novels and to challenge cultural norms about women's lives and women's work while still moving, indirectly, toward the conventional outcome. Working with the double-proposal plot, authors create stories that, instead of conforming absolutely to the predetermined courtship mold, hold out more than one narrative trajectory for their heroine at the crucial point when the hero proposes. Through this doubled narrative structure, the novels comment on alternatives to marriage and contribute to cultural dialogue on the nature of romance, courtship, and marriage.

Notes

1. Collins's article not only testifies to how frequently double-proposal novels were written but also highlights the link between British and American literary discourses because it was first published in *Household Words* in England and reprinted in *Littell's Living Age* in the United States. The writer (identified as Collins by Richard Lettis 38) poses as a member of a self-styled group of eager novel readers he terms the "Disreputable Society," a group containing himself, his wife, his daughters, and his nieces (the society does not apparently include his son, although that "character" appears later in the article). As a man publishing in a popular journal, in charge of his family, and directing his "Disreputable Society," he speaks from a position of triple authority. He opposes his "Disreputable Society" to other reading groups, most notably the "respectable and dull" people who believe novel reading to be a "dangerous luxury and an utter waste of time" (180), the librarians who bow to the respectable people and relegate novels to the end of their booklists, and the critics who "may say that one novel is worth enjoying, and that another is not" (181). As a writer of sensational fiction, Collins does not himself fit any of these posited groups, and one can only speculate on the source of his irritation with the new breed of novels he identifies. Evidence from Collins's fiction reveals he also experimented with gender roles and created transgressive female characters, and I would not venture a guess as to his intentions in writing this humorous column about his female competitors' work. Collins's own "sensational" novels have recently been analyzed in terms of their intriguing treatment of gender. Donald E. Hall finds that "gender fluidity abounds" (154) in Collins's work and that "gender subversions are rampant, though not necessarily welcomed in a univocal, uniform fashion" (174).

2. Laws of coverture effectively make the wife a piece of property, a slave to her

husband. According to William Leach, "feminists saw in the slavemaster, and later in the capitalist, the figure of the economically rapacious patriarchal husband who robbed his wife of her just remuneration, threw her into extremes of 'parasitical' degradation, bound her to narrow patterns of behavior, and prevented the 'growth, maturity, and health' so typical, they thought, of egalitarian relationships" (192).

3. The plot can, simply by having the heroine recant, of course be turned to reactionary as well as progressive purposes; such conservative renditions include Alfred Tennyson's *The Princess* and Henry James's *The Bostonians;* such texts are clearly in dialogue with other voices on women's issues and are considered in later chapters.

4. This motivation has become apparent only in recent years. The first twentieth-century critics to study nineteenth-century women's novels apparently did so at least partly to justify excluding those novels from the canon. In any case, their work did not encourage or lead to additional work (Brown; Cowie; Papashvily). The few published dissertations that perfunctorily surveyed a popular writer's work and described her biography (one each on Southworth and Evans) also failed to provoke ongoing interest. Feminist critics began more promising avenues of research when they found evidence of feminist impulses in the texts of Victorian writers, of awkward tensions and contradictions, of pregnant silences, of self-conscious rescriptings of male narratives, of struggles within writers' dual lives as women and as writers, and of outbursts of anger at woman's condition (Gilbert and Gubar; Miller; Kelley). This criticism, however, ignores much of what nineteenth-century women writers produced because most of that work is too conventional to appeal to feminist critics, who prefer to study novels that obviously break with generic and societal dictates. Among the first American women's novels to be reprinted were Kate Chopin's *The Awakening*, whose heroine rejects her dual roles as wife and mother, Elizabeth Drew Stoddard's *The Morgesons*, which features an iconoclastic heroine, and Elizabeth Stuart Phelps's *The Story of Avis*, which examines a struggling marriage. Feminist interests led critics to valorize those books whose female protagonists are crushed in the machinery of the male system (Edith Wharton's *House of Mirth*, Chopin's *The Awakening*) and to brush aside those in which the protagonist is integrated happily ever after (the bulk of women's novels). Critics celebrated fictions that depict strong women in solitude (Sarah Orne Jewett's *The Country of the Pointed Firs*) and set aside more conventional texts. Furthermore, in rereading canonized novels such as *Jane Eyre,* critics focused on elements such as repressed anger or problematized sexuality that can be read as implicitly criticizing the courtship plots in which they were developed. Much of this earlier feminist criticism on nineteenth-century novels assumes that female freedom is incompatible with a marriage closure. Novels with a focus on courtship and an ending in happy marriage remained frustrating to critics who searched for protest and raised consciousnesses in earlier women writers. A happy ending in marriage was frequently perceived as capitulating to patriarchy, as marrying "in defeat" (Spacks 158). On the whole, women writers who stayed within the confines of the marriage plot were viewed as hopelessly conservative, as complicit

in the patriarchal domination of family and society and therefore as less interesting to study that their openly rebellious contemporaries.

5. The critical discourse that has proven most fruitful for studying the large body of popular novels by American women was generated by Nina Baym's *Woman's Fiction*. Instead of searching for the exceptional feminist text, she studied the mainstream popular works that women were writing and reading in the midnineteenth century. In the process of studying the genre in its most popular form, Baym uncovered a strong undercurrent of interest in women's issues. Building on this historical work, critics have begun developing ways to analyze and interpret woman's fiction as a product and an agent of its historical context, by, for example, examining the "cultural work" that texts do (Tompkins) or finding through formal analysis protofeminist critiques of male-centered institutions (Harris, *Nineteenth-Century American Women's Novels*). Tompkins and Harris use formal analysis combined with reader-response approaches to illuminate how novels might have been read or might have influenced readers or might have engaged their historical moments. Harris's readings of several women's novels are based on the contention, now accepted by many critics, that early readers could "read on more than one level, could penetrate beneath the novels' 'covers'" (14). Erica R. Bauermeister argues that we are now prepared to move beyond categorizing women's novels by their adherence to a common genre and to "look more closely at the differences between works in order to see the richness of and variety among the ever-increasing number of newly rediscovered texts, and to help substantiate the autonomy of individual works" (17). Indeed, many critics now agree with Barbara Bardes and Suzanne Gossett, who maintain that "nineteenth-century fiction provides an extremely rich and complex set of sources for understanding the cultural changes that brought woman into the public sphere" (5). A work that manifests this richness and complexity is Lora Romero's *Home Fronts*, which examines the figure of the domestic woman in order to challenge the binary nature of our thinking about power relations: "Instead of a monumental and centralized struggle between mind-numbing popular doctrine and demystifying marginal critique, *Home Fronts* describes different horizons of representation on which struggles for authority played themselves out in the antebellum period: the middle-class home, the frontier, African American activism, social reform movements, and homosocial high culture" (7).

6. Twentieth-century critics readily assume that *Jane Eyre* influenced popular American fiction, although no one has systematically studied that impact. Fred Pattee refers to *Jane Eyre* several times in discussing the excessive emotionalism (as he sees it) characteristic of the 1850s. He says that realism must have seemed "out of place in romance that was to be read by the women who had reread *Jane Eyre*" and later announces that Augusta Evans's *St. Elmo*, "in out–*Jane Eyreing* even *Jane Eyre*" with its "gorgeous ultra-romantic atmospheres," featured a "Byronic, Mr. Rochester–like hero [who] bowled over a whole generation of romantic school-girls" (111–12, 125). William Perry Fidler compares Wilson's characters to *Jane Eyre* counterparts, not-

ing the similarities between St. Elmo Murray and Rochester and between Beulah and Edna Earl and Jane Eyre (187). Baym documents critical treatments of *Jane Eyre* in *Novels, Readers, and Reviewers* (see in particular 266–69), but no one else has studied the impact of Brontë's novel on American literature. However, the collection of essays entitled *The Female Gothic,* edited by Juliann E. Fleenor, reveals how *Jane Eyre* became the female gothic prototype. Several contributors discuss its influence on the popular gothic (Joanna Russ in "'Somebody's Trying to Kill Me and I Think It's My Husband': The Modern Gothic" and Kay J. Mussell in "'But Why Do They Read Those Things?': The Female Audience and the Gothic Novel"). *Jane Eyre* is also discussed in Fleenor's introduction and in many of the other essays (for example, see "Monsters and Madwomen: Changing Female Gothic" by Karen F. Stein, "Terror-Gothic: Nightmare and Dream" by Ann Ronald, and "Place and Eros in Radcliffe, Lewis, and Brontë" by Nina da Vinci Nichols), testifying to its formal and thematic influence on "serious" as well as popular female gothic. Baym suggests that the gothic plot derived from *Jane Eyre* may have been "instrumental in destroying woman's fiction by undercutting some of its basic premises" (*Woman's Fiction* 30). *Jane Eyre's* influence on the popular gothic has received much closer attention than its influence on other forms of women's writing.

7. Popular twentieth-century gothic/courtship novels, which are frequently seen as *Jane Eyre's* descendants (authors include Victoria Holt and Phyllis Whitney), borrow only this first part of the plot, along with gothic characters and situations, from *Jane Eyre.* They are generally not as engaged in developing characters and analyzing proposed unions as are double-proposal novels.

8. Barrett Browning claimed to have forgotten *Jane Eyre's* plot when she wrote *Aurora Leigh,* although she had read and enjoyed Brontë's novel. But she insisted the fate of her hero was significantly different. Romney is blinded, but not disfigured, a distinction she maintains makes a difference (Mermin 185; Cooper 189–90). But critics, in common with Barrett Browning's earliest reviewers, consistently find that Brontë was a crucial inspiration for her. For example, Mermin notes that *Aurora Leigh,* "as the fictional autobiography of a woman by a woman," has its "only significant Victorian counterparts" in *Jane Eyre* and *Villette.*

9. Julia Kavanagh (1824–77) was born in Ireland, was raised in France, and then moved to England in 1844. She set novels in both France and England and probably influenced Charlotte Brontë and George Eliot (*Nathalie* [1850] provides a model for *Villette,* and *Rachel Grey* [1856] is considered an influence on Eliot). She also wrote biographies of women designed to correct the silence of male historians, including *Woman in France during the Eighteenth Century* (1850), *Women of Christianity* (1852), and *English Women of Letters* (1863). Her biographer reports that Kavanagh's "work was popular, reaching a large audience through both serialization in periodicals and publication as multi-volume novels" (Todd 277).

10. A number of courtship fictions were also written by black authors, who adapted and subverted marriage plots using different strategies than those employed by white

women writers, who almost never overtly factored race into their courtship equations. Anne duCille's *The Coupling Convention: Sex, Text, and Tradition in Black Women's Fiction* explores these strategies: "Making unconventional use of conventional literary forms, early black writers appropriated for their own emancipatory purposes both the genre of the novel and the structure of the marriage plot" (3). This appropriation did not include the double-proposal plot until the twentieth century, when it appears in Jessie Redmon Fauset's *There Is Confusion* (1924). Fauset employs the plot in conjunction with a development plot featuring a heroine who courageously pursues a theatrical career while resisting marriage (see duCille 74–78).

11. Critics have consistently focused on locating connections between courtship novels and the social matrix, social realities, or social meanings. Alfred Habegger maintains that "women's fiction was a material aid for the enjoyment of a certain complex fantasy with a strong erotic component" (*Gender, Fantasy, and Realism* 6), but also says that, "turning from this body of fiction to the actual social matrix, one is at once struck by the mounds of magazine articles and books dealing with domestic and marital concerns and changing norms of behavior for young women" (viii). Nancy Miller argues that "because the novel, more than any other form of art, is forced by the contract of the genre to negotiate with social realities in order to remain legible, its plots are largely overdetermined by the commonplaces of the culture" (157–58). And Rachel Blau DuPlessis notes that "one of the great moments of ideological negotiation in any work occurs in the choice of a resolution for the various services it provides. Narrative outcome is one place where transindividual assumptions and values are most clearly visible, and where the word 'convention' is found resonating between its literary and its social meanings" (3).

12. Boone perceives narrative structure as determined by social structure, and his study "explores the complex interchanges whereby ideological structures of belief— of which the ideal of romantic wedlock is a prime example—are translated into narrative structures that at once encode and perpetuate those beliefs" (2). Some critics argue from a Marxist perspective that the courtship-marriage plot demonstrates one way ideology defines and constrains the middle class. Tony Tanner sees the institution of marriage as "the all-subsuming, all-organizing, all-containing contract" for bourgeois society, "the structure that maintains the Structure, or System." The bourgeois novel, by extension, is "coeval and coterminous with the power concentrated in the central structure of marriage" (*Adultery in the Novel* 15). The marriage plot, therefore, becomes the vehicle that maintains the structure of the bourgeois novel. The institution of marriage determines the pattern of life for the middle class, and the convention of the courtship plot determines the pattern of narrative for the middle-class novel.

Working from a feminist perspective, DuPlessis argues that courtship fiction reproduces social structures: "The romance plot separates love and quest, values sexual asymmetry, including the division of labor by gender, is based on extremes of sexual difference, and evokes an aura around the couple itself. In short, the romance plot, broadly speaking, is a trope for the sex-gender system as a whole" (5). Annis Pratt attacks "novels of marriage" because, she argues, marriage brings repressed intelligence, limited freedom, submission, and diminished eroticism for the female heroes "that split these heroes' personalities between authentic selfhood and social dictates for femininity" (51). DuPlessis also insists that marriage endings countermand the individual growth of heroines: "In nineteenth-century narrative, where women heroes were concerned, quest and love plots were intertwined, simultaneous discourses, but at the resolution of the work the energies of the *Bildung* were incompatible with the closure in successful courtship or marriage. . . . We learn that any plot of self-realization was at the service of the marriage plot and was subordinate to, or covered within, the magnetic power of that ending" (6).

13. For DuPlessis, "writing beyond the ending means the transgressive invention of narrative strategies, strategies that express critical dissent from dominant narrative . . . [and] produce a narrative that denies or reconstructs seductive patterns of feeling that are culturally mandated, internally policed, hegemonically poised" (5). Boone similarly describes a countertradition that developed in response to the courtship tradition: "There have emerged texts whose dismantling of the patriarchal implications of marriage and marriage plots have gradually opened up the closed field of romantic representation, and which have constituted a vital counter-tradition in Anglo-American fiction" (19). Boone's countertradition texts either attacked the tradition by "exposing the dangers of its socially constructed myths by following the course of wedlock beyond its expected close and into the uncertain textual realm of marital stalemate and impasse" or by inventing "fictional trajectories for the single protagonist, male or female, whose successful existence outside the convention calls into question the viability of marital roles and arrangements" (19). And in her study of how women appropriate traditional narratives, Nancy A. Walker draws a distinction between "disobedient" narratives that "expose or upset the paradigms of authority inherent in the texts they appropriate" and more typical works that "endorse instead of challeng[e] the assumptions of the original" (7).

14. One such approach treats the plot as incidental to other textual elements that appear to challenge the message of the courtship plot. Harris argues that happy endings were part of "textual restraints" that acted as "a cover—or cover-up—for a far more radical vision of female possibilities embedded in the texts" (*Nineteenth-Century American Women's Novels* 12–13). Another perspective valorizes the courtship plot itself as a vehicle of women's choice rather than women's oppression. Katherine Sobba Green believes that early British women novelists, drawing on the concepts of individual rights and companionate marriage that were gaining currency in eighteenth- and early nineteenth-century England, used the courtship form to promote women's well-being. Green finds that the heroine is empowered when love becomes the ideal basis of courtship: "Women, no longer merely unwilling victims, became heroines with significant, though modest, prerogatives of choice and action" (2).

15. The courtship studies by Lystra and Rothman rarely distinguish between North

and South. The letter writers studied by Lystra "were a geographically dispersed lot, which included southerners, but perhaps best represented the West, Midwest, and Northeast" (5). The story of courtship uncovered by Lystra was apparently consistent between representatives of these different regions, but she does not generalize about geographical distinctions as she analyzes the letters. Rothman's study draws on evidence from "white, Protestant middle class [letter writers] living in the settled areas of the North" (6).

16. Degler flatly claims that "if a woman wanted a career she had to forgo marriage." As one example of a professional group of single women, he cites academic women: "Three quarters of all women who earned Ph.D.s between 1877 and 1924 remained unmarried. And the census in 1920 revealed that only 12 percent of all professional women were married" (385).

ONE

Caroline Hentz:
Counterplots in the Old South

IN the introduction I argue that the double-proposal plot is inherently likely to destabilize readers' notions of love and marriage, since by its very structure it calls into question easy clichés of "the right suitor" and "true love." And I argue that women writers of double-proposal novels were, in general, interested in reform of courtship and marriage and in expanded opportunities for women outside of marriage. How, then, to explain the appearance of this supposedly progressive plot in works by Caroline Hentz and Augusta Evans, avowedly conservative writers of the American South who wrote polemic novels defending a culture that founded itself on the assumption of white male supremacy? Historians and literary critics have argued that southern women experienced internal conflict about the racial and economic hierarchy that provided them with privilege even as it deprived them of full autonomy. Perhaps the double-proposal plot provided writers a suitable vehicle with which to express, albeit cautiously, the dissonance between their conflicting desires for literary success and for the perpetuation of the social system that was founded upon slavery. For a combination of literary and ideological reasons, these writers deployed the double-proposal plot simultaneously and paradoxically to defend the southern polity and to imply that privileged white men should share power with privileged white women.

Even though only a small percentage of people were actually part of the elite class, the plantation system personified the South in literary and cultural rhetoric, and southern apologists scrutinized publications, even domestic novels, for ideological conformity. And because of southern elitism, sensitivity, and vulnerability, authors working there labored under an awkward

double burden: anything written about the South might be rigorously tested on ideological grounds, yet critics embraced such elite intellectual values
that they did not take fiction, especially domestic fiction by women, at all
seriously as literature. Nineteenth-century rhetoric often aligned feminists
with abolitionists, and defensive southern eyes were wary of any "strong-
mindedness" that might encourage rebellion in their own women. However
much Hentz and Evans worked to pretend otherwise, any challenge of gender
roles necessarily called into question race roles, since the hierarchy of race,
gender, and class was an interlocking system resting under the capstone of
the white planter. The antebellum South was not merely a distinct region
within the United States but a subculture whose economic and social reli-
ance on slavery brought it under attack at home and abroad: "The rest of
Christendom stands united against us, and are almost unanimous in pro-
nouncing a verdict of condemnation," a writer for the *Southern Literary
Messenger* frantically declared, irrationally blaming the situation on southern authors for failing to defend the South vigorously ("The Duty of Southern Authors" 241).

Southern double-proposal novels illuminate the complex literary and
political influences under which antebellum women writers worked. The
different groups of readers they catered to had disparate expectations and
demands. Writers had to sell their manuscripts to northern publishers, pla-
cate southern critics who screened novels for ideological conformity, and
entertain the popular reading audience throughout the United States. The
domestic novel that sold best was generally characterized by strong heroines
who made their own way in the world (the plot delineated by Nina Baym in
Woman's Fiction); thus, to sell to northern publishers and readers, southern
writers presumably needed to create strong heroines. But those strong heroines, however "moderate, or limited, or pragmatic" their feminism (*Woman's Fiction* 18), were out of place in the American South, where a southern
belle could not even make the initial move of a woman's fiction heroine (to
escape from or be abandoned by her family) without being thrown entirely
out of her sphere. The southern planter society was structured in ways fundamentally different from northern middle- to upper-class families, and if
class and race distinctions were to be maintained, the woman's fiction plot
had to be altered to fit a southern setting.

Caroline Hentz discovered in the double-proposal plot one means for
having it both ways.[1] In the rejected proposal and interproposal space, her
southern belles could temporarily assert their independence from their parents and, by extension, from southern culture itself. Yet in the accepted pro-

posal, the marriage originally desired by suitor and parent(s), modified by the actions of the heroine and the character change of the hero, takes place after all and therefore simultaneously palliates any critics who disapproved of the earlier rebellion and asserts that stronger women could and would act through marriage to protect and perpetuate the elite family unit. So even as Hentz argues for privileged women's increased participation at the peak of the social pyramid, she cements ever more firmly the racist ideology that buttresses wealthy white entitlement. In her novels Hentz argues that privileged women should be trusted because their interests are aligned with those of their men and not, most definitely, with those of blacks or lower-class whites. In Hentz's fictional world, where love is conveniently defined and women are loyal to their class, fears that resistance will seep down from planter women to their subordinates are shown to be groundless. When Hentz's elite women are allowed to assert their autonomy and to choose their own mates, the patriarchal elite is strengthened rather than threatened. But notwithstanding such disingenuous denial, any argument for increasing women's autonomy or for developing more companionate models of marriage, however subtly and carefully offered, questioned the supremacy of the planter, which depended on the submissiveness of his women as well as on the subservience of his slaves.

But the double-proposal plot must have looked like typical courtship fiction to reviewers who read the novels only hastily and partially, because the southern belle eventually married the appropriate suitor. Reviewers, as the gatekeepers, consistently and predictably trivialized both writers and readers of women's novels. A reviewer for the *Southern Literary Messenger* describes Hentz's popular audience in 1855 as a "great mass of readers" for whom "the lines between right and wrong, vice and virtue cannot be made too plain" ("Notices of New Works," rev. of *Robert Graham* 328).[2] Given the arrogant assumptions of the critical press, women writers could produce potentially subversive material if they stamped it with the hallmarks of happy endings and generally proper didacticism. The *Southern Literary Messenger* offered this particularly condescending review of *Robert Graham* (1855): "This is one of Mrs. Hentz's picturesque and entertaining stories, and as far as we have read, seems to be similar to, and perhaps as interesting, as her other works" ("Notices of New Works" 328). A writer for the *Southern Quarterly Review* commented with somewhat less superciliousness on *Rena* (1851): "Mrs. Hentz is well known and much esteemed, as a writer of popular work. Her stories and sketches are commended by sweetness, propriety, and an easy, graceful style" ("Critical Notices" 264). The same periodical also printed a review of *Eoline* (1852), in which Hentz's "nouvelletes" were summarized as "usually pleasant and piquant—full of the sweetest caprices, that usually end happily at last, with one or more marriages, and to the satisfaction of all the *spectators*" ("Critical Notices" 280). So long as Hentz maintained "propriety" and satisfied the expectation of happy endings, critics did not pay her much attention.

But while the southern critics slighted fiction as literature, they demanded that it protect and defend southern culture. Political surveillance of southern writers by other southerners increased in the years leading up to the Civil War as sectional relations became increasingly strained. The immense popularity of *Uncle Tom's Cabin* (1852) exacerbated and focused the literary conflict, which southern apologists characterized as a battle between popular northern female novelists (Harriet Beecher Stowe in particular) and elite southern male authors (such as George Fitzhugh): "As literature has been the most powerful weapon which the enemies of African slavery have used in their attacks, so also, to literature we must look for the maintenance of our position, and our justification before the world" ("The Duty of Southern Authors" 242). Writing in 1856, this author maintains that a comprehensive history of slavery rather than fiction would provide the best literary justification. After all, southern authors live "in a community in which African slavery subsists. We, of the South, recognize it as a great social, moral and political blessing—beneficial alike to us and to the slave." Among those blessings, this writer notes, is the authors' leisure to write: "While their institution of slavery affords them so much leisure for thought and literary activity, and assures every advantage of order and security, why are our authors oblivious of their duty to the slandered South and to the fame of their fathers?" ("The Duty of Southern Authors" 241, 247). Later the same year, another columnist in the *Southern Literary Messenger* sharply criticized southern literature for aiming "a blow at the existence of the very social fabric which supports it" ("An Inquiry into the Present State of Southern Literature" 387).[3]

The ideological minefield walked by southern writers is demonstrated by the *Southern Quarterly Review*'s reception of Hentz's overtly prosouthern novels, *The Planter's Northern Bride* (1854) and *Marcus Warland* (1852). The reviewer of *Marcus Warland* attacks Hentz and her novel, accusing the story of having "several serious defects," the worst of which is that Hentz fails to "provide the argument in regard to slavery. Slavery is not to be apologized for; to be sustained it is to be justified. . . . No Southron, who knows anything of the subject, argues in this manner" ("Critical Notices" 257).[4] Hentz apparently corrected her argument, for *The Planter's Northern Bride* did not offend in the same way. This time a critic praised her as a northern woman who had learned to "love and honour" southern institutions, which she "desires to sustain"; she is further praised for her possession of "veneration, one of the most precious moral virtues, in which the feminine Uncle Tommys are marvellously deficient" ("Critical Notices" 255).[5] Authors were held to strict standards, expected to justify the customs and institutions of the South or face censure from southern watchdogs.

But while Hentz generally expressed enough "veneration" to pacify the southern press, critics were not her primary audience. She had to sell her manuscripts to northern presses and entertain northern and southern readers; therefore, the portraits she drew of the South had to please in both the North and the South. The double-proposal plot enabled her to write stories that accomplished multiple goals for multiple groups of readers because it allowed her to introduce the woman's fiction plot, with its emphasis on female heroism and achievement, into courtship plots that interrogate the patriarchal system of the South. With the one hand she sustains southern hierarchy, but with the other she carves out a more powerful niche for privileged white women at the top of that hierarchy. What to twentieth-century readers might appear to be artificiality, stiffness, and strain in Hentz's fiction can be traced to her determination to vindicate southern paternalism while pleasing the readers on whom her financial success depended, readers who devoured stories of female heroism and companionate marriage. The popularity of Hentz's novels attests to her overall success in navigating this labyrinth of conflicting interests. In just two years, *Linda* (which like all her novels was published in Philadelphia) was printed in thirteen editions (*Woman's Fiction* 128). Her novels reportedly sold "93,000 copies in three years" (James Hart 97) and remained popular "well into the 1890s" (Wimsatt 161).

Linda; or, The Young Pilot of the Belle Creole (1850), its sequel *Robert Graham* (1855), and a novel published between these two, *Eoline* (1852), deploy double-proposal plots at two levels: for the title heroine and the suitor picked out for her by her parent in the primary narrative and in a secondary narrative used to counterpoint the implications of the primary double proposal.[6] In *Linda* the heroine's widowed father marries a woman who, although she manages the plantation efficiently, treats Linda cruelly and plans for her a marriage of convenience with her son by a previous marriage, the spoiled and hot-tempered Robert Graham. Linda, who is afraid of Robert and in love with the gallant Roland Lee, resists Mrs. Walton's demands and Robert's added pressure, eventually fleeing to avoid a forced marriage. But Linda also refuses a first proposal from Roland because she fears Robert will do vio-

lence to all three of them. The first novel resolves the love triangle in Roland's favor: Robert is converted to Christianity and becomes a missionary, and Linda accepts Roland's second proposal with Robert's blessing. In the sequel, Roland is killed and Linda marries Robert after all, planning to join him in the missionary field. *Eoline* deploys a similar plot, but replaces the Byronic suitor with a phlegmatic one. Eoline Glenmore's father had betrothed his daughter to his neighbor's son Horace when the children were infants, but the heroine spurns a loveless marriage, answering her father's ultimatum to accept the engagement by leaving his house to teach music at a nearby ladies' academy, Magnolia Vale. Horace visits her at school, and they fall in love. Not knowing of the change, Eoline's father relents and allows her to return home on her own terms. He is then rewarded by the delightful news that Eoline and Horace want to marry each other after all.

Hentz's novels show that she was aware that southern planters wanted to control their daughter's marriages as best they could, and she even agrees with the principles they desired to enforce. In several ways, Hentz reconstructs circumstances representative of southern courtship. The potential choice of suitors for the heroine is limited by the small cast of characters, typical of the restricted circle a young plantation woman moved in. In portraying young brides marrying near associates, Hentz met contemporary southern expectations that daughters would marry quite young and frequently wed cousins or neighbors. Thanks to the workings of double-proposal plots, her heroines eventually marry the suitors their families originally picked out for them, but they do so on their own terms, accepting suitors whose characters are improved by, among other things, increased regard for the heroines. Planter daughters will make good marriage decisions—that is, decisions incorporating planter values—on their own. Hentz thus argues in her novels that daughters should never be forced to wed against their will in part by demonstrating that such force is unnecessary.

Using the multiple levels of dialogue made possible by double proposals, Hentz manipulates the southern hierarchy to redefine love and alter suitors' characters; as a result, the endings appear natural even though they paradoxically increase the heroines' autonomy and strengthen the system that confines them. The courtship stories highlight the shift between the two proposals: the first is prompted by the parent's interference, and is thus rejected; the second comes from the suitor himself, who has corrected his character flaws, fallen in true love with the heroine, and thus become acceptable. A more equitable marriage grows out of courtship while remaining compatible with southern hierarchy. This compatibility is made possible by the definition of love that emerges from the double-proposal plots, a definition that will reconcile parent, heroine, and suitor by combining passion (and the thrills of romantic love) with respect, which guarantees class and race solidarity simultaneously with the heroine's own increased power. Furthermore, a heroic path is marked out for the southern belles on which they can cultivate their own individuality while in rebellion from the first proposal. Hentz makes the most of the sharply limited options available, pushing the boundaries of what was acceptable behavior for southern belles: Linda impulsively runs away from her plantation, but her adventures are carefully monitored so that she never loses caste; Eoline rashly undertakes to teach music at a girls' school, risking humiliation for herself and her father, but her status is eventually enhanced by the contrast between her and those of humbler origins with whom she works. Throughout it all, Hentz continually reinforces the racial and social hierarchy, anticipating and curbing any fears that the rebellion might spread beyond the heroine's tier. Rebellious protagonists were a convention of woman's fiction, so when Hentz's southern heroines rebel and confront abusive parental figures they break cultural but not literary expectations, which may have both protected her novels from southern criticism and sold them to northern audiences. However, given the culture's habit of fetishizing southern women, a habit in which she also indulged, this genre-typical female rebellion, despite her constant efforts to gloss it over, creates palpable discomfort in the ideological balance of her novels.

For her novels to accomplish the two-fold goal of venerating and rectifying the South, the settings must be reasonably realistic. Jamie Stanesa argues that setting in Hentz's fiction carries ideological implications even when she is not explicitly defending the South: "Her Southern settings signaled the importance of 'region' itself—not merely as setting, background, or local color—but as the site of particular social and economic relations and certain kinds of male and female, and Southern identities" ("Caroline Lee Whiting Hentz" 134). While Hentz never lived on a plantation herself, and her novels cannot be said to present plantation life in compelling detail, they do capture, despite their use of melodrama and other fictional devices, the household-based economic and social system that was a basic structural unit of the South, a unit that made the South fundamentally different from the North. The North's increasing commercialism (even early in the nineteenth century, before the industrial and urban booms) sharply contrasts with the agrarian South and its widely dispersed plantations.[7] The historian Elizabeth Fox-Genovese describes southern slaveholding society as "a network of households" in which the household was "the dominant unit of production and reproduction." In such a culture, both labor and gender relations are ascribed to the household, whereas people in the North increasingly ascribed them to market and state (*Within the Plantation Household* 38). The plantation's strict hierarchy of race, class, and gender relations determined social as well as labor relations. Each of Hentz's double-proposal novels evolves in a specific household characterized by just such a hierarchy, and even when the action moves outside that household, the primary characters are still members and adjuncts of the home plantation. The heroines are thus bounded by the geographical, social, and economic forces that limited the lives of historical women.

Even slight efforts by a fictional heroine to shift out of her fixed position, efforts which outside the horizon of expectations that bounded antebellum southern women might appear feeble, take on greater impact when read in the context of the position in which the Old South placed planter women. Cultural differences between North and South were particularly evident in the roles women were expected to perform. The southern belle looms large in fiction and legend, yet a southern woman was a belle for just a few brief years between puberty and marriage. The image of the self-confident and self-promoting belle is at odds with the model of the self-effacing southern matron, and young women were required to shift from the "self-promotion" characteristic of the belle to the "self-abnegation of the Christian wife and mother" very quickly (Fox-Genovese, *Within the Plantation Household* 270).[8] The boundaries of a planter woman's life were dictated by both the caste system and the agrarian economy it supported. Northern middle- to upper-class homes did not parallel domestic life for a plantation mistress, whose "home" included not only her immediate domestic circle and house but also her husband's slaves and plantation.[9] While northern women established clubs and other means for associating with each other, in the South they remained distanced from their class and generational peers by miles and from others of their gender by caste.

Creating a heroic southern heroine was additionally complicated by the ideological pressures that southern rhetoric brought to bear on plantation women. Historians of the antebellum South and critics of southern literature argue that, partly in response to northern attacks, literary and polemical southern rhetoric made "woman" into an icon representing the South itself, a phenomenon not paralleled in the North.[10] Southern woman came to embody and ideologically to justify the South, so that any attack on southern woman was an attack on the South. By extension, any effort by a southern woman to challenge the place the culture assigned her threatened the socioeconomic and ideological structure of planter culture and therefore was liable to more heavy censure than an equivalent move might have been in the North. Hentz participates in the idealization of the planter woman even as she writes novels that partially protest her social and ideological entrapment. Throughout the novels, in tableaux such as the following, the heroine's color-coded power to enchant derives from her race and class, and the objectified position she is placed in thus reconstructs the entrapment of southern woman as icon: "Horace had seen Eoline at the harp many a time before, but he felt as if it were the first time he had ever experienced her minstrel power. As she raised her hands to sweep the glittering wires, her loose gossamer sleeves fell back, revealing an arm of unrivalled beauty, both as to form and hue. He thought of Ossian's fair-haired maids, of the white-armed daughter of Joscar, and he thought, too, of the angels, and the golden harps of Heaven" (*Eoline* 177).

How can such a heroine be provided with a range of action that will not cause her to topple from her pedestal? How can she assert not just "minstrel power," but power over her own destiny? One answer, as provided by Hentz's double-proposal novels, is to take control over the moment in her life when self-determination is most crucial: courtship, or the passage from the father's to the husband's plantation. At the site of courtship, the heroine's right to wedded happiness can compete with and overthrow, on moral grounds, the planter culture's need to control marriage in order to perpetuate itself. Courtship customs thus particularly exemplify the restrictions under which a planter woman lived; as she made her transition from daughter to wife, she carried her family's name and a portion of her family's land and slaves with her. Hentz's novels reconstruct circumstances typical of southern courtship. Slaveholders insisted that children should marry within their own class and that marriages should when possible amalgamate rather than fragment property. On average, women married at a younger age in the South than in the North, while men married at an older age. Marriage among relatives, including first cousins, was common. Frequently cousins married to consolidate property; in other instances, they married because the pool of potential mates was so small. Chaperoning was more strict than it was in the North, and courting couples in the South were rarely if ever alone.[11]

The patriarchal dictates governing marriage in the South explain why Hentz chose to revive the plot of daughter against father so belatedly in terms of Anglo-literary history. Many nineteenth-century domestic and courtship novels marginalized or dismissed the heroine's parents, but the patriarchal basis of the southern system Hentz wanted to address suggested a plot model that recalls Samuel Richardson's *Clarissa* (1748), in which the authoritarian father dictates a distasteful marriage for his daughter, who flees rather than submit to his demands. Hentz modernizes *Clarissa* by transforming the forced marriage into a first proposal, developing a triumphant heroine along the lines of a woman's fiction plot, reforming both parent and suitor, and then concluding with a final proposal acceptable to all. Baym states that southern and northern woman's fiction shared a common agenda: to show that "women were strong and that men needed to submit to their influence, to give them in reality the power that was assigned to them in rhetoric" ("The Myth of the Myth" 188). The challenge of conveying this message, however, varied according to the region the author portrayed. Hentz uses the double-proposal structures exemplified by *Pride and Prejudice* (1813), in which an arrogant suitor is humbled, and *Jane Eyre* (1848), in which a Byronic suitor is reformed. She integrates these plot options into novels about antebellum life in the American South, where courtship and marriage were structured by social and economic influences quite different from those that dominated British life and different yet again from those that dominated life in the American Northeast.

In the initial proposal, the daughter defies not merely the suitor but the parent who controls the property, thus directly contesting the system by which class privilege is perpetuated. In *Linda,* the father has abdicated his authority to his second wife and passively acquiesces with her selfish plans: Mrs. Walton "was resolved to unite [Robert and Linda] in marriage as soon as they should return from their respective schools and thus keep the large fortune of Linda from passing into a stranger's hand" (57). Similarly, Eoline's father and his neighbor plan to marry their children to combine their adjoining plantations. When Linda's father refuses to defend her against his wife's demands, his daughter lectures him: "Father, I shall never marry without *your* consent; neither will I marry without my *own.* I know the limits of a parent's authority and a daughter's obedience. . . . As you expect to meet the soul of my mother, at the bar of God, on the great judgment-day, do not destroy that of her child" (115). Eoline, horrified that Horace has coolly "consented to obey" their parents (8), maintains that, for children, "obedience in such a case, instead of being a virtue is a sin. 'Tis sacrilege—and God will judge it so" (9). But her father insists that he knows "of no intentions a young lady can have in opposition to a parent's will" (7) and is stunned that his young, pliant, anxious-to-please daughter should now "undauntedly brave his authority, resist his will, and thwart the favorite plan he had been maturing from her infancy" (11).[12] Each heroine justifies her insubordination by appealing to God, thus defying the myth that the patriarch's power flows from the divine and claiming some of that power for herself: "In a struggle for power," Mr. Glenmore tells himself, "for a father to yield to a child was monstrous, unnatural; it was an outrage upon social regulations, an infringement of the Divine law" (32). But if God is on the side of the daughter, the father's control is seriously threatened.

But as the second proposals demonstrate, this power sharing will not endanger the status quo after all, because the daughter is fortunately a trustworthy guardian of class interests. When they at length accept proposals from the suitors they had originally fled from home to avoid marrying, the hero and heroine, rather than the parents, are the primary actors in the courtship scene, but they are acting in accordance with the parents' original wishes. As Horace insists to Eoline's father, "We love each other as we always would have done had we been left to our own free will" (*Eoline* 250). A brief subplot in *Linda* extends the thematic contention that privileged young women have their class's, as well as their own, best interests in mind. In one of the abbreviated conflict and resolution incidents typical of Hentz's fiction, Linda's schoolmate Emily is caught in a clandestine correspondence with "a young man whom she had known from earliest childhood, but to whom her father objected, because he was not rich" (85). Three brief paragraphs (one year) later, the schoolmistress, Mrs. Reveire, convinces Emily's father to relent because of the "extreme worth, growing reputation, and constant attachment" of the suitor (87). Even the limited space given to this courtship demonstrates that Hentz is willing to break social expectations in asserting the primacy of the woman's right to choose; her choice, however, never threatens her household's well-being. Emily's suitor is acceptable by class and because he is a long-standing acquaintance, and even the initial objection to his lack of "wealth" is overcome by the young man's "growing reputation." Emily has made a good choice. Breaking cultural but not literary expectations, Hentz invokes the conventional novel trope of the clandestine correspondence to maintain that privileged Southern women have good sense even in matters of love. The heroines confirm that they can preserve both their personal prerogatives and their class entitlement; their families need not force them to be objects of exchange in marriage.

While the daughters affirm class and race values, they insist on controlling their own futures by introducing the requirement of "love" into their courtships. "Love" is a privatized emotion impervious to the imperatives of duty, and so it draws the parents' scorn and fear. Mr. Walton is impatient when Linda insists she cannot marry Robert without loving him: "Your foolish romance about not loving him, when you have lived as long as I have, you will know what nonsense that is" (114). Mr. Glenmore similarly mocks Eoline's ideal of love: "He is willing to marry you—and that is a sufficient proof of his love. . . . If you expect the fooleries and raptures of which you read in novels, you may be disappointed, and deserve to be so" (9). But, the story will argue, the raptures of novels can indeed coexist with fitting marriages if the couples share true love, here deliberately defined to include both romance and respect. In Hentz's stories "love" partakes of the thrills of fictional passion without becoming a random force that might jeopardize class interests. As the courtships are renegotiated along the lines of this specialized version of "love," the heroine's longing for both increased autonomy and wedded happiness becomes compatible with the planter aristocracy's desire for expedient marriages.

Although one is aggressively intrusive and the other strictly well-mannered, neither suitor is fit for marriage because neither sincerely respects the heroine. Linda's rejected suitor, Robert Graham, labels his frantic desire to possess Linda as "love," but his willingness to coerce her into submission exposes his lack of respect. Although Robert's conscience creates a "fearful warfare" within him, he hopes to win Linda's forgiveness for the forced marriage by promising "an eternity of love and devotion" (180–81). Robert is a seductive character, but Linda dreads his dark passions and violent possessiveness. She knows she would be miserable with someone she cannot trust. Explaining her repugnance, Linda tells her father, "You do not speak of his fierce passions—his fiery temper. Oh! father, they would make me wretched." She does not want, she says, "to mould others to *my* will" and so she will consent to marry only "one who can guide and sustain me in my life's journey, one whom I can respect as well as love" (114). The pride and self-control Hentz depicts as inherent in the plantation woman insulate her from the passion that weakens Jane Eyre and other double-proposal heroines vulnerable to the magnetism of untrustworthy Byronic heroes.[13]

Horace Cleveland's faults are the inverse of Robert Graham's. Horace is willing to have his father arrange a marriage even though, or perhaps because, he feels "indifferent, blind, stolid, perhaps" about the proposed bride (*Eoline* 107). Despite Horace's gentlemanly manners, he does not truly respect Eoline because he does not value women as individuals: "He had seen her a beautiful and accomplished girl, but he deemed it a matter of course that all young ladies must be beautiful and accomplished, and it excited in him no especial emotion. He had seen her surrounded by admirers in her father's drawing-room . . . and he had thought her frivolous, as he took it for granted that all young ladies were" (60). Presumably it makes little difference whom you marry if women are all beautiful, accomplished, and frivolous. Eoline senses his patronizing attitude and scorns him as approaching marriage "like a victim to the slaughter, never dreaming that a poor weak girl would have courage enough to resist an authority to which his stronger will has bowed. If he does not love, he shall at least respect me" (29). In Hentz's judicious vision of courtship, mutual respect must lay the foundation for true love.

As the suitors' emotions and characters are reformed during the inter-proposal counterplots, Hentz implicitly critiques certain gender assumptions and the courtship practices they underwrite. Robert is seductive and predatory whereas Horace is patronizing and chivalrous, and neither respects the heroine's autonomy. Hentz rejects both views of women: that they are sexual property to be "possessed" or that they are indistinguishable embodiments of beauty and frivolity meant to decorate drawing rooms. A marriage with a suitor acting under either assumption would bring neither safety nor happiness to the woman. The double proposals reveal that women should reject marriages based on these flawed and dangerous attitudes and instead should work toward more companionate unions. With the father removed or relegated to the position of spectator, the courtship renegotiations demonstrate that love, properly defined, can be rapturous without transgressing class obligations. Furthermore, and not, in these tales, coincidentally, the renegotiated alliance preserves some of the autonomy the heroine so staunchly protected when she rejected the first proposal. Robert's passion is tempered by religious conversion and years of internal struggle, and when he proposes for the final time, language of romance mingles with that of religion, and possessiveness is replaced with respect: "Years of happiness may be ours, if we now take each other by the hand, with chastened hopes and heavenward faces, as fellow pilgrims to an immortal goal" (248). For Horace, indifference gives way to respect, and then respect engenders love: "When he learned of her flight and banishment, her noble self-reliance, to avoid a hated wedlock, though the object of hatred was himself, he felt a thrill of admiration, such as the history of heroic deeds inspires" (60). The "thrill of admiration" is followed by a burst of passion: "He was as one waking out of a deep sleep, by a flash of conviction, intense as the lightning, and almost as scorching" (174). As a counterpoint to the primary proposal plot, Eoline's lack of respect for another suitor, St. Leon, extinguishes a brief infatuation while the regard she develops for Horace during his support of her flight eventually generates love: "What Promethean fire had suddenly kindled that cold eye, and given it such strange fascination?" (187). The changed suitor exhibits increased respect for the heroine, and by extension, a willingness to admit the justice and wisdom of the heroine's own perspective. Magically, along with respect comes romance, guaranteeing a more companionate marriage.

But the proper alchemy of love is not Hentz's sole concern; she also tries to prove that women can be heroic and therefore worthy of increased freedom. Given the formidable restrictions that bounded planter women's lives, what could a heroine do to manifest her individuality without losing status? Linda simply runs away, putting herself at tremendous risk as she has to be rescued by male protectors from male predators. Although she is primarily reacting to circumstances rather than fashioning an active role for herself, she has "many misgivings as to the propriety of the steps she had taken in leaving the paternal roof," fearing that even her beloved Roland might "look coldly on the wanderer, doomed to such strange vicissitudes, through what he might deem her rashness and imprudence" (230). Eoline, in contrast, actually goes to work as a music teacher, but she imagines venturing on a more ambitious career; given the restrictions of her society, even her fantasy gets her into trouble. In the opening scene, she tells her father of a compliment from "Mr. Leslie, the European traveller." Eoline's speech reveals both her pride in her musical skill and the restrictions imposed on women by wealth: "He said he wished I were the daughter of a poor man, so that I might be compelled to give my voice to the world; that nature never bestowed such a treasure for the benefit of the domestic and social circles alone. Think of that, father—a prima donna! Would it not be magnificent?" (6); Mr. Glenmore thinks it unlikely she would be "reduced to such an alternative" (6), but when shortly thereafter Eoline announces her intention to leave him rather than submit to a marriage to Horace, he throws the idea back at her: "I should like you to tell me, Miss Eoline Glenmore, what you intend to do, when you launch out into the world—a prima donna, perhaps. That will be admirable. I dare say you will find some itinerant Italian to take charge of you, and give éclat to your debut?" (11). When Eoline auditions for a teaching job by performing, the narrator envisions Eoline as a public star: "No Italian Prima Donna ever had a more clear, brilliant, powerful voice than Eoline. . . . Mr. Leslie had said truly, that she would make her fortune on the stage" (51). But such a public career can be no more than a dream for the planter daughter, and Hentz's heroine settles for the still shameful option of teaching. Mr. Glenmore's conviction that Eoline embarrasses the family mirrors the scorn of planter society toward a privileged woman's ventures outside the household. Horace also demonstrates this disgust when he visits Magnolia Vale, although he does not extend his contempt to Eoline: "What a place for the daughter of Mr. Glenmore!" (62). Unlike other double-proposal heroines, then, Hentz's protagonists cannot prove themselves by pursuing challenging careers that showcase their intellectual and creative abilities.

Female heroism is a consistent theme in American double-proposal novels beginning with Hentz, who portrays her southern belles as heroically as she can within class expectations, and growing stronger and more central in later writers. Miss Manly, who manages the school at which Eoline teaches, demonstrates the turn from male heroic idols to female ones that will be developed more fully by Evans, Bullard, Southworth, and Phelps. Students at Magnolia Vale practice their conversational abilities by discussing "Great Men" at dinner, but by the end of the book Miss Manly has become more respectful of her own gender and less "manly" herself: "She still kept up her literary banquets, but she no longer confined herself to heroes who had won the honors of the *Great*. She even condescended to bring forward the good and gifted of her own sex, as models for imitation" (257). Later double-proposal novelists write their heroines into successful careers as writers or artists, but Hentz, bound to the planter ideology of the antebellum South, makes the most of the sharply limited options made available within its restrictive geographical and cultural limits. Read through the lens of the historical setting, without which the heroines' actions appear unremarkable and stilted, the counterplots between the proposals are filled with partial stories of female ambition and triumph.

Linda and Eoline need someplace to go and something to do that will approximate the successful quests by which heroes prove their mettle, but without pushing boundaries too far. To solve the problem, Hentz transforms the affective realm of private relationships into a site of struggle, conquest, and renunciation, thus constructing a heroic battlefield on women's conventional turf. During their exploits on this modified field, the maturing heroines develop from inexperienced and pampered belles into confident women who have experienced something of the world outside the plantation, learned to rely more on themselves (though they occasionally need to be rescued), and proven they can balance the demands of social responsibility and hard-won autonomy. As the protagonists overcome some of the egotism they have absorbed from their lives of privilege, they build toward their most heroic moments: renunciation of self-fulfillment. The ultimate test of heroism is to refuse a proposal in service of a higher ideal than domestic bliss.

Having rejected abhorrent proposals on moral grounds, the heroines later refuse welcome ones because they believe acceptance would render them liable for the death of another person.

When the emotional stakes of the experiences are elevated, her heroines triumphantly confront life and death challenges within the accepted confines of southern womanhood and domestic fiction. Linda refuses to marry Robert; but to prevent the hemorrhages and violence his excessive passions cause, she agrees not to commit herself to anyone else, either. Because of this promise, she declines Roland's first proposal, although the narrator declares it the happiest moment of her life: "Though there was sorrow behind her and darkness before, she had touched one bright, luminous point—one dazzling focus of bliss—where her spirit fainted from the excess of joy and light" (144). Although she assures Roland of her love, she declares, "While Robert lives, I never can wed another. . . . The guilt of murder would be on my soul!" (145). Linda's heroic status is established by this renunciation, which she believes will save Robert from killing all three of them: "He would pursue you with unrelenting vengeance to the world's end. A three-fold sacrifice would be the awful result. . . . I can love you—live for you—die *for* you, Roland, but not *with* you" (145). In a similar spirit of glorious self-sacrifice, Eoline rejects Horace's (as opposed to her father's) first proposal, although by then she desires to accept it. She has pledged herself to the critically ill St. Leon because the physician persuades her that "she held perchance in her hands the life of a human being," and despite grave misgivings, she is "all but willing to immolate herself, rather than destroy him who hung trembling on her decree" (183–84). When St. Leon, thriving on the anticipation of life with Eoline, unexpectedly recovers, she stands by her promise even though she would now prefer to marry Horace. She criticizes Horace for seeing the future as full of "disappointment and misery": "This is unworthy of yourself, Horace, and of me. Great minds never despair—they struggle with destiny, and triumph in the conflict,—it is the weak only who yield. Let the selfish live for their own happiness. Let us live for something noble, Horace,—the happiness of others" (197). For Eoline, a "great mind" has no gender, and self-sacrifice, born of strength and action rather than weakness, is heroic in man or woman. (Circumstances rather than selfishness bring the heroines their desired marriages after all. Robert is converted to Christianity and blesses Linda's union with Roland, and Eoline is saved from marrying St. Leon when she discovers he is guilty of duplicity; she insists that he marry Amelia, whose life he has damaged by thoughtless flirtation, thus leaving herself free to marry Horace.)

Hentz ensures that we will not mistake such courageous acts for conventional feminine passivity by contrasting active sacrifice with mindless submission. The subplot of *Eoline* is a cautionary tale directed overtly at parents and more subtly at youth, clearly delineating Hentz's belief that women should choose their husbands and simultaneously demonstrating the dangers that may derive from a woman's passivity. Amelia, her father tells Eoline's father, was "ever swayed by the will of others, ever sacrificing her own wishes to those around her" (113), declining even to tell her father whether she wished to marry a certain suitor, an eligible man with "cold, reserved manners" (114). Once married to this suitor, Amelia had "no will but his," and he turned out to be selfish and cold, condemning her to a "living death" (115). She becomes melancholic and almost insensible, responding to nothing except direct addresses. Amelia's father exhorts Mr. Glenmore to appreciate Eoline's strong will, amazed that he would have discarded such a "glorious girl" because she "dared to be the judge of her own happiness; dared to assert the supremacy of conscience, honor, and truth, over parental authority" (116). Self-sacrifice must be an action born of strength, not a mindless, undiscerning habitual behavior. The active heroine who chooses her own destiny wins respect, love, and happiness; the passive woman who allows others to choose for her is victimized.

The shocked reactions of both Mrs. Walton and Mr. Glenmore when the heroines reject their authority suggest that a heroine's power of refusal, in undermining the parent's control, could reverberate throughout the household. If the daughters refuse to marry as directed, thereby sabotaging their parents' control of land and slaves, other acts of obedience dwindle in significance. The interdependence between female submission and black enslavement was not lost on contemporary observers. A correspondent for a British periodical, writing after the Civil War about the unsettling forwardness of American women, exempts southern women from his critique: "The South is eminently conservative; and even the institution of slavery, while it lasted, helped to maintain, not only the subordination of the inferior to the superior race, but of the weaker sex to the stronger" ("Women and Children of America" 83). Northern feminists and abolitionists pooled their reform efforts, a fact not lost on the defenders of the South. Southern apologists intensely loathed the women's movement and were conscious of the parallels drawn between the position of women and the position of slaves: "To confront women's status would have called into question all that the South embraced, including slavery. Challenging the status quo would have jeopardized a society that prided itself on slaveowning and male authority" (Mc-

Millen 9). No doubt conscious of southern sensitivity, Hentz uses dialogue and incident to deny that her heroines could ever identify with slaves. Only privileged white women are meant to have the increased freedom she advocates. Hentz's novels portray people of color as willing servants of privileged whites: her slaves are childish and content, and a Native American couple instinctively recognizes their own racial inferiority. Scenes such as the following cater to racist ideology and soothe white fears. Having been rescued by Tuscarora (identified only as a "Christian Indian"), Linda falls asleep as his wife, Naimuna, brushes her hair: "Naimuna looked down upon her, as she lay like a weary child slumbering on its nurse's arm, with feelings resembling worship. She longed to kiss the rosy lips whose pure breath stole so softly over her cheek, but there was such an angelic innocence diffused over her face that she would have deemed it profanation in one of darker hue to approach them. Long she remained in her kneeling position" (220–21).

Especially at moments when the heroines most aggressively assert their rights, as in the scene above when Linda has run away from her oppressive parents, Hentz insulates the rebellion by affirming white superiority. Even as the heroines protest against injustice, they reinforce the very values that make that injustice possible. The point of disagreement—who has rights over the heroine's will and body—is put into perspective when the characters concur that the will and body of others, particularly slaves, is to remain subdued. But in the very process of establishing this perspective, Hentz inevitably gives voice to potential rebels. Both Mrs. Walton and Linda invoke slave relations as they argue over Linda's proposed marriage to Robert. Linda refuses to be "bought and sold like a negro slave" and announces, "You ruled me with a rod of iron, and I did not complain. But I will bear no more. I will not be trafficked away in this vile manner" (105). Mrs. Walton responds with, "I took you away from the negroes, and made you sit by my own side; and now . . . you look as if you would trample me under your feet, and address me as you would not dare to do a single slave on the plantation" (106). Although Linda is gracious to her slaves, she is never "familiar" with them. Mrs. Walton's accusation that Linda was too friendly with her slaves implies that the heroine was not taught a proper understanding of her own status. But Linda's responses suggest she needs no instruction from Mrs. Walton about class and race relations. Mrs. Walton and Linda demand consideration from one another partly because of their assumed racial superiority, a move that affirms the novel's unified stance on race and class hierarchy and tries to deflect fears that the privileged woman's protest could be echoed by other groups. *Eoline* similarly bounds the rebellion scene with dialogue that reinforces racial hierarchy. As Eoline prepares to leave her father's home, her slave Gatty criticizes Mr. Glenmore in support of Eoline, but the daughter interrupts her midsentence: "You must not speak disrespectfully of my father, Gatty; I cannot allow it. . . . You must not suspect, you must not think, you must not speak" (27). How power is to be distributed within the ruling race is the issue, and Eoline cuts short her slave's attempt to identify with her. But by explicitly attempting to silence the implication that the daughter's disobedience could inspire disrespect in her slaves, the novel draws attention to the possibility.[14]

Hentz further certifies that her heroines harbor no democratic sentiments by sketching their interactions with whites of lower classes, but the upstart class is thereby given a voice that overtly challenges aristocratic presumption. In Hentz's novels, even the best refining influences cannot elevate vulgar white characters, embodied by the obnoxious Jerusha Spots in *Eoline*. Once Eoline leaves the plantation, she becomes the "Queen" of the school, attracting adoration because of her beauty and the privileged heritage it represents. Jerusha's infatuation with Eoline, combined with her stupidity, especially her inability to learn refined manners and speech, argues for a difference in white classes that education cannot begin to overcome. Jerusha believes that class is a mere matter of wealth—"Pa's as rich as any body, and has got as many niggers, too" (122)—but the chasm between the woman of lower-class stock and Eoline cannot be hurdled simply because the Spots family has acquired money and slaves. This single sentence of Jerusha's dialogue demonstrates the hopelessness of her immersion in her caste. No refined woman in this novel's world would shock listeners with the term *nigger,* refer to her father as "Pa," allude to the degree of her family's wealth, or deliver ungrammatical phrases such as *as any body* or *has got.* Here is Jerusha at home after a term at the young ladies' school: "It was a stout coarse-looking girl, in a blue-checked bib apron, with short sandy hair, that fell over her eyes like a thick, flaxen fringe, holding in her hand a long green pickle, whose truncated end exhibited the print of her incisors" (224). Although she tries to be gracious, Eoline never overcomes her disgust for Jerusha. When her father meets the crude pupil, he is outraged that Eoline could allow "such vulgar familiarity. If such are the associations you have been forming, you have, indeed, disgraced your family forever" (226). Far from defending Jerusha, and thereby suggesting that her sympathies extend beyond her class, Eoline is distressed that her father has gotten "wrong impressions of the beings with whom she had been associated" (227). Jerusha is sacrificed to renewed solidarity between plantation master and daughter: "'Foolish child!'

said he at length, putting his arm round Eoline, and drawing her towards him, 'when we once reach home, all will be well'" (227). By affirming class supremacy, Hentz endeavors to show that increased freedom for privileged women will not threaten the status quo, but in the process she exposes the elite as vulnerable to encroachment.

Hentz's conscientious and cautious representation of race and class suggests that it would be eminently reasonable if planter men permitted their own women greater freedom. Yet the artificiality and potential fragility of Hentz's immaculately tended world is sometimes exposed. Even if readers accept its disingenuous assumptions, such as that refined women "naturally" will not fall for men they do not respect or that people of color "naturally" will kneel to and be silenced by their innate reverence for wealthy whites, the partial leveling of power among those at the top still unsettles the structure as a whole, as the discordant voices of Gatty and Jerusha suggest. Another crack in the ideological facade emerges in a secondary double-proposal plot in *Robert Graham*. Nora Marshall speaks clearly what a model representative of the planter class could not say herself. Even though Hentz warns the reader that "Nora Marshall was, perhaps, the last person" a mother would choose as "the companion of her daughter" (48), and she "always seemed treading on the very verge of propriety" (103), the lively character charms other characters and, probably, readers because of her humor, intelligence, and bravery (she seems better adapted to an E. D. E. N. Southworth adventure plot than to a Hentz novel). Her boundless energy and unpredictability attract an eligible suitor hopeful of taming her wild spirit, but she rejects his first proposal. The hierarchical values Nora has internalized are incompatible with the personal autonomy she prizes: "The man who tried to govern me, I should hate; the man who allowed me to rule him, I should despise. The man who permitted me to have my own way, I could not respect, and, therefore, could not love,—and yet my own way I must have" (155). Nora's speech pinpoints a central contradiction in the ideology that forms the basis for Hentz's construction of love and courtship: respect in this imaginative world is largely based on a response to superiority, and all relationships, apparently, must be formed hierarchically. But if both partners are to command respect, then who will rule? Nora "could not respect and therefore could not love" any man who did not exert authority over her, yet she "would hate" any man who insisted on curbing her. Nora's initial solution to this dilemma is not to marry at all, for she is convinced that men would gain and keep the upper hand: "Men are all tyrants—all Napoleons in their way: some wrap their sceptre in down, and twine it with flowers, but it is, nevertheless, the rod of empire, and wo [*sic*] to the wife who disputes its awful sway" (155). Nora's protests set up apparently insuperable obstacles to companionate marriages in the planter class. How can an independent and proud woman find satisfaction with an independent and proud man, especially given that men are habitually domineering?

Yet Nora ends up marrying her suitor. As in the primary plots, scope of feeling is called on to replace scope of action, and the death of a character who is both Nora's friend and her suitor's sister shocks and humbles the estranged couple and draws them together again. Nora's independent spirit is undermined as she confronts the reality of death and of her need for others, but Henry is also more subdued: "As it was then, so it is now,—only I have more need of the boon I asked, and feel that I could prize it more" (191). Nora does not recant her earlier heterodoxy, but she accepts the renewed offer of marriage. Profound emotions are credited with the change: "Sorrow is a miner,—it digs deep in the heart, and finds its embedded gold," we are told. "It is a diver, and brings up the ocean pearls. It is a high priest, and consecrates the sacrifice it imposes." In other words, experiencing loss and sorrow deepens the character and lays a foundation for a stronger future because it creates a companionate bond between the characters: "Their hearts were more united, more melted in one, by the mutual sorrow and sympathy which had unveiled them to each other, than they would have been in years of gay, mirthful intercourse" (191). Companionate love language glosses and idealizes the hierarchical relationship, and the paradox Nora had identified is not solved, but only blurred.

By dutifully reinforcing southern institutions and creatively deploying literary conventions, Hentz marked out where she wanted to challenge antebellum southern culture and where she wanted to support it. White upper-class women, her novels argue, should have more autonomy, especially in the area of self-determination in marriage; for this goal to be achieved, the privileged men who control the South (both fathers and suitors) must learn to respect women and to concede to them a larger share of their own power. Marriage must be based on both respect and love, projecting possibilities of more companionate, if not yet egalitarian, unions. Although the renegotiated marriages are described with hierarchical rhetoric, Hentz's double proposals redistribute conventional feminine and masculine attributes. Women become stronger and more active, manifesting their independence through both self-assertion and self-sacrifice. Men, on the other hand, maintain their traditional active virtues, but also learn to sacrifice, thus taking on a feminine attribute. The marriages are, therefore, more companionate than they would have been as first proposed while still meeting the expectations of a stratified society.

As twentieth-century readers, once we unpack the plotting, reconstruct some of the historical framework, and read closely between and through the proposals, the internal contradictions and ideological manipulations in Hentz's novels become painfully apparent. The novels' almost exclusive focus on women of privilege reveals self-serving expedience, the definition of "love" is surely wishful thinking, and the denial of the broader implications of any protest of oppression must be willfully blind.[15] But even though the emergency ideological brake remains set, progressive impulses within Hentz's fiction tug at male prerogative, pointing out how a woman might effectively challenge a patriarch's authority by demanding control over her courtship. In the conclusion of her story, Eoline plays a trick on her father, asking him to approve of her chosen suitor before revealing she has selected Horace. Responding to the joke, Mr. Glenmore ventures a partial apology for his earlier coercion: "We fathers may have erred in judgment as to the best way to accomplish our wishes, but you must acknowledge we were right after all." In lieu of any direct acknowledgment, Eoline explains, "You have been so long plotting against us, I thought I would get up one little counterplot, to wind up the last scene of the last act of the drama" (249). The heroine's self-reflexive voice hints at the narrative strategy of the novel as a whole: the paternalistic system that dictates the script of women's lives is vulnerable to strategic counterplotting aimed at the crucial passage of courtship.

Hentz's conclusions contain within them denials and contradictions, the seeds of additional problems to be raised and debated by succeeding writers. A love ideal of mutual respect and passion promotes a companionate concept of marriage, yet as Nora recognizes, a hierarchical marriage may be incompatible with mutual respect. The dialogue of question and answer through each of her novels, and through the succession of novels, reveals increasingly more direct challenges to patriarchal authority in the South and increasingly more probing questions about the domestic ideal of marriage. In *Linda,* the Byronic hero is tamed and the unflaggingly well-behaved hero is awarded the heroine. The criticism of Linda's father is relatively indirect; his sin is weakness, while Robert's mother's sin is wickedness. In *Eoline* Hentz directly criticizes the father and corrects his judgment even as she provides him with the marriage he desired. Eoline actually works outside her home, a prospect Linda never even imagines. In *Robert Graham* Hentz removes parents from the picture, renegotiates the courtship between Linda and Robert, and closes by sending the couple away from the South. This missionary exodus does not openly threaten the southern polity, but Linda's language suggests her ambition to do something greater than be the mistress of a plantation: "This new-born heart pants to share your higher, nobler destiny" (249).

Hentz uses the double proposal to negotiate with the southern system on behalf of privileged women but also to reinforce the crucial values of that system. Her manipulation of plot and character, which creates continual tension between the elite conservatism of the system she endorses and the independence for women she projects, creates a series of additional questions and problems. Subsequent double-proposal novelists less constrained by the rigid hierarchies of class and race to which Hentz was committed investigate the problems she ignores. Evans, for example, recognizes that respect may not "naturally" coexist with romantic love and explores how a heroine can deal with passion when it conflicts with her reason, when she is attracted to a man she cannot respect. Southworth admits that marriage is conceived and institutionalized to allow the husband to dominate the wife and criticizes the conflict between companionate ideals and marriage laws of coverture.

And all of the later American double-proposal writers develop their heroines' desire for personally fulfilling work. Eoline longed to be a performer, to share her musical artistry with the world, but was scarcely allowed even to dream. Linda finally chooses the mission field because it provides her with excitement, travel, supreme service, and sacrifice. Over the course of the double-proposal tradition, authors explore more fully the dissonance between ambition that requires self-promotion and marriage that demands self-effacement. Double-proposal novelists continued for several decades to search for answers within renegotiated marriages, reluctant to challenge the efficacy of marriage itself.

Notes

1. Born in New England in 1800, Caroline Hentz adopted the South after her marriage in 1824 to Nicholas Marcellus Hentz, who became a professor at the University of North Carolina in 1826. After leaving Chapel Hill in 1830, the Hentzes lived in Kentucky, Alabama, and Georgia, where they operated young ladies' academies. Hentz had good opportunities for observing the class of women she wrote about, although she herself was never part of a plantation household. She began her publishing career in 1831 with an award-winning play, and she wrote two more plays,

poetry, several volumes of short stories, and at least eight novels before her death in 1856. Profits from her novels, mostly written between 1850 and 1856, provided needed support for her family during her husband's extended illness.

2. When *The Planter's Northern Bride* was recognized by southern reviewers in 1854 as a potentially positive ideological influence, reviewers divided northern and southern reading groups, suggesting a concept of a somewhat more mature reading audience than that posited by reviewers of domestic novels devoid of obvious political intent. A critic for *DeBow's Review* (published in New Orleans) praised the novel as follows: "The author is a Northern lady who has long been a resident of the South. She speaks with eloquence, truthfulness, and vindicates the character of her adopted home from the vile aspersions of the ignorant and deluded of other quarters" ("Book Notices" 443). In a similar vein, a writer for the *Southern Quarterly Review* announced that "her book will be found of grateful reading in the South, and may become of great Christian utility in the North" ("Critical Notices" 255). However, when treating the domestic novel three years before, a critic for the *Southern Quarterly Review* refers to Hentz's probable audience as "most readers, who prefer a natural and lifelike picture to a strained and extravagant romance" ("Critical Notices" 264). Here is more evidence of how gatekeepers patronized both writers and readers of domestic novels, but also evidence that such patronizing was based on assumptions about reading audiences that could quickly shift depending on the material the novel was presumed to be presenting.

3. The demand for sectional loyalty was extended to readers as well as to writers. The resentment in the following excerpts testifies to the dominance of northern presses and the popularity of northern writers in the South. In 1851, an editor for the *Southern Literary Messenger* criticized southerners who subscribed to northern publications: "We must say that we hold that Southern man utterly without excuse who passes by such literary issues as the Gazette, the Commercial and Quarterly Reviews, or our own magazine—all representing the Southern mind and devoted to the support of Southern institutions, to take Northern works in no degree superior and often full of rancorous hostility to our social system" ("Editor's Table" 519). This theme is echoed a decade later by a writer for *DeBow's Review,* which condemned southerners for buying "Yankee rubbish" and the "ephemeral trash of the North" ("Disenthralment of Southern Literature" 353, 356) instead of supporting southern publications; this writer (in the first year of the war) correlates literary publishing with armed conflict, and blames laxness in the antebellum period for southern dependence on northern publications: "Capable of the highest achievements in literature, the South should have striven to acquire the prestige which attends excellence . . . yet she has not only suffered her own armor to rust in permitting her literature to languish, but, by buying and reading Northern publications, has strengthened the arms of her adversary" (349).

4. *Southron* was a regional variation of *southerner* that was later used in Confederacy rhetoric. Thus, it probably carries an insider connotation that emphasizes Hentz's outsider status.

5. I do not mean to suggest that Hentz's endorsement of southern paternalism was insincere. See Jamie Stanesa's discussion of *The Planter's Northern Bride* for an evaluation of Hentz's "deep belief that the system of chattel slavery was the only truly moral system on earth, the best possible social system for all civilization" ("Caroline Hentz's Rereading" 241).

6. Hentz's last novel, *Ernest Linwood* (1856), uses a similar plot in that it follows a troubled marriage through a break and reconciliation (another method for negotiating the emotional terms of a marriage by juxtaposing two versions of the same couple's union). In *Ernest Linwood* Hentz leaves behind the special problems of the South to examine the fate of a young dependent heroine who chooses to marry a passionate Byronic hero. The hero's jealousy, a product of his passion, nearly destroys their marriage, and only when there is a decisive break, separation, and reconciliation does the relationship begin to heal. Thus in *Ernest Linwood* Hentz explores some of the same problems double-proposal authors do. For a discussion of Hentz's work with seduction and domestic plots in that novel, see Elizabeth Barnes's analysis of the connections between mother's and daughter's narratives.

7. Gordon S. Wood argues that before industrialization, urbanization, and mechanization began their rapid growth the early republic was characterized by buying and selling even where the North was still largely rural. Northeasterners in particular were inspired by the prospects of commercialism (313). Wood contrasts the North with the South several times, arguing that the South "with its leisured aristocracy supported by slavery [came to seem] even more anomalous" (277) as the young republic began to act on its creed of egalitarianism.

8. Fox-Genovese suggests that southern women read works that would help them negotiate their passage from belle to matron, a passage that demanded a fragile balance; perhaps Hentz's novels were adapted to this purpose, among others. In Hentz's novels, young belles mature into strong women before they marry, a growth calculated not only for their personal benefit but also, the novels suggest, for the good of the households with which they are associated.

9. Catherine Clinton's research shows how domestic challenges differed in the South. The plantation mistress had to oversee the clothing, feeding, and nursing of family and slaves in addition to undergoing more frequent pregnancies than her middle- to upper-class northern counterpart; to complicate matters further, she often married quite young and had not been expected to handle such responsibilities when in her father's household (*Plantation Mistress* 18–29).

10. Anne Goodwyn Jones states that "the southern lady is at the core of a region's self-definition; the identity of the South is contingent in part upon the persistence of its tradition of the lady" (4). Anne Firor Scott discusses how the mythology of the southern belle and the southern lady affected the lives of actual southern women and suggests ways in which this myth may have been a response to the ethical problems presented by slavery (4–21). Clinton devotes a chapter to examining the "moral bind" in which plantation society placed women, concluding that women were forced into "rigid and exacting roles. [They were] protected, yet at the same time

confined, by interlocking systems of patriarchal authority. Men further confounded women with contradictory and often hypocritical challenges: to fulfill the belle ideal, to ensure the spiritual welfare of all plantation dwellers, to turn a blind eye on male transgressions. Myth, ideal, and duty weighed heavily on plantation women" (*Plantation Mistress* 109).

11. For information on the courtship and marriage practices of white southerners, see Wyatt-Brown 201–17; Clinton, *Plantation Mistress* 59–86; and McMillen 15–40.

12. The different roles of the fathers in *Linda* and *Eoline* may suggest Hentz's growing willingness to directly criticize a patriarch. Linda argues with both her stepmother and her father about marriage with Robert, but it is Mrs. Walton who forces the issue. Mr. Walton, like many a Jane Austen father, is directly guilty of weakness but only indirectly guilty of warping his daughter's life. In *Eoline*, the father himself attempts to coerce his daughter into marriage. Mr. Walton's marriage provides a counterpoint to the novel's marriage theme. He marries a woman who is an excellent manager (she runs both her own and Mr. Walton's plantations at a good profit), but he does not love her. Hentz does not link Mrs. Walton's efficiency with her "unwomanly" behavior toward Linda. In fact, Linda herself is described at the end of the first novel as arranging her own extended household: "Never did a young bride commence such a patriarchal establishment" (274).

13. In the first novel Linda feels that Robert is her brother although he is not a blood relation; marriage with him "seemed more than unnatural—sacrilegious in her eyes" (103). This objection to Linda and Robert's union conveniently disappears in *Robert Graham*. The discrepancy helps one guess about the composition of the two novels. *Linda* never hints that Linda and Robert might get married after all. Hentz thus decided on doubling the proposal after writing the first novel, and the sequel was published five years later. Perhaps the increasing fascination with the Byronic hero influenced Hentz's decision to drop Roland from the story and marry Linda to Robert, or perhaps reader pressure influenced her to shift from the safety of the heroine's marriage to a gallant brother figure to the gothic excitement of her marriage to a reformed Byronic hero. *Eoline*, published between the Linda and Robert stories, also reveals Hentz's increasing interest in the Byronic figure. Eoline, distressed at St. Leon's weakness and timidity, tells her friend Louisa, "I said I am wicked, because I feel as if I could really admire a man more, who is capable of some great crime nobly repented of, if he have corresponding greatness of character, than one amiably weak and constitutionally timid" (161). Neither St. Leon nor Horace is at all Byronic, but in *Robert Graham* Linda experiences Eoline's fantasy, loving a regenerated villain who has "nobly repented" of the crime of attempting to marry her against her will.

14. In a study of how "sentimental patterns can evoke a terror as well as a tear," Jan Bakker similarly concludes that Hentz's fiction problematizes southern culture even as it purports to defend it. In a study of how Hentz addresses "her contemporary Southerners' obsessive, unspoken fear of servile insurrection" in her first novel,

Lovell's Folly (6), Bakker finds that even though the temporarily rebellious slave "tear-fully apologizes" and is reconciled with his mistress, the sentimental pattern has been twisted "to reveal some unpleasant truths" about southern life (12).

15. Robert Hunt's analysis of how Hentz represents slave-master relations offers another detailed investigation of the intersections of literary technique, historical setting, and cultural connotation. Whereas Hunt is interested in political economy and I am studying courtship patterns, we both find Hentz to be ingenious in her literary technique and given to fantasy about cultural realities.

TWO

Augusta Evans:
Ambition and Commitments

THE capacity of the double-proposal plot to give voice to conflicting views of women's roles, to generate intertextual dialogue, and to mediate varied social conditions is manifested with particular clarity in Augusta Evans's double-proposal novel *St. Elmo* (1867), which incorporates literary critique, direct quotation, and overt allusion to previous double-proposal texts as she negotiates between British versions of renegotiated courtship and her partially disguised allegiance to the American South. During a dinner table conversation concerning woman's suffrage and the equality of the sexes, the heroine Edna Earl, a popular author of novels that parade their learnedness (much like Evans's own), is asked what she thinks of "the comparative merits" of Tennyson's *The Princess* (1847) and Barrett Browning's *Aurora Leigh* (1856). Edna believes Tennyson to be the better judge of the "womanly nature" even though she would "yield to no human being in admiration of, and loving gratitude to Mrs. Browning." She regards "the first eight books of 'Aurora Leigh' as vigorous, grand, and marvellously beautiful," but yet, she adds, "I cannot deny that a painful feeling of mortification seizes me when I read the ninth and concluding book, wherein 'Aurora,' with most unwomanly vehemence, voluntarily declares and reiterates her love for 'Romney.' . . . It is because I love and revere Mrs. Browning, and consider her not only the pride of her own sex, but an ornament to the world, that I find it difficult to forgive the unwomanly inconsistency into which she betrays her heroine" (*St. Elmo* 255). Edna prefers the ending of *The Princess*, whose heroine is "more feminine and refined and lovely than 'Aurora'" (255). Tennyson's treatment of "the woman question," a double-proposal narrative itself, was published the same year as *Jane Eyre;* Princess Ida is betrothed as a child to the Prince and rejects this betrothal to pursue her dream of governing an all-female university. In Tennyson's ending, Princess Ida recants her feminism, pronounces herself a failure, and yields to the hero, who has conquered her domain by deceit and violence but who promises her a visionary marriage: "In true marriage lies / Nor equal, nor unequal. . . . The two-cell'd heart beating, with one full stroke, / Life" (284–89). With Edna's story (the heroine's name itself might be derived from "Ida") Evans attempts to weld Tennyson's ending onto Barrett Browning's plot, to celebrate the development of the successful woman author while clinging to a hierarchical and sentimental marriage ending. The final words of her novel are directly quoted from *The Princess* by the hero St. Elmo: "My hopes and thine are one. / Accomplish thou my manhood, and thyself, / Lay thy sweet hands in mine and trust to me" (367). Yet even this final endorsement of Tennyson's vision is altered by St. Elmo's, or Evans's, deletion of the imperious and perhaps indelicate command "Come, / Yield thyself up" (342–43) from the middle of the quotation.

The inherently dialogic nature of the double-proposal plot becomes particularly apparent when we study works in which authors attempt to turn back, not merely silence or modify, the progressive impetus generated by the heroine's initial refusal to marry her destined mate. The contradictory movements of the plot lines draw from readers and critics sharply varying responses and interpretations of the appropriate roles for women and the best model for marriage. By directly invoking Tennyson's and Barrett Browning's endings, Evans enters an ongoing literary and critical conversation of just this sort. From the first reviews of *The Princess,* some readers found it an "eloquent and effective" defense of women's rights, a view echoed by several twentieth-century critics who, as Donald E. Hall reports, "'hear' Tennyson critiquing and repudiating some of the fundamental assumptions of Victorian patriarchy" (45). But many other readers agree with Hall's own argument that Tennyson's work "is reactionary . . . a relentless process of silencing self-interested women and quelling agitation that disrupts patriarchal order" (46). Elizabeth Barrett Browning was apparently in the second camp; she wrote that she was "disappointed" by *The Princess,* and according to Gardner B. Taplin, she "directly challenged" Tennyson's conservative view of women when she wrote *Aurora Leigh* (xiv). Critics continue to compare the treatment of women in the two poems much as Edna Earl did at her dinner table. Marjorie Stone argues that both writers "were engaged in subverting gender and genre distinctions" (103) but concludes that "despite its subtle explanation of gender inversion reinforced by genre subversion, *The Princess* is a conservative poem" (112), whereas Barrett Browning "is more subversive in *Aurora Leigh*" (115). Cora Kaplan similarly finds that "where Barrett Browning quarrels with Tennyson is over the concept of ideal marriage as gender complementarity" (27) but suggests that "her silence about the central polemic in *The Princess,* the recuperation of an autonomous woman's movement into a liberalized version of kinship and marriage structures, can be reckoned as a kind of agreement" (28).

From the earliest reviewers to the most recent critics, readers have participated in a dialogue about *The Princess* and *Aurora Leigh* as well as Charlotte Brontë's *Jane Eyre* (1847): "[Reviewers] wanted the plot [of *Aurora Leigh*] to be either more realistic or more allegorical—either *Jane Eyre* or Tennyson's *Princess,* not both at once" (Kaplan 12). Some of the intertextual references linking *Aurora Leigh, The Princess,* and *Jane Eyre* are outlined by Stone, who notes that Romney's first proposal to Aurora revises images from *The Princess:* "[Aurora's] response to Romney's invitation to 'come down' and allow her woman's heart to 'melt' in passion is very different from Ida's final response to the Prince. In terms reminiscent of Jane Eyre's spirited rejection of St. John Rivers, she rejects Romney's bid" for a helpmate wife (119). In *Aurora Leigh* Barrett Browning responded to *Jane Eyre* and *The Princess,* revising both St. John Rivers's and the Prince's offers into Romney's first proposal; Aurora's refusal to marry opens an interim in which she develops as an artist and renegotiates the marriage offer into "a reversal of the usual Victorian domestic contract" (Stone 122). Like *Aurora Leigh, St. Elmo* celebrates a heroine who claims independence through rejecting a proposal and successfully pursuing literary fame, but like *The Princess,* it refuses to relinquish—as the renegotiated marriage shows—the sentimental ideal of a refined woman serving as helpmeet to her husband. The double-proposal plot as Evans works with it in *St. Elmo* and the earlier *Beulah* (1859) seeks to accommodate both an ambitious vision of women's intellectual capabilities and a conservative, even reactionary, model of their social and political roles.

Evans's double-proposal plots celebrate both women's aspirations and women's dependency because she wanted to defend the South's sociopolitical institutions while insisting that women's intellectual capabilities were equal to men's. Her stance is like that of Caroline Hentz, whose southern novels attempted to negotiate the same conflicting drives. Evans tries to disguise her southern allegiance by labeling her political views "American" rather than more specifically "southern" and by dressing her gender politics in sentimental and religious idioms, yet she pushes boundaries for women much further than did Hentz; in her novels she therefore struggles harder to reconcile the divergent plots. Evans's heroines seek success in the literary marketplace but accept hierarchical marriages; they experience sexual desire (reserved by Hentz for men) but are not allowed to express it. Inviting women to become desiring subjects while insisting that they accept the object status conferred on them by southern ideology, Evans constructs female subjectivity as a site of turmoil and anxiety.

Born in Columbus, Georgia, in 1835, Augusta Evans (later Wilson) lived most of her life in Georgia, but during her childhood her family resided briefly in Texas. Although she was "descended on both sides from prominent South Carolina families," she grew up amidst economic uncertainty because of her father's fluctuating fortunes and amidst political uncertainty because of the steadily increasing tensions between the South and the North (Faust, Introduction ix). During the Civil War Evans committed herself unreservedly to the Confederacy. She met and advised Confederate leaders, nursed wounded soldiers, and wrote *Macaria; or, Altars of Sacrifice* (1864) to inspire Southerners and justify the southern cause.[1] Whereas Hentz's double-proposal novels were written when she could still imagine promoting sectional reconciliation, *Beulah* was published under the shadow of conflict, and *St. Elmo* after the defeat of Evans's beloved Confederacy.

Both of Evans's double-proposal heroines, Beulah Benton and Edna Earl, are torn between the drive toward individual expression and the desire for domestic safety. They are gifted intellectuals but are not, the novels make clear, "those unfortunate, abnormal developments, familiarly known as 'strong-minded women'" (*St. Elmo* 254). They write about sociopolitical issues to instruct and edify a large reading public, yet they disdain women who want to vote. Better educated and more intelligent than virtually all of their acquaintances, male and female, they still maintain that a woman's highest duty is service in the domestic sphere. They passionately love flawed and skeptical heroes, yet remain passive within courtship. The eponymous heroine of *Beulah* is an orphan who works as a nursemaid until she falls ill; the Byronically attractive physician Guy Hartwell rescues her, makes her his ward, and sends her to school. Beulah accepts his help only until she graduates and can support herself, rejecting first his plan to adopt her and later his marriage proposal in favor of an independence achieved by teaching and writing. Obsessed with finding empirical evidence to support Christian revelation, she ventures into the wilds of skepticism, returning to the church and accepting Guy's second proposal after exhausting all hope of finding human explanations for divine activities. Edna Earl of *St. Elmo,* also an orphan, is taken in and educated by the wealthy Mrs. Murray. Edna goes to New York to pursue a literary career in spite of Mrs. Murray's offer of continuing support and her errant son St. Elmo's offer of marriage. She becomes a famous writer and travels overseas, rejecting proposals from prestigious men because she cannot overcome her love for St. Elmo; meanwhile, St. Elmo reforms and is ordained a Christian minister, and Edna can finally trust him enough to accept his marriage proposal.[2]

Critics have already noted that Evans is committed to women's right to higher, even the highest, education and that she is convinced that women's minds equal men's in the capacity to absorb and propound erudite subjects. Nina Baym notes that, among woman's fiction authors, "only [Evans] found such excitement in pure ideas; only she believed so passionately that women could feel with their minds as well as their hearts" (*Woman's Fiction* 282). Evans's heroines specialize in male-dominated discourses: Beulah tackles metaphysics and theology, while Edna masters ancient languages and classical mythologies. These intellectual quests drive the character development plots. Elizabeth Fox-Genovese traces Beulah's progress "through the thickets of nineteenth-century science and skepticism finally to end upon the rock of Methodist conviction" (Introduction xix). Susan K. Harris describes Edna's intellectual progress as a "struggle to grasp verbal power and to create a feminine mythology" and comments, "It would be difficult to imagine a more radical appropriation of elite male intellectual culture than Edna achieves" (*Nineteenth-Century American Women's Novels* 66, 67).

While the intellectualism of these heroines might suggest a progressive view of women, Evans vehemently condemns women's rights activists, especially suffragists, and warmly endorses a limited, domestic role for women. Readings of Evans must confront what to us appear to be glaring inconsistencies between character development and courtship plots. Anne Firor Scott finds Evans's position hypocritical, noting that Evans "was not the last woman to achieve an enviable emancipation herself while denying that it was appropriate for others" (76). (But in fact upon marriage Evans did devote herself mainly to domestic pursuits, writing only in her spare time.) Anne Goodwyn Jones thinks the conclusion of *Beulah* "does not just turn the tables; it turns back the forward motion of the novel, denying the implications of the previous 430 pages rather than fulfilling them" (57). Harris writes that "to have Edna's hard-won career thus abruptly terminated, and for her to offer no resistance, constitutes an ending that amounts to a lie" (*Nineteenth-Century American Women's Novels* 73). The development plots tell an aggressive story of a woman's individual achievement; the double-proposal plot, even while renegotiating the marriage between the proposal scenes to strengthen the heroine's position, seems to tell a contradictory story of a woman's necessary subordination. In short, Evans's double proposals show how marriage might accommodate an independent woman, but do not draw the conclusions of their own implications. Evans challenges gender hierarchy by demonstrating that women and men are intellectual equals and should marry as intellectual equals, yet she maintains that the marriage relation itself should be hierarchical. The tension produced by such discrepant convictions is more apparent to twentieth-century critics than it was to nineteenth-century readers, yet the pressure exerted by the simultaneous assertion and denial of female autonomy is also indexed in the text, particularly in the language of illness and death with which Evans conveys her heroines into marriage.

Twentieth-century critics label Evans's marriage endings compromises, lies, denials, or dilemmas, but those endings were much less likely to provoke frustration from nineteenth-century readers than were endings that, to us, grow more "naturally" out of a plot of the heroine's independence. The contrast between early reviewers' responses and more recent critical assessments suggests just how different our horizon of expectations is from that of the original readers. When Evans kept her independent heroines single, as in *Macaria* (1864) and *Vashti; or, Until Death Us Do Part* (1869), early readers and reviewers were displeased. *Macaria* and *Vashti* tell much the same story of female heroism as *Beulah* and *St. Elmo*. In *Macaria* a heroine remains single because the hero is killed in battle, whereas in *Vashti* the protagonist, belatedly freed by the death of her estranged husband, dies moments before her suitor comes to offer her a second proposal. Both *Macaria* and *Vashti* sold well, but neither was as popular as *Beulah* or *St. Elmo;* readers and reviewers alike seemed to prefer the domestic endings of the double-proposal narratives to the unconventional outcomes of these two novels.[3] *Macaria* "received some highly critical notices from reviewers objecting to Evans's abandonment of the domestic plot," including one that accused her of doing "no inconsiderable violence to our just expectations" and another who believed that "if many heroines like Irene should appear, 'the world will need the new classification of men, women and Irenes'" (Faust, Introduction xxiv–xxv). *Macaria* diverged too markedly from readers' expectations; while its heroine is no more learned or independent than Beulah and Edna, her failure to marry and cut off the development plot fundamentally altered reviewers' responses. As for *Vashti,* the diarist Isabella Maud Rittenhouse describes it as "the funniest thing I ever saw": "The main object of the writer seems to be to compose a book as entirely different from anything else ever written as possible and I think in that she succeeds. . . . Everybody in the book save one old maid is in love, not a person finds that love reciprocated, everybody dies but two, one the hero, whose 'true love' has died, the other a glorious girl, hopelessly in love with aforesaid hero, nobody gets married, and the book stops without really ending" (26).

Evans's message of female heroism and independence challenged the expectations of her readers; she sold it most successfully when she "really ended" the novels; in other words, when she closed with a marriage. The double-proposal plot served to conclude the novels with marriage after all without giving up the plot of the woman who rejects her eventual husband to pursue her own goals. I have located no complaint from the midnineteenth century resembling those of critics today concerning the double-proposal novels' endings. Evans's marriage conclusions break our horizon of expectations because we do not anticipate a plot about a protagonist's successful battle for independence to end in her capitulation to a hierarchical marriage, the previous rejection of which was a crucial element in making her development possible. But such a capitulation would have appeared more "natural" than "strained" to nineteenth-century readers who expected marriage endings in novels and who were not yet prepared, as twentieth-century literary critics are, to imagine a woman's life plot fulfilled outside of marriage.

The double-proposal plot allowed Evans to explore competing ideologies of women's social and political roles without "doing violence" to readers' expectations. In a culture dealing with multiple responses to "the woman question," neither Evans nor many of her contemporaries would have registered the contradiction that we now see between development plot and courtship outcome. The fluid concepts of "women's rights" and "women's sphere" were not yet rigidly defined along the lines with which we have become familiar. "Women's rights" did not always link higher education to suffrage to married women's property rights, and "women's sphere" was not always strictly limited to the domestic. Evans steadily attempts to show that genteel women could claim intellectual independence without sacrificing the privileges they already had. When Beulah graduates from the public school she delivers a valedictory address that conveys Evans's views on women's rights and women's sphere. Beulah's "predicate" is "that female intellect was capable of the most exalted attainments, and that the elements of her character would enable woman to cope successfully with difficulties of every class." Having proven woman's capabilities by arguments from "the fertile fields of history," Beulah then defines woman's "peculiar sphere, her true position" in conservative terms, exhorting her classmates "to prove themselves true women of America—ornaments of the social circle, angel guardians of the sacred hearthstone, ministering spirits where suffering and want demanded succor" (140). Edna similarly explains that God and nature define women's rights as "the right to be learned, wise, noble, useful, in woman's divinely limited sphere. . . . But not the right to vote; to harangue from the hustings; to trail her heaven-born purity through the dust and mire of political strife; to ascend the rostra of statesmen" (301).[4] Edna's "divinely limited sphere" includes the worldwide literary market, but not the polling booth.

Because Evans was so committed to the South, she sharply distinguished her work from nineteenth-century women's rights discourse, which often asserted that women's mental equality and consequent right to higher education justified their demands for increased participation within the public sphere, particularly the right to vote. Furthermore, in northern reform movements feminists often joined forces with abolitionists, so that increased freedom for women was linked with freedom for slaves. Evans opposed any extension of suffrage: women should influence men, not compete with them. In her wartime correspondence, she attacks John Stuart Mill's doctrine of universal suffrage as an "effete theory" (see Fidler 118); in St. Elmo she propounds the same view. St. Elmo says: "The clearest thinkers of the world have had soft spots in their brains . . . and you have laid your finger on the softened spot in Mill's skull, 'suffrage.' That is a jaded, spavined hobby of his, and he is too shrewd a logician to involve himself in the inconsistency of 'extended suffrage' which excludes women" (168). St. Elmo, at this point in the novel a committed misogynist, assumes that Mill supports woman's suffrage only because it is a necessary corollary to his doctrine of extended suffrage for men. St. Elmo rejects the entire package: "When I read his 'Representative Government' I saw that his reason had dragged anchor, the prestige of his great name vanished, and I threw the book into the fire and eschewed him henceforth" (168). Edna echoes St. Elmo's views about Mill when she denounces the women's rights movement—linked here with Mill's "theory of Liberty and Suffrage"—as the "most loathsome of political leprosies . . . the ridiculous clamour raised by a few unamiable and wretched wives, and as many embittered, disappointed old maids of New England" (253). She associates women's rights activists with "amazonian legions" of England and old maids from New England, pitting them against the "truly refined American woman" (by the process of elimination, implicitly the southern woman typified by Edna) who is satisfied with the political status quo.

The apparent contradictions in Evans's progressive view of women's minds (which she elaborates in the development plots) and conservative

attitude toward women's social role (which she asserts through the courtship plots) express her version of what Eugene D. Genovese has labeled the
"slaveholders' dilemma." Genovese locates a contradiction in educated antebellum southern discourse between commitment to modern ideas and
support of slavery. Genovese argues that southern intellectuals tried to articulate "an understanding of freedom and progress as grounded in—not
opposed to—slavery as a social system" (10–11). The slaveholders' contention
that freedom and progress for the privileged race depended on continued
subservience of a lower race involved them in irreconcilable contradictions
because "they could not deny that the material progress they celebrated
flowed from the performance of the societies that were not merely expand-
ing freedom but eradicating slavery" (40). Evans similarly celebrates progress
for women in education, the arts, and commercial literature while insisting
that this progress can best be achieved within a hierarchical system. She ignores the fact that all her admired female intellectuals are from England and
New England, the very places she also identifies with radical political views.

Evans attempts to resolve her dilemma by clothing progressive ideas in
conservative terms; in particular, she alters the concept of refinement to make
it fit her purposes. Middle-class values of achievement through self-educa-
tion and hard work are "classed up" by being designated "truly refined," while
the snobbish behavior of the *beau monde* is "classed down" as "falsely refined."
The narrator of *Beulah* breaks out early in the novel: "Ah, this fine-ladyism,
this ignoring of labor, to which, in accordance with the divine decree, all
should be subjected; this false-effeminacy, and miserable *affectation of refinement*, which characterizes the age, is the unyielding lock on the wheels of
social reform and advancement" (33; my emphasis). While lazy and affected
"fine ladies" hamper true progress, a well-educated, hard-working woman
benefits society and is therefore truly refined. Evans ties this progressive,
indeed New Englandish, definition of refinement to political and social conservatism. Gaining an education does not, Edna insists, make a woman potentially "dangerous":

> Erudition and effrontery have no inherent connection, and a woman has an
> unquestionable right to improve her mind, *ad infinitum*, provided she does
> not barter womanly delicacy and refinement for mere knowledge. . . . Does
> it not appear reasonable that a truly refined woman . . . should increase her
> usefulness to her family and her race, by increasing her knowledge? A fe-
> male pedant who is coarse and boisterous, or ambitious of going to Con-
> gress, or making stump-speeches, would be quite as unwomanly and unlovely
> in character if she were utterly illiterate. (254)

A refined woman may become well educated and therefore more useful "to her family and her race," but she will not demand direct political representation. Education, properly administered, will not change her politics or her essential character, but rather will make her more useful to the polity.

In her double-proposal novels Evans tries to associate her political views with "America" and not with the South explicitly. Evans knew the North was prejudiced against southern literature and no doubt wanted her own novels to rise above the second-class rating often given southern productions. Elizabeth Moss, who examines a series of articles Evans wrote for the *Mobile Daily Advertiser* (in October and November 1859), summarizes Evans's argument: "By encouraging southerners to write exclusively 'southern' literature, northern publishers consciously repressed the development of southern genius and ensured that the South would remain inferior to the North in the world of national and international letters" (164). But the southern press also pressured writers to pen "southern" literature, though for different reasons (see my discussion in chapter 1). Despite such pressures, only in *Macaria,* as a Civil War novel, does Evans make a point of southernism. Still, Evans's identity as a southerner was always linked with her work. Southern periodicals were proud to claim her (even when they also criticized her), while northern reviewers were apt to patronize. In 1860 a reviewer for the *Ladies' Repository* (published in Cincinnati) makes a point of citing the "letter sheet of recommendations, chiefly from southern pens" that arrived with *Beulah.* One of these, the reviewer maintains, makes the novel "the occasion for a regular fire-eater's onslaught against all who do not swear by the 'peculiar institution'" while another "exults that 'the south' could produce so much excellence" ("New York Literary Correspondence" 125). A writer for the same periodical, when reviewing Mary Forrest's *Women of the South Distinguished in Literature,* singles out the entry on Evans as partially confirming the speculation that *Beulah* is autobiographical. The concluding sentences of that review, written early in the critical year 1861, underscore both regional division and the literary dominance assumed by the North: "Since our southern friends like to see themselves by themselves, I do not see that we outsiders have any right to object, especially while they allow us to enjoy with them the pleasure which such an exhibition affords; and I am certain that the best way for us to avenge ourselves will be to imitate the Roman youth with the Sabines by seizing the volume and its fair occupants" ("New York Literary Correspondence" 60). By smugly coding the North as successful male warrior and the South as conquered female even before the onset of the Civil War, this reviewer reveals that regional prejudice could combine with gender prejudice in such a way as to doubly demean southern women writers. The pattern of northern superiority and southern adulation continued after the war. In 1867 a northern reviewer of "Southern Books by Southern Authors" noted with some amazement that "there are a good many people in the North who read Miss Evans's volumes" while laughing at a southern commentator who suggests that admiration of her should inspire "this unconstitutional and radical Congress [to] forthwith reconstruct [her home] State of Alabama" (232).

Not surprisingly, then, in Evans's double-proposal novels regional sympathies are apparent only in closer readings. *Beulah* suggests fear of the political tensions of the late 1850s when the heroine proclaims that gifted statesmen are desperately needed: "To such the call will be imperative; America needs such men. Heaven only knows where they are to rise from, when the call is made!" (142). Edna's violent language as she bemoans the fate of the "stabbed constitution" refers to the defeated Confederacy: "Statesmen were almost extinct in America. . . . Republicanism was in its death-throes, and would soon be a dishonoured and insulted ghost, hunted out of the land by the steel bayonets of a centralized despotism" (300). These gestures of Confederate loyalty failed to console one southern reviewer, who criticizes the novel because it fails to paint "a picture of true Southern life ere the rude hand of Radicalism completely obliterates the delicately tinted lights and shadows. . . . The society to which we are introduced is scarcely a fair sample of the manners, customs and conversation of our people" ("Miss Evans— St. Elmo" 270).[5] One reference to the Civil War in *St. Elmo,* occurring seven pages from the end, announces Evans's political position outright and dates the book explicitly: "Only one cause of disquiet now remained. The political storm of 1861 alarmed her, and she determined that if the threatened secession of the South took place, she would immediately remove to Charleston or New Orleans, link her destiny with the cause which she felt was so just, so holy, and render faithful allegiance to the section she loved so well" (360). Almost immediately after this reverie, St. Elmo comes to claim Edna and return her to the South. The impending Civil War thus provides an additional reason for Edna to accept the final proposal. At least one of Evans's contemporaries read the ending of *St. Elmo* through the lens of the Civil War. In *St. Twel'mo* (1868), his parody of *St. Elmo,* Charles Webb constantly mocks Evans's southernism, revealing that Evans's original readers were attuned to sectional differences. Webb links "Etna's" acceptance of St. Twel'mo with the imminent war: "The war breaking out just then, Etna determined that St. Twel'mo should not be at peace, and married him. She knew that the cause of the South was pure and just, and that they had a right to forts, arsenals, territory, and things which they had not paid for, and she was perfectly willing to sacrifice her best beloved to establish the sincerity of her convictions" (58).

Given the publication dates of *Beulah* and *St. Elmo,* given the fact that her southern identity would inevitably frame readers' reactions to her novels, and given Evans's strong sectional commitment, one understands why her heroines' ambitious careers must appear to pose no threat to existing political and social institutions, must in fact seem to validate and promote them, must have no connection to northern reform movements that helped to overpower the South, must, in a word, be refined. But the literary ambitions of her heroines are nevertheless ill-fitted to the hierarchical, interdependent social structure Evans wished to protect, and thus she separates her protagonists from that structure while they are pursuing careers. The demands of the southern worldview made it particularly difficult for her heroines to claim profession and marriage simultaneously, and Evans resolves this conflict by giving her heroines first an individual quest and then a marriage. By denying herself a place in a kin structure that would bind her to family obligations Evans was unprepared to question, the protagonist can fulfill a heroic destiny and then set it aside to retire into marriage.

In an attempt to muffle the discord created by her dual endorsement of intellectual independence and social dependence, Evans orphans her heroines. To be sure, orphans populate much woman's fiction of the North and South, but Evans makes special use of the convention. Not only is an Evans orphan motherless and fatherless, but she is also without siblings or more distant kin, without any relative who has a right to dictate to her. Inadequately protected orphans must become strong, must make their own way in the world, must pursue the upward course that Baym shows is the dominant trajectory of woman's fiction. Orphanage is the common way to "deprive the heroine of all external aids and to make her success in life entirely a function of her own efforts and character" (*Woman's Fiction* 35). In Evans's double-proposal fiction, orphanage carries additional meaning because of the significance of kinship in the American South. Jean E. Friedman maintains that "the importance of kinship cannot be underestimated in the Victorian South. . . . The South derived its unique identity not only from slavery but from . . . interdependent kin connections" (3).[6]

Only as an orphan can the heroine pursue her ambitions without challenging the interdependent social system, and thus Beulah and Edna refuse offers of adoption and of marriage to maintain their independence. A "true woman," as defined by Evans herself, could pursue extensive learning and literary fame only if she was herself outside of a southern household and had to anticipate earning her own living. Fox-Genovese reports that "women who contemplated a career normally encountered fierce parental opposition and risked community disapprobation" (*Within the Plantation Household* 258–59). Beulah and Edna insist on contemplating careers even when their guardians offer them financial dependence in exchange for a commitment. Both suffer loneliness and meet disapproval as they struggle toward literary fame, but they face no parental prohibition. Accepting the sponsorship of people who rescue them from poverty, Beulah and Edna insist that they be allowed to pay back the costs their guardians incur in educating them.[7] Beulah rejects Hartwell's offer of adoption: "You knew that I came here only to be educated. . . . Will you urge me to remain, when I tell you I cannot be happy here?" (144). Edna similarly refuses Mrs. Murray's offers to support her or to hire her as a companion: "I have never expected to live here longer than was necessary to qualify myself for the work I have chosen." "I could no longer preserve my self-respect or be happy as a dependent on your bounty" (183, 182).[8]

The heroines refuse to be bound by family until they have accomplished their individual goals. Before accepting Guy, Beulah finds the answer to her spiritual search—her primary quest—and is satisfied with the writing fame she has received: "She had been ambitious, and labored to obtain distinction as a writer; and this under various fictitious signatures, was hers" (379). She also has some financial security, as an "increased salary rendered rigid economy and music lessons no longer necessary," but she continues to write "to warn others of the snares in which she had so long been entangled" (379). Beulah also overcomes her self-consciousness, her conviction that she is too ugly to be lovable, when she is courted by Reginald Lindsay, a man she admires and respects: "I do not know his superior" (413). All other goals accomplished, she acknowledges her love for her guardian and prays daily for his return.

Edna's desire for literary immortality is as strong as Beulah's need to discover metaphysical truth: "To possess herself of the golden apple of immortality, was a purpose from which she had never swerved" (151). Edna, however, pushes boundaries further than does her predecessor. Beulah is satisfied with fame "under fictitious signatures," but Edna becomes so public a figure that St. Elmo can buy her photograph. The "world honoured her," and she also had "the precious assurance that her Christian countrywomen loved and trusted her" (360). She is qualified to earn her support even if she must return to the South. "She knew that she could easily obtain a school, or support herself by her pen"; she also has accrued "a very respectable amount—the careful savings of sums paid by her publishers" (360–61). She accepts the reformed St. Elmo only after achieving a satisfactory degree of fame and financial independence.

The character development plots of *Beulah* and *St. Elmo,* narratives of obscure orphan girls who become well-known writers, demonstrate individualism triumphing over self-abnegation, as critics have noted: the heroines "internalize . . . the values of self-reliance, of liberal individualism, which the dominant culture valued in men" (Voloshin 109); or, again, the plot develops "the theme of individuality, of power in and of the self, of energy fuelled not by sexual love but by self-love" (Harris, *Nineteenth-Century American Women's Novels* 64). The courtship plot, on the other hand, maps out a path for renegotiating proposals by reforming suitors who tyrannize over the heroine and abuse the superior power the hierarchy grants them. The renegotiated proposals are offered by suitors who have become less dictatorial, and the heroine accepts a dependent marriage role with the assurance that her husband will not abuse his power.

While the interproposal intervals are primarily occupied with the heroines' personal growth, Beulah and Edna also try to reform southern aristocratic male society. In this reformist activity, Evans shows how a refined woman, especially one who has no family duties, can influence the polity. *St. Elmo* indicts dueling, and *Beulah* features a temperance subplot. According to Bertram Wyatt-Brown, few southern families were entirely free from alcoholic diseases (278–80); he argues that drinking, an exclusively male recreation, played a decisive role in "the struggle over which would be the greatest commitment, the husband's loyalty to male friends or to his wife" (278). Dueling, as a ritual of honor, carried even greater significance to southerners. Steven M. Stowe reports that, after 1800, "duelling rather swiftly came to be perceived as a southern phenomenon by southerners and northerners alike" (*Intimacy and Power* 16). Dueling was "the most visible part of the affair of honor, a masculine ritual that went deeply into the reaches of authority and manhood in the planter elite" (5). Portraying drinking and dueling as behaviors that involved a loss of control, Evans categorizes them as forms of male excess rather than vehicles to display male pride and honor. She exposes the dangers of male tyranny and self-absorption, prescribing a solution consistent with her ideal of true refinement.

Beulah slowly loses respect for her childhood sweetheart, Eugene Graham, when he abandons plans for a political career, begins to drink, and treats her more dictatorially and less lovingly. Beulah had treasured his guidance during the early part of their friendship, but resists being tyrannized over by a man she does not respect. Her lectures wound his pride and estrange him. Still, when he is badly injured while driving horses under the influence, she nurses him because his fashionable and heartless (that is, "falsely refined") wife will not. Under Beulah's guidance, he reforms and begins to struggle again toward the lofty ideals of his youth. Evans here criticizes men who are insufficiently self-controlled, women who fail to do their duty, and the *beau monde* whose "false refinement" has encouraged both Eugene and his wife Antoinette to stray. Like Hentz, Evans does not criticize hierarchy itself but rather abuse of privilege within that hierarchy. She also levels the power relationship between the sinning man and the caring woman; Eugene, humbled and reconciled after Beulah nurses him back to health, acknowledges the value of her guidance.

As a critique of traditional male behaviors, dueling is even more telling in *St. Elmo.* In the first scene of the novel, the young Edna is shocked out of an innocent pastoral idyll when she witnesses a fatal duel and watches the victim's wife die of grief the next day. She remembers her shock and horror throughout the novel, snubbing the man who won the duel when she meets him at the Murrays' estate. St. Elmo, hearing her scathing announcement that duelers should be "shunned as murderers," despairs of winning her love because he has also killed a man in a duel. Edna rejects St. Elmo largely because of that duel, provoking criticism from his mother: "The world sanctions duelling . . . and you have no right to set your extremely rigid notions of propriety above the verdict of modern society. Custom justifies many things which you seem to hold in utter abhorrence" (307). Edna believes she should challenge society's "verdict" and publishes a story critical of dueling: "The principal aim of the little tale was to portray the horrors and sin of duelling . . . but well aware of the vast, powerful current of popular opinion that she was bravely striving to stem, and fully conscious that it would subject her to severe animadversion from those who defended the custom, she could not divest herself of apprehension lest the article should be rejected" (235). Her editor publishes the "little tale" although he does not agree with all of her arguments: "It will, of course, provoke controversy, but for that I presume you are prepared" (238). By criticizing ritualized violence and excessive drinking, Evans argues that southern men ought to be more controlled, more attentive to the needs of their families; she recommends, in short, that they adhere somewhat to the refined standards of behavior they expect of women. She also establishes her conviction that women can and should use the public medium of print to condemn male weaknesses and push for reform.

In addition to using the bifurcated structure of double-proposal novels to develop independent heroines willing to challenge customary male behaviors, Evans deploys the courtship plot for a dialogue about love and marriage. Within each courtship plot, Evans considers how the flawed marriage that would have resulted from the initial proposal can be renegotiated so that the heroine will accept it. Head and heart are continually at odds with each other, first in the battle between ambition (the drive to display intellectual skills and excel individually) and desire for a family (the need to subsume the self in meeting the needs of others); and second in the battle over the courtship, in which respect and trust (the consent of the head to the union) and love (the involuntary capitulation of the heart to one man) continually conflict. In Evans's taxonomy of each heroine's psyche, the "head," which includes mind and will, is ruled by moral conviction. The "heart," on the other hand, comprises the conventional feminine attributes of emotion and intuition, but seems to be ruled by sexual desire. The "love" a heroine must feel for a hero before marrying him has to include emotional and physical attraction, but also be sanctioned by the mind. Evans depicts each woman's will as ruling her behavior although it cannot rule her heart; for Hentz respect and love, in the case of privileged heroines, grow together naturally. Evans's heroines, in contrast, bewail their unfortunate fate when they respect suitors they cannot love and then love suitors they cannot respect, leaving all suitors unfit marriage candidates. When Eugene asks her why she does not love the irreproachable Reginald Lindsay, Beulah suggests that love and reason have no necessary connection: "A strange question truly. My heart is not the tool of my will" (377).

Evans's novels, which reveal the influence of Romantic thought in their portrayals of characters responding to nature, music, and art, also manifest the concept of love that Karen Lystra connects to Romantic individualism (see especially 28–55). Love is irrational, spontaneous, mysterious, an "uncontrollable and baffling force" (29). Evans makes physical response part of her heroines' romantic love and opposes it to the will, but she avoids disruptive potential by showing how a refined woman's behavior will obey conservative social dictates. Evans undertakes to legitimate a definition of woman's "heart" that will include her sexual response without sacrificing her claim to the privileges conferred upon traditional womanliness. For Evans as for others in her culture, women could be pure without being passionless: "In nineteenth-century American culture, purity did not mean the absence of all sexual activity; it meant legitimate sexual expression" (Leach 76). But while Evans portrays physical desire in her heroines, she denies them the privilege of expressing it.

In his history of nineteenth-century marriage reform William Leach argues that feminists distinguished romantic from sentimental love and condemned both. The former celebrated the autonomy of the self's emotion and "potentially promised bold and . . . even revolutionary behavior" (111); the latter "portrayed women as idealized objects and the passive recipients of masculine affections" (100) and supported the status quo (111). He observes that "both could coexist uncomfortably or even tragically in a single consciousness or at different points in the lifetime of a single person" (112) and points to "rational love" as the feminist thinkers' antidote to the other two: "Rational love did not emerge from ignorance, subterfuge, and momentary dalliance, but only after an extended period of mutual self-scrutiny and revelation, and equal development of both sexes" (124). Evans was no feminist, yet her novels reveal her awareness of competing definitions of "love." Beulah and Edna are virtual textbook examples of uncomfortable conjunctions among the three conceptualizations detailed by Leach. Evans struggles to draw something from each. She wants women to maintain their idealized sentimental status so as not to compromise their class position. Furthermore, a sentimental pedestal may be a platform for influencing the world, as demonstrated when Beulah and Edna assume moral superiority to criticize men who drink and duel. Evans also believed, however, in the Romantic individual self that could intuitively respond to beauty or feel romantic love without the mediation of a rational, socially conscious self. A good marriage, Evans's novels suggest, will emerge from a fortuitous and perhaps rare combination of all these elements: the mysterious response of one heart (or body) to another, the protection of the ideal of morally superior womanhood, and the approval of the rational mind, the knowledge that the loved one will be a worthy intellectual companion and a moral exemplar.

Beulah and Edna reject the heroes' first proposals in part because they are not satisfied with the love they feel or the love expressed by their suitors; the second proposals by contrast articulate an ideal combination of romantic, sentimental, and rational love. *Beulah*'s courtship plot demonstrates some of the problems in approaches to love, while *St. Elmo* portrays in detail a solution to them. The growth of love between Beulah and Guy is represented in encounters that are alternately stifled and explosive, perhaps because both characters are confused about their own emotions. Guy admits that he "did not know my own heart" when he asked Beulah to be his adoptive daughter, and when Beulah at last accepts him, she confesses that she had loved him "longer than I knew myself" (412). The consistent theme is gratitude versus love; Hartwell tries to manipulate Beulah by playing on her gratitude, inviting her to discharge her debt by submitting to him: "Now Beulah, I have saved you, and you belong to me" (56). When she is seventeen Beulah's feelings for Hartwell are described as "more earnest gratitude than genuine affection" (112), and he wants her to accept adoption because, he says, "I think you owe me something for taking care of you" (143). Later, she rejects his first marriage proposal, maintaining that she does not love him although she admires and is grateful to him: "You would despise a wife who was such only from gratitude. Do not ask this of me; we would both be wretched. . . . I reverence you; nay, more, I love you, sir, as my best friend; I love you as my protector . . . but I cannot marry you" (328). Beulah will not confess to any romantic love for her guardian, notes the age difference between them as a barrier, and does not believe he loves her either. Neither gratitude nor respect is enough.[9]

In *St. Elmo,* Edna studies and understands her desires, and romantic love becomes a part of her acknowledged experience. She is "disquieted and pained" when she discovers that St. Elmo's face "possessed an attraction—an indescribable fascination—which she had found nowhere else." While attempting to "analyse the interest she was for the first time conscious of feeling, she soothed herself with the belief that it arose from curiosity concerning his past life" (95). But eventually Edna has to admit that her heart indeed ignores the dictates of her mind: "Hitherto she had fancied that she thoroughly understood and sternly governed her heart—that conscience and reason ruled it; but within the past hour it had suddenly risen in dangerous rebellion, thrown off its allegiance to all things else, and insolently proclaimed St. Elmo Murray its king" (138). This realization shocks Edna out of her previous complacency, an understanding of love that might have been learned from Caroline Hentz's fiction: "Love could only exist where high esteem and unbounded reverence prepared the soil" (138). Edna finds this romantic love "contemptible and . . . unwomanly" and vows to "crush out the feeling at once, cost what it might" (139, 138). She initially refuses to call her attraction to St. Elmo "love": "It is not love; for esteem, respect, confidence belong to love: but I cannot deny that he exerts a very singular, a wicked fascination over me" (214). Edna reconsiders the relation between love and trust when she is tempted by an offer of marriage from Mr. Manning, a magazine editor. Now she labels her feelings for St. Elmo "love": "Edna was weary of battling with precious memories of that reckless, fascinating cynic whom, without trusting, she had learned to love; and she thought that, perhaps, if she were the wife of Mr. Manning, whom without loving she fully trusted, it would help her to forget St. Elmo" (276). But finally she cannot accept the offer: "Oh! why cannot my weak, wayward heart follow my strong, clear-eyed judgment?" (276). However insistent a woman's "weak, wayward heart" may be, Evans suggests her mind, her will, ought to be stronger, ought to rule her conduct; unloving women are monstrous women, but women who give in to unseemly desires are also unwomanly.[10] This conflict between respect and love thus establishes both the heroine's womanliness and her mental strength. Conveniently for the contradictory imperatives of the development plot and the courtship plot, even as the heroine achieves her (potentially unwomanly) career ambitions, her struggle with love reminds us of her traditional feminine side.

Evans joins Brontë in using the first proposal to rewrite the conventional seduction plot that featured a Byronic hero taking advantage of a heroine's involuntary sexual attraction to him. When the seduction plot is recast, the woman no longer loses because she no longer yields to her desire for the hero. The double proposal thus both acknowledges physical response and puts it in its place. *St. Elmo*, like *Jane Eyre*, demonstrates that a woman may be a sexual being and yet not be out of control; on the contrary, her self-control is stronger for having withstood severe temptation. When the second proposal is accepted, the hero does not use sexual attraction as leverage. The two meet on more equal ground. For Evans and Brontë, rational love merges with romantic attraction; in *St. Elmo*, sentimental love joins them as Evans endeavors to fit the double-proposal love ideal into a conservative worldview.

Edna does not succeed in crushing her attraction to St. Elmo, but she controls her actions. In the first proposal scene, St. Elmo tries to manipulate Edna's feelings to coerce her into acceptance. Instead of urging gratitude like Hartwell, he marshals the forces of romantic and sentimental love against Edna's reason, casting the scene as an attempted seduction as well as a marriage proposal. Having recited the history of his sinful life and subsequent rejuvenating love for Edna, St. Elmo arrogantly claims her love: "'I know you do not want to love me. Your lips cannot dissemble. I know it; you are struggling to crush your heart. You think it your duty to despise and hate me. But, my own Edna—my darling! my darling! you do love me! You know you do love me, though you will not confess it! My proud darling!' He drew the face tenderly to his own, and kissed her quivering lips repeatedly, and at last a moan of anguish told how she was wrestling with her heart"

(210). In addition to this appeal to Edna's sexual desire, St. Elmo tries sentimental pleas, deferring to Edna's superior purity and piety: "My precious Edna, no oath shall ever soil my lips again; and the touch of yours has purified them. . . . With your dear little hand in mine, to lead me, I will make amends for the ruin and suffering I have wrought, and my Edna—my own wife—shall save me!" (211). Edna rejects the romantic and the sentimental appeals, basing her actions on her rational convictions: "Mr. Murray, I can never be your wife. I have no confidence in you. . . . I can neither respect nor trust you" (211). Edna clings to her conviction in the face of great temptation, as Jane Eyre had done before her: "Laws and principles are not for times when there is no temptation: they are for such moments as this, when body and soul rise in mutiny against their rigour" (*Jane Eyre* 344). In Brontë's novel, the first proposal is equated with seduction when the wedding is interrupted and Rochester pressures Jane to become his mistress instead of his (bigamous) wife. Evans suggests in her novel that even legitimate courtship can be motivated by dangerous impulses. Had Edna given in to St. Elmo, she would have been, even as a wife, a sexual prey much like the objects of his earlier seductions.

In entering the dialogue on the role of romantic love in courtship, Evans exploits the popularity of Byronic heroes, capitalizing on the fascinating dangers of romantic love before reforming the hero. Webb suggests the degree to which the trope of the intelligent heroine attracted to the Byronic hero was considered characteristic of novels by women: "The moral that women with 'intellect into them,' can be best won by pelting them with vituperation and junk-bottles instead of with bon-bons, and telling them to go to the devil instead of to Delmonico's, where anything they choose to fancy in the way of lunch awaits them, I do not believe, and do here resolutely refuse to accept, though all the authoresses in Christendom and out of it are leagued together to persuade me to the contrary" (25). Both Guy Hartwell and St. Elmo Murray could be accused of "pelting" women with "vituperation." Both also share, though in different degrees, the telling characteristics of Brontë's hero, summarized by one exasperated reviewer of *St. Elmo* as follows: "He is a very bad person. His brow is white, but the lower part of his stern face is bronzed with exposure. He has magnetic eyes. He has not been inside of a church for nearly twenty years. . . . [His] physical strength is great, his wealth is boundless; he has roamed all over the world; he despises the conventionalities of society; he is 'quite the gentleman' when he likes, and is particularly clever at a profound, perfectly polite, but mocking bow, which he alone can do. In short he is a very stupid copy of Rochester" ("Southern Books"

233). But Evans's Rochesters are also adapted to the antebellum South; they are slaveholding gentlemen, town dwellers who own plantations. Each attempts to dominate the heroine, bringing all the force of physical presence, emotional manipulation, and intellectual brilliance to bear in the effort to coerce her into marriage.

While engrossed readers registered their approval by making *Beulah* and *St. Elmo* best-sellers, gatekeepers objected. Several southern reviewers disdained the reappearance of the Byronic hero and made clear their preference for heroes who would not require reformation. The *Southern Literary Messenger* reviewer prefers either Eugene Graham or Reginald Lindsay (both conventional chivalric characters) to Guy Hartwell and professes dismay at Eugene's dissipation, which spoils his chance to marry Beulah. This reviewer, miffed that Evans would have failed to reward the more conventional heroes, betrays an interest in the characters that reveals engagement in the world of the novel rather than an objective critical stance; Eugene, the reviewer suspects, succumbed to "the earliest temptation to crime, that more favoured personages may occupy the high places of the novel unrivalled" (Rev. of *Beulah* 244); in this case, the "more favoured personage" would be Guy Hartwell, who, the reviewer claims, is "the chief error of the whole 'novel'" (244, 245).[11] The reviewer also derides Beulah's rejection of Reginald Lindsay—"a hero worthy of the highest place in any novel, whose character is more happily drawn than any other in the plan of the work"—and sighs over Reginald's fate: "He rises to great worldly distinction, but his heart . . . was destined to pine in gloomy disappointment" (247). A critic for the *Southern Review* similarly ridicules the reappearance of the Byronic hero in St. Elmo, "the scoffer, the cynic, the misanthrope whose heart has been cankered and hardened by one treason, the restless wanderer upon the earth who has exhausted life at the age of thirty-four" ("Book Notices" 494). A reviewer for *DeBow's*, identified as "a young lady of Virginia," complains of St. Elmo's sinfulness, cruelty, cynicism, and pedantry, dubbing him "a cross between Rochester, Bruno and Byron" instead of the "chivalrous, high-toned Southern gentleman" who might have been portrayed instead ("Miss Evans—St. Elmo" 270). The reviewers do not consider the hero's reformation when complaining about a heroine's romantic love for a flawed hero. Perhaps the danger of the romantic love story, of the rewritten seduction makes a stronger impression than its didactic revision, or perhaps reviewers preferred that women writers represent their heroes as flawless from beginning to end. St. Elmo, and to a lesser extent Guy Hartwell, overcomes the threatening elements of Byronism before marrying, but these reviewers prefer the hero to be chivalric from beginning to end.

Of course, the refusals also open the path to the heroines' ambitious careers, a fact the reviewers ignore but Webb's parody exploits. He renders
Etna's refusal of the first proposal in these terms:

> The only wonder is, that Etna had not married, out of hand, this chivalric
> Chattanoogian. Seducing the sister, by way of getting even with her broth-
> er, certainly commends itself as an original enterprise, which should have
> stirred the depths of a refined and cultivated woman, emulous of elevating
> her kind by writing for the fashion magazines, to love and admiration. How-
> ever, Etna declined the honor of a betrothal. . . . O the feminine bosom! is
> it not fearfully and wonderfully made up! . . . She did not wish to incur the
> risk of having a "hemorrhage of *blood*" and besides, ambitious of authorship,
> she was determined to do it or die. (48–49)

Webb's treatment bares the truth that the heroine must reject marriage in
order to pursue her career, a point that the courtship plot itself, with its
emphasis on reforming suitors and defining ideal love, tends to obscure.

Evans's novels *Macaria* and *Vashti* attest to her resistance to conventional
marriage endings, but if marriage endings helped the books to sell, Evans
reached more readers with her messages of women's intellectual capabilities
and the superiority of a refined social and political order when she married
off the heroines. Evans self-consciously adapted plot and genre to suit her
didactic agendas and created a heroine, Edna Earl, who did the same.[12] In
St. Elmo, Edna's speeches and experiences defend Evans's approach to fiction.
Edna's editor, who is defined as a paragon of the severe yet fair critic, casti-
gates her for her unwavering didactic view of fiction: "You indulge in the
rather extraordinary belief that all works of fiction should be eminently didactic, and inculcate not only sound morality, but scientific theories. . . . You
entirely misapprehend the spirit of the age. People read novels merely to be
amused, not educated; and they will not tolerate technicalities and abstract
speculation in lieu of exciting plots and melodramatic *dénouements*" (237). Mr.
Manning doubts that Edna's plan to subvert genre boundaries by incorporating an intellectual treatise into a novel will work. When people want to
learn about science, he explains, they look in textbooks rather than in novels. But Edna wants to reach the popular novel reader, who, she points out,
is not generally a textbook reader as well. Edna is sure that the novel form is
the best vehicle for educating the popular reader and believes that a novel
can be both interesting and didactic: "In order to popularize a subject bris-
tling with rocondite [*sic*] archaisms and philologic problems, she cast it in
the mould of fiction" (108).

While Evans was conscious of what her popular audience expected and understood that plot was the means to interest while educating, she also recognized the role played by reviewers. In *St. Elmo* Evans scorns critics who attack Edna for pedantry (the attacks and Edna's responses might be drawn directly from Evans's experiences), but she also recognizes their gatekeeping mission. The "marvellously perfect intellectual automaton" (236) Mr. Manning explains that mission: "Review writers now serve the public in much the same capacity that cup-bearers did royalty in ancient days; and they are expected to taste strong liquors as well as sweet cordials and sour, light wines. Moreover, a certain haze of sactity [*sic*] envelopes the precincts of 'Maga,' whence the incognito 'we' thunders with oracular power. . . . The credulous public fondly cling to the myth that editorial sanctums alone possess the sacred tripod of Delphi" (238). Edna, like her creator, wanted to be successful with the critical elite, whose approval could win her the literary immortality she desired and whose criticism would interpret her work "with oracular power" for "the credulous public" she wanted to influence, but she also invited conflict with them. The preface to Edna's first novel, borrowed from *Aurora Leigh,* is a passage addressed to "My critic Belfair," which points to the impossibility of pleasing critics who demand "A striking book, yet not a startling book" (*St. Elmo* 285).

Evans encountered criticism for every novel she wrote, most drawn by her unrelenting use of obscure allusions and learned debates. A writer for the *Southern Review,* whose 1867 notice of *St. Elmo* primarily critiques its style, illustrates Evans's negative press. The reviewer claimed to have "read the novel from beginning to end, and as attentively as human frailty would allow. Following the author's advice, we have also taken great pains 'to inform ourselves;' nor shrank from procuring and using the ponderous apparatus necessary for that purpose." This reviewer finds that "Edna Earl, the heroine, is our old friend Beulah, with the difference that instead of fathoming the depths of philosophy and theology, she ransacks the domains of classic literature, archaeology and science" ("Book Notices" 493–94). And a reviewer identified as a "young lady of Virginia" complains that "the few original ideas in the book" are lost "in a sea of classical quotations, while page after page is but a compilation of every philosophical, metaphysical and religious treatise that has been thrown to the surface since the days of Roman grandeur and Athenian eloquence" ("Miss Evans—St. Elmo" 269). Webb, in his description of the childhood of Etna, writes that "her discovery of a dictionary" was "a triple calamity, for she acquired in consequence a fatal fondness for polysyllables, a trick of speaking them trippingly, and a contempt for common English, from which she never recovered" (10–11).

But not all reviewers dismissed Evans's learned style, complained of her pomposity, or claimed that she used encyclopedias rather than original sources. At times she received glowing praise, some of it (from southern sources) placing her in the highest ranks of novelists. Mary Virginia Terhune, another southern novelist, praised *Beulah* without qualification: "I pronounce it the best work of fiction ever published by a southern writer. No American authoress has ever published a greater book" (*Mobile Register,* Oct. 7, 1859, qtd. in Moss 173), and a reviewer for *DeBow's* wrote that *Beulah* "may be considered one of the best American novels" ("Editorial Miscellany" 490). A critic for the *Southern Literary Messenger,* the journal so patronizing to Caroline Hentz a few years before, argues that *Beulah* should be recognized as a flawed but promising beginning to a great southern literature. The writer treats Evans's intellectual arguments seriously, although claiming that Beulah's character is distorted by "a philosophic dictum residing everywhere, and pervading every department of the work" (Rev. of *Beulah* 246). This reviewer engages Evans in several of her learned arguments, contending at one point that nature may be itself a source of revelation (Evans accepts only the Bible) and later taking her up sharply for her treatment of the philosopher Cousin. This reviewer also fears that, in detailing Beulah's struggles with skeptical thinkers, Evans might have made "dangerous and seductive theories of metaphysics and theology still more attractive to the enquiring mind" (247). For the most part, however, Evans was praised for the moral worth of her novels. Even the sarcastic critic of *St. Elmo* for the *Southern Review* notes that "the moral tone and teachings of the story are unexceptionable" ("Book Notices" 496), and the writer for *DeBow's Review,* also primarily critical, acknowledges that "the purity of thought, the elevation of purpose, displayed in her writings, cannot be too highly commended" ("Miss Evans—St. Elmo" 269).

Throughout the course of her career, then, Evans drew mixed reviews for the intellectual elements of her novels, for the scholarship that the development plots aimed to display and promote. But Evans hoped to reach popular readers, not just critics, and to inspire them to improve themselves. According to the typical profile of the popular fiction audience, including the one contained in *St. Elmo,* readers ought not to have been enchanted by overwritten novels; they were supposed to read for light amusement only. Edna calls this approach to fiction the "hasty, careless, novel-reading glance" and tries to reassure the "dear reader shivering with learning-phobia" that a difference in knowledge is to be overcome, not feared (333). Evidence from involved readers, spotty though it is, suggests Evans was sometimes successful in inspiring her readers with both the intellectual and the love plots. Isabel Maud Rittenhouse, who found *Vashti*'s plot so funny, wryly admits to having learned from the novel: "I suppose it did me good for it kept me running to the Dictionary or to an encyclopedia to see who Joubert is, or where the 'cheerless temple of Hestia' stands or stood, or to find what 'a wan Alcestis' and 'a desperate Cassandra he had seen at Rome,' indicated" (26). Mary Forrest found the development plot of *Beulah* interesting but the courtship plot less so. She reports in *Women of the South Distinguished in Literature* that Beulah's intellectual quest is the "intensely vitalized action of the book . . . its grand feature and fulcrum; effecting more than whole folios of mere argument" (331); but she expects Guy and Beulah's love plot to disappoint many readers: "They make a grim pair of lovers enough, and throw into spasms of impatience all who are wading through 'ontology,' 'psychology,' 'eclecticism,' etc., merely for some green isle of 'billing and cooing'" (331–32). As her double proposals demonstrate, Evans was conflicted over how to consign an intellectually vital woman to marriage, but she had no qualms about maintaining that a woman should become as educated as possible. Despite continuous pressure from critics, she never backed off from writing learned, heavily allusive prose. Like her heroine Edna, she "continued the hydropathic treatment" of pumping "spring water" (334) on her readers' nerves (yet another allusion to *Aurora Leigh*) because it was good for them. While she experimented with different love plots, her commitment to challenging her readers intellectually never altered.

In her diary, Anna Maria Green recorded that she did not "fancy" *Beulah* or *Macaria* (52), but enjoyed *St. Elmo;* her enthusiasm for education is stronger than Rittenhouse's, and her style appears to reflect the inspiration she describes: "I have been reading Miss Evans last work St. Elmo. I know nothing of the rules of critticism *[sic]* and am incompetent to pronounce upon it as a critic, yet found the book deeply interesting, and think it calculated to do good, by its tone of exalted female heroism. I feel so deep a desire to improve my talents and acquire useful information I have resumed the study of my latin—and enjoy it thus far I am studying without assistance. I wish I could devote myself to unremitting labor in literary pursuits" (111). Green's diary as a whole suggests she might be exactly the type of reader Evans sought to reach and inspire, more interested in love than in learnedness, but receptive to Evans's intellectual message and inspired by "exalted female heroism." In many entries Green discusses men she finds interesting, but in her response to *St. Elmo* she discusses not its love plot but the inspiring effect of its development plot. In her diary Green experiments with both development and courtship plots for herself, but the realities of her life made the courtship outcome almost inevitable. She provides an interesting test case of a con-

temporary reader who imagined a development plot for herself that the realities of her life prevented her from pursuing.[13]

Evans the southerner tries to portray renegotiations in the final proposal that do not overtly compromise the pride of either hero or heroine. Cautious in suggesting that the heroes have been humbled, she implies that their
pride will be redirected; they will cooperate with, rather than tyrannize over,
the heroines. When Beulah rejects Guy's first proposal, he does his best to
wound her verbally, then vindictively vows that she will never see him again:
"I am going very soon, and this is our last meeting. . . . I asked your heart;
you have now none to give; but perhaps some day you will love me, as de-
votedly, nay, as madly as I have long loved you . . . but *then*, rolling oceans
and trackless deserts will divide us" (329–30). Guy announces proudly, "Once
resolved, I never waver," but several years later he reappears. Declaring, "I
don't want a grateful wife," he implies that he now refuses to use Beulah's
debt of gratitude to manipulate her. His joyful response when Beulah accepts
him suggests he recognizes that this is a fairer, and happier, emotional contract than was his first proposal: "I shall be happy in my own home; shall have
a wife, a companion, who loves me *for myself alone*" (413; my emphasis). His
harsh nature continues to soften after the wedding.[14]

Edna, certain that marrying the embittered and sinful St. Elmo would
endanger her own spiritual welfare, is not persuaded by his improvement until
he becomes a minister, at which point "a glory breaks upon the future" (358).
St. Elmo's violence and tyranny are controlled, and trust and mutual respect
have been added to their relationship. Rather than humbling St. Elmo, Evans
recasts his pride into a respect for, rather than a domination over, Edna: "He
stood within two feet of her, but he was—too humble? Nay, nay, too proud
to touch her without permission" (363). In the second proposal, St. Elmo no
longer appears in the character of seducer. The Byronic hero has been reformed and reclaimed by the double-proposal text.

The double-proposal structure that brings together elements of romantic and rational love with conventional sentimental love implies that the
heroine will, indeed, have more independence in the renegotiated marriage
than she would have had in the first proposed marriage. While the conclusions employ conventional marriage rhetoric, Evans suggests elsewhere in
the novels that she entertains an ideal of marriage that will offer intellectual
companionship, hinting that a wife may fully participate in her husband's
public life. While John Stuart Mill is castigated in *St. Elmo* for his position
on suffrage, Edna quotes approvingly, even longingly, his "glowing tribute
to the intellectual capacity of women," written in memory of his wife:

To the beloved and deplored memory of her who was the inspirer, and in
part, the author, of all that is best in my writings, the friend and wife whose
exalted sense of truth and right was my strongest incitement and whose
approbation was my chief reward, I dedicate this volume. Like all that I have
written for many years, it belongs as much to her as to me. . . . Were I but
capable of interpreting to the world one half the great thoughts and noble
feelings which are buried in her grave, I should be the medium of a greater
benefit to it than is ever likely to arise from anything that I can write un-
prompted and unassisted by her all but unrivalled wisdom. (169)

Mill appears to idealize both his wife's "sense of truth and right" and her
active intelligence. When Edna permits herself to fantasize about what life
with St. Elmo would have been like had he been trustworthy, her thoughts
recall the ideal marriage of "the friend and wife" who was coauthor of Mill's
writings, although she casts her vision of mutual work in Christian terms:

A vision of a happy, proud, young wife reigning at Le Bocage, shedding the
warm, rosy light of her love over the lonely life of its master; adding to his
strong, clear intellect and ripe experience, the silver flame of her genius;
borrowing from him broader and more profound views of her race, on which
to base her ideal, aesthetic structures; softening, refining his nature, strengthening her own; helping him to help humanity; loving all good, being good,
doing good; serving and worshipping God together; walking hand in hand
with her husband through earth's wide valley of Baca with peaceful faces full
of faith, looking heaven-ward. (326–27)

This idealized picture begins in the domestic circle of Le Bocage, but broad-
ens to include an active intellectual life that recalls Mill's words. Evans implies that a wife could continue to write, to "base her ideal, aesthetic structures" on the "more profound views" contributed by her husband. The
remainder of the vision moves outside the home, as the husband and wife
do God's work together. Edna's vision suggests a sharing of gendered traits,
as the husband is "softened" and "refined" while the wife is "strengthened";
each partner becomes more balanced in a manner characteristic of double-
proposal fiction. Evans's renegotiated marriage, like Hentz's, involves an
adjustment of masculine and feminine qualities between the couple, as the
hero becomes less dictatorial and overbearing and the heroine enters the
marriage as a successful career woman rather than as a dependent girl.

    To what degree do the renegotiated marriages in *Beulah* and *St. Elmo*
meet Edna's ideal? Evans insists that the domestic calling demands the same
heroic dedication the heroines invested in their writing careers. Beulah's
"work" will be to convert the still-skeptical Guy Hartwell (note the parallel

to the announced task of *Beulah*, to combat skepticism in the world); Edna, refusing to marry St. Elmo while he was a skeptic, will now assist him in his duties as a Christian minister. Like Hentz, Evans finds that the transcendent reach of Protestant Christianity offers women the chance to emerge from a restricted domestic sphere. Linda leaves her plantation to work with Robert in the missionary field, and Edna will join forces with St. Elmo in nurturing his congregation through, presumably, the horrors of the coming Civil War.

Neither heroine states whether she will continue to write or not, and the novels are ambiguous on this point. Beulah still uses her learning after her conversion and her marriage, drawing on metaphysical and scientific arguments to win Guy away from skepticism. He is listening to her with respect, seeming to "ponder her words." Beulah is the teacher: "You plunge into a deeper, darker mystery, when you embrace the theory of an eternal, self-existing universe, having no intelligent creator, yet constantly creating intelligent beings" (419–20). St. Elmo, disturbed when Edna collapses on their wedding day, attributes his bride's illness to working too hard and announces that he will "snap the fetters of your literary bondage. There shall be no more books written!" (365); Edna neither assents nor objects. I suspect Evans, unsure whether a refined woman could continue her literary pursuits after marriage, was reluctant to portray either the unequivocal retirement of the heroines or the action of their continued writing.[15]

The heroines occupy far stronger positions within their marriages than they would have held under the terms of the heroes' first proposals, but as they enter marriage, they become more passive, drawing attention to the void created when they abandon their proud independence. Rather than being untried, economically dependent young women, they have achieved fame that helps them compel respect as well as love from their reformed suitors. The heroes no longer attempt to manipulate them into submission either emotionally or physically. But notwithstanding such adjustments, as Beulah and Edna shift from active, desiring subjects to relatively passive dependents, the novels register their distress.

Although Beulah and Edna enter marriages in which they have more influence than they would have had before, and although both announce they have accomplished the goals set for their single life, the tension in the marriage endings is undeniable. The rhetoric of death and illness signifies how difficult it was for Evans's independent heroines to submit even to renegotiated hierarchical marriages. Although both Beulah and Edna are sometimes ill while single because they deny themselves sleep in order to work, both feel particularly wretched on their wedding days, their bodies registering the pain they feel in giving up their hard-earned autonomy to enter hierarchical southern households that will thereafter dictate their roles.

Beulah, who was once so opposed to marriage that she exclaimed, "I would rather die! I should be miserable as your wife. . . . Oh, no, no! a thousand times, no!" (328), interprets her body's wedding-day dis-ease as fear: Beulah "was very pale; now and then her lips quivered, and her lashes were wet with tears. . . . Much as she loved him, she could not divest herself of a species of fear, of dread. . . . The future looked fearful" (416). Evans resolves Beulah's quandary with a miracle of sorts: "She saw the expression of sorrow that clouded his face; saw his white brow wrinkle; and as her eyes fell on the silver threads scattered through his brown hair, there came an instant revolution of feeling; fear vanished; love reigned supreme" (417). The evidence of vulnerability in Hartwell (his graying hair) appears to reassure Beulah.

Whereas Beulah exclaimed, "I would rather die!" in apparent hyperbole, Edna seems literally about to die. During her development plot, her occasional fainting spells are attributed to a heart ailment, and the doctor holds out no hope of a cure; he advises her to rest and give up writing. She refuses, declaring, "I would rather die working than live a drone." She reveals, "More than once I have had, a singular feeling, a shadowy presentiment that I should not live to be an old woman, but I thought it the relic of childish superstition, and I did not imagine that—that I might be called away at any instant" (282). Edna stubbornly continues to write and to deny herself rest, and her health continues to decline. Mrs. Murray exclaims, "You are a mere ghost of your former self" (303), and Mr. Manning mourns, "To see you dying by inches is bitter indeed," pleading with her "not to continue your suicidal course" (331). Edna's retirement from New York society is couched in language that could suggest her impending death or her impending marriage. The day St. Elmo returns, Edna has "held her weekly reception as usual, though she had complained of not feeling quite well that day" (361). Her friends, we are told, "little dreamed that it was the last time they would spend an evening together in her society" (361). In sentimental novels, the presentiments of heroines are usually fulfilled, and *St. Elmo* hints that Edna might die rather than marry until the final two pages of the novel. When Edna returns South to marry St. Elmo, the act almost kills her: "The orphan's eyes were bent to the floor, and never once lifted, even when the trembling voice of her beloved pastor pronounced her St. Elmo Murray's wife. The intense pallor of her face frightened Mrs. Andrews, who watched her with suspended breath, and once moved eagerly toward her. Mr. Murray felt her lean more heavily against him during the ceremony; and, now turning to take her in his arms, he saw that her eyelashes had fallen on her cheeks—she had lost all consciousness of what was passing" (365). Edna, like Beulah, miraculously recovers once the wedding is behind her: "Yes, love; the pain has all passed away. I am perfectly well again" (365).[16] In the penultimate paragraphs Evans describes both Beulah and Edna looking "reverently up" into their husbands' faces. They have survived the harrowing transition to marriage and are prepared to take on the role of wife. The magical transformations necessary to bring Beulah and Edna safely through their wedding days accentuate the difficulty Evans faced in consigning her heroines even to renegotiated marriages.

Evans's double-proposal novels embody her version of what we could call the "slaveholding woman author's dilemma": the difficulty of promoting women's progress in literary and artistic fields while still maintaining that their greatest social good relied on a stratified society that denied them full participation. Evans cannot allow her heroines to satisfy ambition and love simultaneously because the egalitarian marriages that would result might threaten hierarchical society; double-proposal authors without her political commitments do not have to be so cautious. *Aurora Leigh* concludes with a radical social vision as Romney comes to appreciate and endorse Aurora's artistic aspirations. Their ideal union transcends the possibilities of the current society, as Barrett Browning's closing allusion to the book of Revelation suggests. As Marjorie Stone demonstrates, Aurora and Romney's marriage inverts the usual Victorian marriage arrangement because Romney "dedicates himself to the service of her art" as well as to Aurora herself (122). Evans does not endorse such a reversal of social hierarchy.

Jane Eyre proclaims that she and Rochester have a perfectly compatible and equitable marriage: "I am my husband's life as fully as he is mine" (475), but to achieve this union, Jane and Rochester separate themselves from society. This Edenic, antisocial solution is as impracticable for Evans as *Aurora Leigh*'s millennial vision. For Evans, marriage reflects the larger social order and draws much of its meaning from its potential to benefit society. Because she can neither retreat from the present world nor envision a new one, Evans tries to portray her marriage conclusions as somehow in harmony with the social order she defends. To refine the marriage plot without altogether denying the development plot, Evans stitches a *Princess*-like conclusion onto a narrative that otherwise invokes both *Aurora Leigh* and *Jane Eyre*, muffling some of the subversive possibilities in her texts.

Because of her entrenched conservatism, Evans does not allow a heroine to take control of her love plot as Brontë and Barrett Browning do. While Edna is assertive in the public realm as a writer and a scholar, she is determinedly passive in the private sphere of courtship. As we saw at the outset of this chapter, Edna was dissatisfied with *Aurora Leigh*'s second proposal because Aurora announces her love for Romney before he declares himself to her again. Aurora realizes she is breaking convention, but insists on her right to be heard: "And yet what women cannot say at all, / . . . I love,— / I love you, Romney. . . . and when a woman says she loves a man, / The man must hear her, though he love her not" (340). And Aurora "voluntarily declares and reiterates her love for Romney" for three or four pages before allowing him to respond. In deliberate contrast, Edna avoids the "unwomanly inconsistency" into which she believed Aurora was betrayed. She merely "glides" into St. Elmo's arms as she accepts him, quoting a chorus from *The Princess:* "Ask me no more, thy fate and mine are sealed" (363). St. Elmo directly requests that she speak her love—"Why won't you say, 'St. Elmo, I love you?'" (363)—but Edna insists that her silent compliance is enough.

Evans courts the ideal of an intellectually productive and companionate marriage that would allow women to continue to express and develop their talents after the wedding, but in deference to the South, she portrays a more conventional union. Each heroine adopts the passive position of idealized sentimental object when accepting the hero's proposal, a role through which she awkwardly navigates the passage from autonomous career woman to dependent wife. Evans may have satisfied her contemporary audiences, but subsequent readers have found it hard to forgive her for the "unwomanly inconsistency" into which she betrayed her heroines.

Notes

1. William Perry Fidler's biography details Evans's wartime activities, which included nursing, an activity many women undertook during the war, as well as the far more unusual task, particularly for a woman, of advising Confederate leaders (84–127). See Elizabeth Moss for another reading of the same events; Moss portrays Evans as opportunistic and self-promoting as well as patriotic (175–83).

2. Both *Beulah* and *St. Elmo* stress the conversion experience and the salvation of the individual soul through Christ's sacrifice. Thus, the "church" appears to be evangelical Protestant, although Evans does not make a point of the denomination. She herself was Methodist.

3. Evans admitted that "the result of her first effort [*Inez: A Tale of the Alamo*] was not very encouraging, as the sale was quite limited" (Derby 389), but it was the precocious production of a teenager. *Beulah* was an instant hit, and *St. Elmo* was one of the nineteenth century's best-selling novels. *Macaria*, Confederate novel that it was, found success in the North and South during the Civil War, and each of the novels Evans produced after her marriage sold well, though never so well as *Beulah* or *St. Elmo*. Although few hard figures are available for comparing the sales of Evans's novels, *St. Elmo* was undoubtedly her greatest popular success, and *Beulah* was probably second. Of all Evans's novels, John S. Hart lists only these two in his catalogue of nineteenth-century best-sellers.

4. Baym points out additional reasons why educated women did not always desire suffrage. If women writers were "to succeed in public advocacy of sentimental values [they] must not engage in behavior that construes them as men." Furthermore, "antisuffrage, to both proponents and attackers, did not equal antipolitical; it involved strategic answers to the question of how women might be politically effective" (*Woman's Fiction* xxxii). These arguments certainly apply to Evans, whose personal involvement in politics during the Civil War is well documented. Beulah argues that women should be "qualified to assist in a council of statesmen, if dire necessity ever required it" (140). Both Beulah and Edna are deeply interested in politics and fantasize about inspiring men they care for to be American "statesmen" (in Evans's work, this word always carries an aura of almost reverential distinction, to be contrasted with terms such as *black republican* and *howling demagogue*). Evans's despair about the direction American politics took is perhaps revealed in the failure of both of these protegés to enter politics. Beulah's friend Eugene Graham takes to drink and chooses a bad marriage, but may, at the end of the novel, be struggling back toward Beulah's original ideals for him. In the postwar *St. Elmo*, however, Edna's statesman-to-be Felix Andrews dies in his teens.

5. This criticism of *St. Elmo* reveals how southern pressure on writers continued after the war, as reviewers began pushing writers to help construct an idealized Old South rather than overtly to defend slavery and the southern way of life it supported. Suzy Clarkson Holstein argues persuasively that in *Macaria*, Evans diminished the ambiguity characteristic of her other fiction to write more effective propaganda: "As the myth of the Lost Cause crystallizes, so too does the idealized identity of Southern womanhood that supports that myth" (115); as a result, "the woman of the defeated South was called upon to sacrifice her independent intellectual and emotional life" (125). In *St. Elmo* Evans clearly returns to the antebellum ambiguity that in *Macaria* she had sacrificed in the interest of the war, and Holstein's argument may further explain why Evans stopped that novel on the eve of the war, as Edna sacrifices her independence in part to support the South.

6. Friedman examines how evangelical church communities in the rural South operated as extended families, exerting authority over the kin groups within its congregation and becoming stronger as people in the church community intermarried.

7. Most woman's fiction details how the guardians who take control of the unfortunate orphan abuse or neglect her: "Home life is not happy, the child is not loved or valued, those who should love and nurture her instead exploit or neglect her" (Baym, *Woman's Fiction* 37). Evans's orphans experience an odd inversion of the woman's fiction theme, for their protectors love and value them, desire to adopt them or marry them, but the orphans stubbornly maintain their independent, although excruciatingly lonely, status. In Evans's novels, the would-be guardians feel neglected and unloved by the orphans, not the other way around.

8. Family ties were crucial to a Southern woman's sense of identity and purpose. Beulah and Edna sacrifice a great deal when they reject would-be families to hunt for identity and purpose through their writing. Edna especially thinks about how her work serves as her child, and her readers as extended family. Both Friedman and Fox-Genovese (*Within the Plantation Household*, see especially 11–15 and 242–89) examine the significance of family connections to a Southern woman's identity.

9. Beulah's confusion about the significance of an age difference may reflect conflicting attitudes in Evans and in the society at large. Apparently marriages between people of widely disparate ages, while unusual enough to provoke comment, were not rare, especially in the case of a man's second marriage. Evans herself chose to marry a man slightly older than her father—to her father's dismay—and the characterizations in her novels must have been affected by her preferences. If one was to submit to a hierarchical marriage, perhaps it made sense to choose a husband whose age and experience vouched for his reliability. For a different reading of the age disparity, see Goshgarian.

10. Heartless women do a great deal of harm in Evans's fiction. The first Mrs. Hartwell, Creola, married Guy for money and catapulted him into years of despair. Antoinette Dupres, Eugene's fashionable but unfeeling wife, is related to Creola by family and character. St. Elmo, like Guy Hartwell, is started on the path of Byronism by the falseness of his first love, the reprehensible Agnes Powell. Agnes's "stony, gray, Gorgonian face, and writhing lips, and blue *chatoyant* eyes" glare from behind tombstones upon Edna's and St. Elmo's wedded bliss at the end of the novel. Heartless women are denied the salvation achieved by the men they provoke into despair.

11. A Baltimore reviewer perhaps also responds to the Byronic heroes of *Beulah* when he announces that that novel is a "very humble and feeble and intellectually unremunerative imitation of *Jane Eyre*" (*Baltimore Daily Exchange*, Sept. 27, 1959, qtd. in Fidler 80).

12. Elizabeth Fox-Genovese discusses several letters from Evans to her friend Rachel Lyons that outline an approach to writing fiction that will convey a didactic message (Introduction xx–xxii).

13. The journal begins when she is seventeen and ends with her engagement. Green reveals frequent anxieties about falling in love, often imagining that some young man she meets is the "right one" and portraying her feelings in novel-like language. She runs through several infatuations before becoming engaged, but she seems to be try-

ing to place this transition state of her life into a courtship novel form. The journal covers the period of the Civil War, but Green's interests remain personal throughout (to the frustration of its editor, James C. Bonner, who judged "a third of the original journal . . . too trivial for reproducing" [6]). Bonner notes that "when her betrothal was accomplished, Anna Maria bade adieu to her journal, as if the sole purpose of her life had been fulfilled" (4).

14. As with so many double-proposal novels, the concluding marriage has generated critical debate. Goshgarian announces that Hartwell's "iron spirit is quite innocent" of compromise, while Jones finds it "difficult to see mutual compromise dramatized in the final scenes of *Beulah*" (99). The evidence of Hartwell's return and his rejection of "gratitude" suggest, however, that Baym is right in concluding that "Hartwell is prepared to compromise at last" (286), although his continued insistence on calling Beulah "child" and his undiminished autocratic tone inform us that his character has not changed extensively. The changes Evans presents in St. Elmo suggest that she had thought further about how a suitor could rise to the heroine's standards without overtly compromising his manly pride.

15. Several years after Evans's marriage, a writer for the *Ladies' Repository* reported that "they say" Evans "has promised her husband (she is now Mrs. Wilson) to write no more, and that she has realized $30,000 by her pen. Mr. Wilson deserves the thanks of all lovers of good literature for the extraction of the promise" ("Women's Record at Home" 461). But Evans did continue to work, although slowly. She published *Vashti* (1865) six months after the wedding, *Infelice* in 1875, and *At the Mercy of Tiberius* in 1887. After her husband's death in 1891, she published *A Speckled Bird* in 1902 and the novella *Devota* in 1907, less than two years before her death. In *Devota* she returned again to a modified double proposal, portraying the belated reconciliation of two proud characters whose betrothal had been broken when the heroine believed a false report about the hero's character.

16. In the University of Alabama Press edition of *St. Elmo* (which is a facsimile of an 1896 edition), Edna refers to St. Elmo as "love" in this speech and in another on the following page: "O love! do not think of it" (366). In every other text I have seen, Edna says "O sir." "Sir" is far more consistent for Edna, who thinks of her husband as "Mr. Murray." Apparently someone was dissatisfied with the degree of "love" expressed in the final pages of the novel.

THREE

Laura J. Curtis Bullard and
E. D. E. N. Southworth:
Courting the "Women's Rights Woman"

NEITHER Laura J. Curtis Bullard (of Maine) nor E. D. E. N. Southworth (born of southern parents but a critic of slavery and a supporter of the Union during the Civil War) was bound by loyalty to the southern polity as were Caroline Hentz and Augusta Evans; in fact, both criticized it. The relative freedom available to novelists working in and writing about the North is demonstrated in how Bullard and Southworth use both courtship and development plots. They deploy double proposals to reformulate the language of sentimental novels, particularly the rhetoric of domestic ideals and religious commitment, constructing a bridge that might allow a reader immersed in such discourses to cross—if only briefly—into progressive, even radical, territory. Each created one heroine who was both recognizably a woman's fiction protagonist and a women's rights advocate. Using double proposals, both writers also stress the potential value of a single life for a woman and negotiate marriages that will be companionate, even egalitarian, as well as beneficial to society.

To create heroines who demonstrate women's unexplored potential, antebellum writers maneuver within limited options. They rely heavily on writing and teaching to prove the capacities of their heroines and they extend the influence of the domestic sphere to include the community, the nation, perhaps the world. Talented and ambitious heroines, however, eventually arrive at an impasse, dressed for action with nowhere to go. The antebellum novels to be discussed in this chapter demonstrate such frustrating limits: Bullard's *Now-a-Days!* (1854) and *Christine: or, Woman's Trials and Triumphs* (1856) and Southworth's *Vivia; or, The Secret of Power* (1857).

Laura J. Curtis Bullard set her two novels largely in her home state of Maine, although much of the later action of *Christine* takes place in New York. Little biographical information is available on Bullard, but she was connected with the feminist movement and enjoyed financial independence. William Leach, who quotes her work occasionally in *True Love and Perfect Union,* refers to her as a "wealthy Brooklynite" (253), and Diane Price Herndl indicates that she made a fortune with a patent medicine, Dr. Winslow's Soothing Syrup (*Invalid Women* 228n13). Unlike most novelists who wrote for popular audiences, she openly advocated universal suffrage as well as educational and legal reforms on behalf of women. In June 1870 she acquired Susan B. Anthony and Elizabeth Cady Stanton's feminist periodical *Revolution* for one dollar, leaving Anthony to work off its ten-thousand-dollar debt (Masel-Walters 250). Bullard edited the *Revolution* for about eighteen months, writing occasionally about the need for courtship and marriage reform and publishing a few of her own short stories with similar themes. She later translated, with Emma Herzog, a romance by Maurice Jokai entitled *A Modern Midas* (1900?). David S. Reynolds describes her as "a pioneer in the women's club movement, which was intended to bring suffragists together with other women of all callings and professions," and as a feminist with a "breadth of vision . . . manifested in her dedication to a uniquely varied range of women's activities, including the advocacy of women's rights abroad" (392). But Bullard was apparently not among the most radical of the feminists. Anthony and Stanton were displeased with the direction she took the *Revolution* after acquiring the paper; Anthony wrote, "It will seem pretty tough to see it fall so below its old standards" and "According to the new regime, publishers and editors must be thrown overboard" (Barry 223). Stanton wrote to Anthony that she refused to write for the new editors: "And think of our sacred columns full of the advertisements of quack remedies! The present owners have asked me and urged me a dozen times to write for them. But I do not feel moved by the spirit. . . . Remember that you did not sell my pen in your transfer of the *Revolution.* I am not to be bought to write at anybody's dictation" (Stanton and Blatch 126). Notwithstanding this tension, Bullard wrote an adulatory biographical sketch of Cady Stanton for *Our Famous Women* (1884), clearly considering herself at one with the suffrage movement and proudly mentioning her connection with the *Revolution.* She ends that piece by cautiously predicting the eventual triumph of the woman's suffrage cause.

Both Bullard's feminism and her willingness to compromise or to be patient in awaiting reform are evident in her fiction. Her novels were self-conscious experiments, which may or may not explain why they failed to find a wide readership (they were published by different houses, and neither was reprinted).[1] In the preface to *Now-a-Days!* the (then anonymous) author explains her intentions to write a realistic and natural account of life in Maine and thus offer a "new thing to the novel-reading public" (vi). She suggests that the public taste is "growing weary of murders, and wars, and rumors of wars, and she has preferred to leave these trite themes to some more fiery pen, and to paint . . . real life, New-England life" (vi).[2] The second novel is ambitious in a different way; Christine Elliot's aspirations as a feminist writer suggest Bullard's own goals. Christine hopes to use the novel form to advance the cause of women with readers who would never examine essays or tracts on the issues: "I will write in a form that will bring my words to all. . . . I will whisper lessons so gently that they cannot offend, and yet, that may bear with them seeds which may spring up in the heart" (150–51). Toward this end, Bullard uses the sort of dramatic plotting she avoided in the first novel, employing sensational tropes including seduction, suicide, and false incarceration to interest the reading public and convey her message. Both novels use double-proposal plotting to emphasize that marriage is a negotiable option in a woman's life and to argue that single women can lead rich and meaningful lives.

The characters of *Now-a-Days!* openly discuss the "propriety of a lady's acceptance of an offer which she had once rejected" (168–69). One stern matron maintains that a woman should "adhere to her first decision," arguing that "no gentleman ever forgets or forgives a rejection" (169), but a more thoughtful character, the heroine's stepmother, Margaret, offers a justification that could speak for most double-proposal texts: "If the lady's first decision was occasioned by some objection which was afterwards removed, I should think it right to accept the lover, but if want of affection for him had been her reason, nothing could be an excuse for her acceptance of him unless it was a change in her feelings" (169). The double-proposal narratives of both Bullard's novels support Margaret's point of view on the ethics of accepting second proposals, revealing where Bullard's understanding of courtship is congruent with that of other double-proposal novelists; in the second novel, the feminism inherent in many double-proposal fictions, including *Now-a-Days!* becomes explicit.

Now-a-Days! has a two-part structure; in the first section the heroine, Esther Hastings, thrown upon herself for support when her father dies in distressed circumstances, takes a job teaching in the Maine backwoods. Bullard uses this recognizable version of the woman's fiction plot to provide a realistic portrayal of the logging community Esther works in along with the familiar story of a young woman earning her way in a strange, though not altogether hostile, environment. The second part of *Now-a-Days!* returns the setting to "civilized" Maine and focuses on the courtships of characters introduced in the opening chapter. These plots include two double proposals that suggest when a woman should refuse the offer of a suitor she loves and how, when the "objections are afterwards removed," she may accept him.

Like many other double-proposal authors, Bullard rejects the notion that a woman can and should "save" a man from destroying himself, arguing (as in, for example, *Jane Eyre, Linda,* and *St. Elmo*), that a suitor should reform himself before expecting the heroine to marry him. Maria Brooks, a secondary character, loves Charles Waldron, to whom her father justifiably objects because of his dissipation and laziness. Charles attempts to persuade her to elope, using the emotional manipulation and physical seduction characteristic of other first proposal scenes. He is arrogantly possessive, claims her cruelty has driven him to drink, and then employs "those soft, low tones, which Maria could never refuse" (263). Maria nearly capitulates, but is saved by Esther's intervention; the heroine convinces Maria that her "first duty" is to her father, particularly since he "is no tyrant" (265); Esther also persuades Charles that he is wrong to pressure Maria. Esther aptly pinpoints the sophistry inherent in the seduction-proposal: "If you love her, as you say, call that strong will, which you now exert to overpower Maria's weaker nature, to aid you in reforming! If you cannot break from your associates without her help, you never can with it! . . . Do not picture your future to her as that of a desolate wretch, which is untrue, but go into the world, and show yourself worthy of her" (269). Inspired, Charles promises to return in four years if he is successful in reforming.

Esther herself is the heroine of the second double proposal. She falls in love with Mr. Templeton, the fiancé of another friend, Emily Sidney, but will not accept him when he suggests rejecting Emily and marrying her. Mr. Templeton, although "noble, good, and generous" (279), employs strategies similar to Charles's in trying to persuade Esther. He triumphantly asserts she loves him, which rouses her pride, and employs emotional manipulation, claiming that it would be a "solemn mockery" if he married Emily while loving Esther and asking, "Is it the sincere and upright Esther Hastings who condemns me to a life of hypocrisy?" (282, 283). But Esther decides that they would both be unhappy if they betrayed Emily: "No, it *is* right for you to marry her, and in the right you will find the only true happiness" (284). Mr. Templeton at length responds to Esther's inspiring advice: "Noble girl! . . . I will follow your counsels. . . . Forget and forgive my mad folly" (284). He marries Emily, and Esther, busying herself with teaching, "soon felt, as she appeared, like her olden self" (287). Much as Esther cares for Mr. Templeton, the novel shows us, marriage is not the only path she can take to a fulfilled and useful life.

In the final chapter of the novel, an epilogue of sorts set years later on Esther's thirtieth birthday, Bullard describes the second-proposal outcomes. The final chapter reads like an extra ending, tacked on after the primary plot is resolved, implying that life can be complete without marriage. Esther has decided that she is, "as I have overheard my pupils call me, an old maid," but determines that "though the duties of wife and mother may not be mine, yet I may fill a place in society equally noble" (303); she remembers the example of the model single woman "Aunt Mary," whose "vision . . . rose before her, pure and holy, dispensing joy wherever she went, soothing the sad, and rejoicing with those who rejoice" (303). But the marriage endings also occur. Esther receives a letter from Maria, now happily married and a mother, in which she describes how much better her life is than it would have been had she eloped: "How different now the confidence that I repose in him, from the trembling fear . . . with which I should have placed my happiness in his keeping. And how different my feelings in that hour when my father gave me, with his blessing, to my husband, from those when I seemed to hear his curse, and to see the look of sad reproach and betrayed confidence with which he regarded me" (304–5). The message of this double proposal is that patience and common sense have brought about a much better domestic conclusion than ever would have resulted from the elopement. Marriage involves much more than the union of the right couple.

Several days later Esther receives a letter from Mr. Templeton (now widowed with two children) proposing marriage; she accepts, resigning her teaching position "for the narrower but delightful sphere of home" (309). Rather than be an old maid, Esther suddenly has a husband and two children. Bullard suggests that Esther would have been content either married or single, that whatever the result Esther was right to have refused Mr. Templeton the first time. "How different," as Maria had written, this result is from what would have been. Both couples are rewarded with good marriages because they refused, when they were younger, to allow passionate impulses to drive them to hasty marriages. Bullard's renegotiated marriages thus illustrate the principles she advocated in her journalism, in which she argued that most people who "fancy themselves" in love merely "imagine the other to possess those qualities which would make a life spent together delightful to both"; such love is merely sensual, and most likely the lovers are doomed to disappointment (qtd. in Leach 116).

Christine's double-proposal story of "what would have been" makes fuller use of the bifurcated plot structure than did *Now-a-Days!* and also makes explicit the implied connection between renegotiated marriage and feminist reform. While wanting to show that Esther could be productive and content as a single woman, Bullard found little for her to do: the heroine draws on her good sense and moral wisdom to guide her friends and make good decisions herself; she is also a successful teacher. As Southworth would discover with a similar character two years later (Vivia), such activities have limited possibilities in narrative, especially when the heroine, already in possession of wisdom and influence, does not need to learn and grow herself. Bullard portrays the development of the feminist Christine Elliot from her early awareness of being "different" from other women to the crucial point when she rejects marriage and commits herself to women's rights through her pursuit of that career and final melding of career and renegotiated marriage. But while focusing on a radical heroine, Bullard also affirms traditional women's roles; as Diane Price Herndl notes, the novel "offers its readers an interesting blend of feminism and domesticity" as Bullard "works at not alienating those women who do not want to lecture or work outside the home, while urging them to be more sympathetic with those who do" (*Invalid Women* 67).

In marking out a career for her heroine as a women's rights lecturer and writer, Bullard places Christine outside the bounds usually allowed the woman's fiction heroine. But through plotting and rhetoric, Bullard attempts to redraw those boundaries to include her heroine, stressing the similarities between Christine and other domestic novel protagonists and suggesting that Christine's overt feminism is but a logical outcome of her participation in the woman's fiction plot and of her entanglement in the more sensational plots of seduction fiction and gothic romance.

The child Christine, inept at domestic chores and partial to reading, is treated as an outsider in her own family, none of whom sympathizes with her idealistic, dreamy nature. Her swings between passionate outbursts and moody introspection recall Jane Eyre, as do her experiences later in school, first as a (falsely accused) classroom pariah and then gradually as an academic standout. Like Jane Eyre and many an American domestic heroine, she is raised partly by an unsympathetic aunt; unlike those other heroines, she has both a mother and a father who cause her trouble when she strikes out on her career as an activist. Like the typical woman's fiction heroine, Christine must fight her way out of an uncongenial environment; unlike the typical heroine, in doing so she must rebel against her immediate family, including her intimidating father, to follow her desires; Bullard presents the obstacles her family and her hostile society place in her path in ways that recall the "trials and triumphs" of both domestic heroines and protagonists of more sensational seduction tales and gothic romances. In so doing, she creates a "women's rights woman" who is also a woman's fiction woman.

To incorporate her feminist project into her novel, Bullard encodes women's victimization in tropes from gothic romance and seduction fiction and then develops a double-proposal plot that includes elements of a woman's fiction story to prescribe how women should combat their oppressors. This literary strategy was an effort to appeal to popular readers while "sowing seeds" that might open their eyes to how society oppressed women; as Christine's speeches suggest, Bullard tried to prepare her readers' minds to accept female activists as "true women." The reforms advocated by her heroine and suggested by her plotting are designed to give women greater control over their bodies and their minds; the links Bullard forges between the plot of her novel and its seduction and gothic episodes connect her text, with the intertexts it invokes, to her historical moment as she attempts to create a fictional world that will influence her readers' lives.

Several sensational episodes in *Christine* "presuppose," in Jonathan Culler's term, the rhetorical strategies of other, mostly earlier, gothic and seduction fiction that expressed—sometimes to exploit and sometimes to critique—the victimization of women. Cathy N. Davidson argues that seduction fiction "becomes a metonymic reduction of the whole world in which women operated and were operated upon" (106). Bullard, writing after the popularity of seduction fiction had given way to woman's fiction, evoked, with a briefly described subplot, the very well-known genre of seduction fiction and the cultural significance that fiction carried. Bullard describes two episodes of seduction, both of which result in the death of the fallen woman and in Christine's heightened awareness of the bond between herself and women who become social outcasts.

The first seduction episode causes Christine to break her engagement with Philip Armstrong, thus linking the seduction and subsequent suicide of Grace Minor with the dominant double-proposal plot. Philip seduces and spurns the innocent working-class orphan Grace, who discovers his treachery when she is hired to sew Christine's wedding clothes. When Christine learns of Philip's infidelity, she refuses to marry him, maintaining that, because Grace should have taken "her rightful place by your side . . . every step to the altar would be through her blood!" (163). (Note that Christine, like Esther, respected another woman's claim on a man she loved.) Philip recognizes that his actions have victimized both Grace and Christine—"He felt that he was [Grace's] murderer—and Christine, too, lay ill. He had killed her, too" (159). But Christine is ill both because of Philip's betrayal and because of her own sense of guilt. Aunt Julia "ridiculed Christine's ideas of her own agency in Grace's fate" but cannot persuade the heroine to accept Philip. "Like all the world," the narrator explains, "[Julia] blamed the victim. . . . How many who may be ready to condemn Mrs. Frothingham as heartless, do not in their secret hearts feel the same?" (164). Christine, in contrast, seems to blame "all the world," including herself, for Grace's death. Having refused Philip's entreaties that she forgive and marry him, Christine dedicates herself to the cause of raising women from their "moral degradation," which she defines broadly: "She thought of all that was pitiful and weak, in her sex; of the worldliness of nearly all about her; of their low and grovelling aims" (171). The term *moral degradation* suggests a continuity between the sexually impure woman and the frivolous and ill-educated society woman with her cramped and "fallen" ideals.

The second seduction episode confirms this continuity, stressing that all women are vulnerable under the prevailing conditions and attitudes of society and that conventional distinctions between privileged (and pure) women and their miserable, "impure" sisters are artificial and fragile. Christine's wealthy classmate Annie Murray, while affectionate and good-hearted, is worldly, thoughtless, and educated only to ornament social circles; in other words, she exemplifies all Christine has labeled "morally weak." Her marriage to the wealthy Mr. Howard, "the matrimonial prize, in the lottery of the last season" (196), turns out badly. Bullard traces the disintegration of the marriage through scenes of psychological warfare between the husband and wife, Annie's flight with her daughter Rosa, her subsequent poverty, and her seduction by a young man who for a time supports her and Rosa but who finally decides to marry another woman. "From that time," the dying Annie tells Christine, "I was utterly lost . . . a vile, vile wretch, with but one spark of virtue remaining, my love for my innocent Rosa" (300). Annie, educated to believe that marrying "brilliantly" would make her happy, reveals that the frivolous woman with "low aims" is vulnerable, under the current legal and social system, to fall into the deepest moral and physical degradation.[3] Davidson argues that original readers of seduction fiction would not, as a modern reader would, view seduction "as a melodramatic plot device" because that plot "set forth and summed up crucial aspects of the society . . . that did not have to be delineated beyond the bare facts of the seduction itself" (106). Bullard, writing for readers who were raised on seduction fiction, could evoke such social conditions with the shorthand of a subplot; she then offers through the main plot a solution that suggests women can empower themselves against institutionalized oppression by promoting their own political and legal rights and by marrying only when they are assured their autonomy will be respected.

While seduction narratives typically show how weak women may become sexual victims, gothic romances portray an isolated heroine who is repressed, confined, and manipulated; she is somehow denied her freedom of action, even her freedom of thought. Davidson suggests that diverse gothic fictions are "unified by a concern (not always the *same* concern) with both individual psychology and the psychology of social relationships[,] . . . with the . . . weaknesses of existing systems, and with the need for social reform" (220). While Bullard's heroine is not exposed to the sexual threat typical of gothic fiction, she is mentally and physically confined, and Bullard is interested in how such repression affects her thoughts, emotions, and behaviors and in what social reforms are necessary to prevent the psychological and physical abuse of women.

In *Christine* Bullard introduces the themes of insanity and confinement in the first chapter and develops them in a gothic episode later, thus linking the domestic imprisonment Christine experiences as a child to her actual incarceration as an adult. In both cases, when Christine refuses to accept a traditional role, insanity threatens her. As a girl, Christine wonders if she is crazy because she does not enjoy domestic chores: "'I am odd, and I don't know but [Mother's] right when she says, I'm "half cracked." Am I crazy? Am I going to be?' and Christine tormented herself with a thousand fearful forebodings" (18). Because the young Christine has no interest in or aptitude for conventional domestic activities, she is treated as a freak and considers herself as such. The psychological repression forced upon her by a family who believes only domestic women are "normal" threatens her mental stability.

When the grown Christine chooses to follow her own path and lecture for women's rights instead of accepting Philip and becoming a wife, her family again labels her insane and physically confines her when they discover that psychological coercion no longer works. Aunt Julia announces, "You are fit for nothing but a lunatic asylum" (175), and when Christine persists in her public reform efforts against the wishes of her family, Julia and her father trick her into entering an insane asylum, where they leave her until, as Julia says, she will promise "never again, by voice or pen, to defend the foolish doctrines of that ridiculous cause which you have espoused" (242). Christine valiantly resists, but in her confinement fears she may become truly insane: "She watched the operations of her mind narrowly, and was startled at the wild fancies that haunted her; she endeavored to control herself, to prevent the wandering of her thoughts . . . and the very effort to do so, seemed to increase, instead of checking the wildness and waywardness of her imaginings" (230). And the narrator describes her in terms that suggest Christine may indeed be vulnerable to insanity: "She paced the floor in agony— she gnashed her teeth—she tore her hair, then suddenly catching a glimpse of herself in a glass, she stood still, horrified" (244). And after her passion and resentment recede, she "seemed sinking into that state, the most hopeless of any kind of insanity, that of a gentle, but settled melancholy. . . . She rarely looked up at any disturbance, never voluntarily addressed any one" (245). Simply because she does not submit to traditional women's roles, Christine is inflicted with a living death that evokes the gothic state described by Davidson, "a nightmare domesticity, a house with doors locked shut from the outside" (222).

Bullard links Christine's childhood fears of madness, fears invoked when she feels trapped on her family farm, forced into domestic duties she hates and is unfit for, with her fears of insanity on being locked into the asylum as a monomaniac who is under the delusion she is (the now famous) Christine Elliot. The parallel conditions of confinement and isolation, of doubting her own identity make Christine ill. Note the similarity of Bullard's descriptions. As a young girl Christine found that "her eager, unsatisfied mind preyed upon her body; she grew thin and pale" (23); as a young woman Christine similarly discovered that "she grew thin and pale . . . and her heart-sickness prayed [sic] on her body" (231). Women need, Bullard suggests, both affirmation of their identity and freedom from imposed domestic bounds to maintain mental and physical health. Christine is punished for her refusal to follow a courtship path, for marking out an independent course instead of following the customary plot.

By creating an intersection with gothic tropes of confinement and insanity, Bullard places her heroine in a lineage of vulnerable gothic heroines, suggesting the dangers consequent when identity and individual freedom are denied and offering, again, an empowering solution: women must claim their right to be free of "nightmare domesticity," must be permitted to choose their own paths. The dangers to women demonstrated by both seduction and gothic plots derive from characters who take advantage of the power allowed them by institutionalized authority and social custom; in other words, the villains are enabled and excused by their social and legal standing: Grace's social inferiority is used as an apology for Philip's behavior by those who would blame the victim. Annie's husband tyrannizes over her under the shelter of marriage laws, which protect his rights over wife and child, leaving Annie only illegal and socially ostracized options for supporting herself and her child. Julia and Mr. Elliot take advantage of a medical system that, as Diane Price Herndl notes, will "lock up a woman solely on her family's word" (*Invalid Women* 72). When women are not validated by the social environment or affirmed by others, the results are alarming: Grace commits suicide, Annie becomes a prostitute, and Christine grows sick in mind and body. If women are to flourish, Bullard implies, they must have meaningful and economically viable life paths outside of courtship and marriage.

While part of the action between proposals reveals the dangers women face in a world that allows them only limited options outside of marriage, the rest focuses on how those dangers could be averted, on how women's problems might be solved. Through Christine, Bullard advocates the social and political reforms that the antebellum women's rights movement was most convinced would improve women's lot.[4] Ellen Carol DuBois states that after 1848 the women's movement began to crystallize its demands around gaining the ballot as the best way to ensure changes even though "public opinion and politicians were more sympathetic to feminists' economic demands than to their political ones" (41). Christine herself believes that the ballot is the cornerstone for social change, although Bullard gives voice to other alternatives and demonstrates respect for women who choose a domestic role and relinquish public involvement. At one point well into her career Christine feels frustrated about the lack of progress in "her darling project, which she deemed at the root of all other demands, the granting of universal suffrage" (288). She fears that it is too difficult to change ingrained attitudes—"ideas which children had imbibed with their mother's milk, were not so easily dislodged from the mind"—and decides that "time alone will bring this matter right—*education* must do the work" (288–89).

Christine has the opportunity to test her theory when she raises Rosa, her adopted daughter, to enlist in the cause as a speaker and to inherit Christine's leadership position. Rosa, happy in domestic pursuits, falls in love with an opponent of woman's suffrage. Although devastated by Rosa's choice, Christine permits the marriage. Bullard thus opens the question of whether nature or nurture makes the differences between the sexes and between individuals of the same gender. Christine herself had no education that would have encouraged her to embrace women's rights, but she did so. Rosa had extensive training to that end, but found herself happier in the home. Bullard offers a dual solution to social ills: on the one hand, the feminist rhetoric and tragic subplotting argues for legal and political reforms that will protect women, while on the other hand, she encourages mutual understanding and tolerance between individuals who are comfortable with traditional values and those who are not. She leaves the nature-nurture question she raises unresolved. Bullard thus both affirms domestic virtues and claims the right of women to choose other roles.[5]

In the effort to enlist domestic rhetoric in her cause, Bullard also aligns her radical heroine with the pious domestic protagonists characteristic of much woman's fiction. Reformers building their argument along lines suggested by William Lloyd Garrison define "true Christianity" as congruent with progressive or radical views, despite opposition from clergy. DuBois argues that the Garrisonian view of religion enabled reformers to break from institutionalized religions while continuing to claim that the Bible supported their position: "Garrisonians' ability to distinguish religious institutions from their own deeply-felt religious impulses was an impressive achievement for evangelicals in an evangelical age" (33). Measured by this internalized rather than institutionalized religion, Christine is consistently pious. She believes that her vow to become a women's rights advocate is a response to God's call: "She would enter upon this great work, and she thanked God for giving her so noble a task, one that would require all her powers—all her soul" (171). She debates another activist, Mrs. Bond, about whether Christianity is an aid or a detriment to their movement. Mrs. Bond takes the position that religion is "superstition," that churches had always been on "the wrong side in all movements of Human Progress" (289–90), and that the Bible was a poor source of authority because it is "so obscure and indefinite that it admits of myriad different interpretations" (290). While Bullard thus gives voice to a radical denouncement of religion, Christine's response aligns her with conventional domestic and sentimental views of women. The heroine maintains that "the church is *not* corrupt or dead, and the religious element in woman is one of the holiest attributes of her nature. . . . Should she ever lose that attribute, Mrs. Bond, she would lose everything. Without the religious element, society would relapse into a state of barbarism, and woman would sink again into ten-fold deeper degradation" (290). This speech might have been uttered by Augusta Evans's Edna Earl, that vehement opponent of woman's suffrage. Bullard thus sketches a version of the domestic ideal that accepts the premise that woman is naturally spiritual, but suggests that the best way to ensure that she maintain her "holy attributes" is to give her more

political and legal control. The granting of universal suffrage thus becomes
a method for defending true womanhood rather than a threat to it.

While the interproposal action of the novel focuses on demonstrating the
dangers society posed for women and the need for legal and political reform,
the courtship plots, in particular Christine and Philip's double-proposal plot,
promote changes in how marriages should be contracted and in how "love"
might be understood. Through the double-proposal plot, Bullard teaches that
marriage can be renegotiated to accommodate a radical heroine and a reformed hero and that the avowed feminist may become a superior mother
and wife.

The first proposal from Philip to Christine culminates a brief courtship
that fulfills Cinderella fantasies. Christine, a poor relation in her Aunt Julia's
fashionable school and an awkward social misfit, attracts the attention of the
wealthy and popular "male coquette" Philip Armstrong. Determined to flirt
with her and force her to fall in love with him, Philip finds himself enchanted
instead and proposes marriage: "She was so far superior to him, so pure, so
good; could she love such a wretch as he?" (138). She could, although she
wonders, "But will he always love me—he, so beautiful, so talented, and I,
so plain, and so far beneath him?" (139). Her friend Mrs. Warner believes,
"You have saved him. . . . Your influence has roused all that was noble in his
nature, and it rests with you to make him all that God intended him to be"
(139). The future, as Philip describes it, is ideal: "They would go to Europe
together; she should see all that was beautiful, in nature and art, in that grand
Old World, all she had dreamed of so often, all that he had described, that
she had read of. After this they would return, and would have a beautiful
home where she should be mistress, and where he should find all the happiness that earth can give" (143).

Christine believes that, though married, she will not "forget my duties
to my fellows in the narrower circle around me" and that she will be able to
write and thus to promote the cause of women in spite of her domestic duties. She tells Mrs. Warner that Philip will be a fellow-laborer for the cause
and imagines that "together he and I will toil on, cheering each other" (150).
Mrs. Warner, who understands the demands of domesticity and traditional
wedlock, doubts this, commenting, "Philip may not wish you to do so" (151).
A reader, noting the difference between Christine's and Philip's idealized
visions of the future, might well doubt it also, particularly if that reader is
conscious that marriage and domestic cares did indeed slow down many a
women's rights woman. DuBois reports that the opposition of "fathers and
husbands on whom they were dependent, reinforced women's lack of public

experience to restrain their feminist activism" (25) and also indicated that feminists were often slowed down by the tax of child care and the struggle to balance motherhood and commitment to the cause (26–28). Christine is enabled to achieve her fame and pursue goals in part because she remains unhampered by a husband, pregnancies, and young children. She builds up a family of her own that demonstrates the benefits of acting upon her radical principles rather than prevents her from promoting them.

The marriage of Christine and Philip as envisioned in the first proposal would have been built on their faulty assumptions about each other and eventually devastated by Philip's shortcomings; fortunately for Christine, she discovers his infidelity before the wedding and so breaks the engagement. Refusing to believe that her love can inspire his reformation, Christine sends Philip into the world to reform and heal himself.

Philip pleads with Christine to marry him even though he betrayed her and drove Grace to suicide; his comments reveal that, in spite of his honest remorse, he is hardly reformed yet. He refers to Christine's compassion for Grace as a "morbid scruple" and claims, "You are breaking the last strand that holds me out of utter ruin. . . . You alone can lead me in the right way" (163). But Christine, arriving at the understanding expressed by Esther in *Now-a-Days!* now rejects that argument, explaining to Philip, "That was my error. . . . I thought to take God's work into my puny hands" (163). To her aunt, Julia Frothingham, who for worldly reasons pressures her to go ahead with the marriage, she offers an additional explanation that reveals how much wisdom she has already gained through her painful experience: "Our union would only bring unhappiness. He has deceived me—*that,* I forgive him, but I could feel no confidence in him, and without that both he and I would be wretched. Then, too, he would cease to respect me, did I yield to his request, and I should lose all influence over him" (164). Christine never pretends that she no longer loves Philip, and she treats him with compassion. In fact, she understands their relationship as continuing, in some sense, although they will not marry. It would kill her, she says, to lose her influence over Philip: "If the knowledge of my love, the memory of what has been, cannot save him, I, weak mortal, could do no more!" (164–65). Philip at length gives up and departs for Europe to drown his sorrows in the time-honored pursuits of Byronic heroes and at length to begin to reform himself. Christine dedicates herself to promoting women's rights.

In the interproposal narrative, in addition to working with the popular discourses of gothic and seduction fiction, Bullard makes striking use of woman's fiction's "network of surrogate kin" that Nina Baym argues "gradually defines itself around the heroine, making hers the story not only that of a self-made woman but that of a self-made or surrogate family" (*Woman's Fiction* 38). In much domestic fiction the heroine, while developing her abilities to look after herself, permits her surrogate kin to help her with this task; the independent Christine becomes a matriarch, the leader of her surrogate family, the proprietor of a Home (with a capital *H*) that she establishes and manages for young single women in New York City. Having been disowned by her immediate family and having rejected a home with Philip, Christine creates her Home in the space between proposals; she creates a family on her own instead of with parents or a husband. She adopts Annie Murray's daughter, Rosa, and employs Annie's destitute friend Martha, saving her from her life as a "sinful wretch." Then, Bullard tells us, "Christine's family circle increased still more" as she offered a temporary home to young women searching for employment, providing them with education and advice: "She had very little trouble in the regulation of her household. She was very systematic; and she arranged everything so that it went on with apparent ease. . . . While all loved her, their affection was mingled with a respectful deference that made all submit readily to her requirements" (305). Christine, though never adept at household chores, proves an ideal household manager.

Seven years later, Christine's home has grown until she "found herself at the head of what deserved the title of an Institution" (308), although it is generally referred to as "the Home." Christine presides with success that any beneficent patriarch might envy:

> Many were the poor and friendless girls who, by means of this Home and watchful friend, had been saved from dangers of which they little dreamed. . . . Many a marriage had been celebrated here in simple and unostentatious fashion. . . . [Christine] endeavored to give those who were to become wives, true ideas of their duties, to render them helpmates, indeed, to their husbands. . . . She was deeply interested in all the affairs of her children, as she fondly called them, and none of the details of life, however commonplace, were indifferent to her. (310)

Without the aid of either father or husband, Christine establishes an ideal Home that furthers the practical and sentimental goals of true womanhood, as she helps her protegées maintain their purity and prepare themselves to be good wives. She also devotes much energy, however, to enabling them to earn their own living: "There were among the number those engaged in every trade that was open to woman, and every year new avenues of employment

were entered by them. . . . There were students of law, theology, and medicine" (309). In time, Christine is reconciled to her original family and has
the pleasure of seeing her protegées and her original family "all chatting together pleasantly under her roof" when they come for Rosa's wedding. In
the final reversal of paternalistic norms, Philip is permitted to join her family and help with her work.

When Philip reenters Christine's life, she is no longer a shy and unsure
dependent or a ridiculed young lecturer, but a famous and widely respected
orator, leader, and writer. Philip calls her to him when he believes he is dying and proposes again: "Be my wife . . . that my wife's hand may smooth
my pillow, my wife's kiss rest on my pale lips, and her hand close my failing
eyes!" (372–73). Christine consents to this extreme version of a second proposal in which the suitor has been weakened and the heroine strengthened:
"It was a solemn sight, that marriage in the death chamber; the pale and
ghastly countenance of the bridegroom, hardly more pale than that of the
bride, as the man of God pronounced those solemn words that made them
one" (373). Philip promptly wills his estate to Christine, proving the gener-
osity of his motives and the depth of his reform: "I read in the papers of your
public life. . . . All your words I read, and gradually your influence, silent but
strong, gained complete ascendency [sic] over me. . . . I lived a secluded life
in the midst of gayety. In my own humble way, I sought to do what would
please you did you see my works" (380).

Bolstered by Christine's nursing and prayers, Philip recovers, and Christine discovers her love for him is unabated: "It was a pleasure to her to feel
that she was so necessary to his comfort and happiness, and his constant
dependence upon her for everything seemed to attach her to him, if possible, even more strongly than ever. . . . Never had she been happier than now,
when, with utter self-forgetfulness, she devoted herself entirely to Philip"
(376). This sentimental rhetoric allies Bullard's radical heroine with conventional domestic heroines. Bullard uses sentimental language to create a portrait of a true woman that is simultaneously a portrait of an activist who returns to her work, with Philip as a helpmate, as soon as he is healthy: "Now
both were absorbed in the enlarging of the Home, for into all her plans for
the establishment of this Institution, her husband entered with zeal equal
to her own. His hand was ever open; his judgment matured, and she found
herself depending on him, as she would hardly have believed herself capable of doing. . . . She quoted Philip's opinions on all subjects, and he was, in
turn, ever ready to defer to her" (383). This marriage demonstrates a princi-

ple Bullard detailed later in the *Revolution:* "Marriage, which is the culmi-
nation of the idea of sex, was designed to make man more womanly, and
woman more manly" (qtd. in Leach 207). Whereas the marriage of Philip
and Christine, had it occurred after the first proposal, would have been
fraught with danger because of his moral weakness and her lack of self-confi-
dence, it is now ideal, for themselves and for society: "Every day they were
more and more closely united; one in heart, one in soul, united in their aims
and aspirations, their lives passed on smoothly and pleasantly. Nor was theirs
a mere selfish happiness; they lived, not for their own present gratification,
but in living for others, in doing all the good in their power, they found their
exceeding great reward" (384). One could argue that this vision, while im-
pressively progressive, is just as fantastical as the projected dreams of Christine and Philip during their first courtship. Later authors do seem to critique
Bullard on this count, problematizing her utopian ideal of the egalitarian,
dual-career union and her optimistic view of the reformed hero. In particular, Elizabeth Stuart Phelps, in *The Story of Avis* (1877), writes a double-proposal plot in which a handsome and vain suitor named (coincidentally?)
Phillip Ostrander persuades the talented artist Avis to marry him, but even
a renegotiated marriage cannot sustain the couple's egalitarian ideals. Also
entering the dialogue is Henry James's *The Bostonians,* in which a friendship
between the established women's rights activist Olive Chancellor and the
protegée she trains to work for the cause, Verena, echoes Christine and Rosa's
relationship. Whereas Bullard's Christine swallowed her disappointment and
allowed Rosa to marry, James's Olive is more autocratic than Christine and
his Verena far more ambiguous about choosing domestic pursuits than Rosa.

E. D. E. N. Southworth's two double-proposal novels are similar to
Bullard's in that the first experiments with an independent heroine without
introducing the subject of women's rights, while the second gives that topic
a central position in the narrative. Esther Hastings is an independent thinker
and a moral exemplar, but she reveals no overt feminism. Two years later
Bullard introduced Christine Elliot, who, while learning many of the same
lessons that Esther taught concerning the roles of work and love in a woman's life, also embraces openly political feminism. Southworth's first double-
proposal novel, *Vivia,* features a heroine who has so much confidence in her
own power and faith that she ignores social convention when she believes it
is right to do so, but after the Civil War Southworth created an avowedly
feminist heroine in Britomarte, the "Man-hater." Britomarte retains Vivia's
beauty, talent, and faith, but is also outspokenly committed to women's rights
and specifically critical of marriage laws of coverture.

Emma Dorothy Eliza Nevitte Southworth, born in Washington, D.C., was among the most popular and prolific American writers of the nineteenth century. She describes her own childhood in terms evocative of Jane Eyre: the child Emma was wild and passionate, a "wierd little elf," and "very much—*let alone*" (Forrest 218–19). She married young and was apparently abandoned by her husband, left with young children to support. Once she started writing, she quickly found success and produced weekly installments throughout most of her life. Her long career as a professional author sharply contrasts with that of Bullard, whose few publications remained obscure. Whereas Bullard consciously experimented with the novel form without apparent need to make money, Southworth, responsible for her own and her children's support, drew on amazing reserves of energy and storytelling talent to produce one popular serial after another, all of which were published as books at the conclusion of their serial runs.[6]

Vivia, like *Now-a-Days!* features two courtship plots that, almost in shorthand, suggest lessons I have found to be typical of double-proposal fiction. The title character, Genevieve LaGlorieuse, orphaned and cheated of her inheritance early in the novel, is raised in a convent and quickly becomes an inspiring influence to all about her, including young Wakefield Brunton, who aspires to fame and fortune in order to win her hand. Theodora Shelley, one of Vivia's protegées, is housed as a poor relation under the roof of a stingy aunt and uncle. Her aspirations as a painter are cut short when she is married against her will to kind but boorish Basil Wildman; although lame and ignorant of farm life, Theodora gradually assumes responsibility for Basil's family farm and after his death achieves some success with experimental agricultural methods. Vivia rescues her from drudgery when she returns from a prolonged journey overseas, and Theodora is able to resume her interrupted artistic career. Both negotiate marriages through double proposals late in the novel.

Wakefield achieves the success he thought would please Vivia, but she rejects his marriage proposal because he has never become his own person: "though I could not create a soul, I developed yours, which, but for me, would have been stunted and dwarfed! I have involuntarily attracted and absorbed that soul, until it is principally by and through me that it lives! . . . The woman should not stand between the Lord and her husband, as in our marriage, I should do" (492). Southworth thus gives an interesting turn to the double-proposal narratives that reject the notion that the love of a good woman can "save" her husband; Vivia refuses to marry the man she not merely "saved" but all but created because that would make the unequal relation between them permanent. In rejecting Wakefield's offer, she rejects a model of marriage that inverts the patriarchal model in which the husband, as head of the wife, takes responsibility for her. Vivia throws Wakefield onto his own resources, and he eventually discovers and proves his own inner heroism, attempting to "purify his soul from pride, anger, injustice, and every form of selfishness" (512). He sacrifices his promising career and gradually becomes poor, fearlessly writing the "truth" instead of what readers want to read.[7]

When Vivia learns of Wakefield's noble but impoverished life, she is delighted, announcing to Theodora that he has renounced "the kingdom of this world" for an empire of "eternity and infinitude" (524). The persistence of religious language in *Vivia* works to frame the title character's independence and unconventionality within traditional boundaries, as the following review from the *Chicago Magazine* suggests: "The secret of power consists in [Vivia's] abiding faith in God and her fellow creatures, and in the charity of life, and hope as the victory. And in the strength of her principles she battles with the powers of the earth, and the temptations of the flesh and the evil spirits" ("Literary Notices" 268). This reviewer implies that the Christian message in the novel is an orthodox one, yet Vivia's faith actually inspires her to break with convention as she takes control of her courtship. Vivia leads her future husband out of poverty and ignorance, ensures him education and social advantages, and then tests him by casting him out on his own before she agrees to marry him. She herself seeks out Wakefield in his humble lodgings and offers the second proposal: "Wakefield, look at me; I am your wife, if you will take me" (528). Vivia is aware that she breaks conventions of womanly modesty in thus offering herself to a man, but implies that she contrasts such conventions to "reason and justice": "I knew that I must come to you, but then a thousand womanly shynesses, unknown before, troubled me; spite of all reason and justice, my cheek burned, and my heart shrank. . . . I, *even I,* was tempted to think that *even you* might misinterpret my act; that you might think my visit unmaidenly or presumptuous" (529). But Vivia and Wakefield are successful in transcending custom, and they contract an ideal marriage; Wakefield now serves "not the time, not fame, nor popularity, nor any other form of selfishness, but the Lord, the truth, and humanity" (529), and Vivia remains "the medium of animating, sustaining, or redeeming life to all within her sphere" (540).

The courtship of Theodora and Austin Malmaison, although resolved very hastily at the end of the novel, is also suggestive of themes that Southworth would explore more fully in *Britomarte, the Man-Hater*. Austin proposed to Theodora early in the novel, but after her unfortunate first wedding; he then makes a bad marriage to Basil's ambitious and coquettish sister, Helen Wildman, who eventually runs away with another man and dies in poverty and obscurity in Paris. To escape the pressures of his difficult and embarrassing domestic situation, Austin immerses himself in politics and begins to drink.[8] When both are single again, Theodora scorns him. Vivia and Wakefield, anxious to help them both, hire Theodora to paint Austin's portrait; in the process of doing so, the artist helps him get back in touch with his more noble self; as Vivia has helped create Wakefield, Theodora helps recreate Austin. At each sitting for the portrait, "Austin's countenance began gradually to lose those marks of excess that had so marred his grace, and to recover something of the old clearness and intellectuality" (538). When the portrait is finished, it is "at once a perfect likeness . . . and a highly spiritualized picture" (539). Austin recognizes that "*It is what I aspired to be!*" and offers Theodora a proposal she accepts.[9]

Now-a-Days! Christine, and *Vivia,* like other antebellum double-proposal novels, registered and contributed to shifts in the overlapping discourses that defined women's roles in midnineteenth-century America. The challenges to rigid gender role distinctions offered by domestic fiction work from within conventional language; instead of challenging a reader with a radical break of expectations, they work from within those expectations and attempt to stretch them. Caroline Hentz's heroine Linda walks away from her privileged life of leisure to join her husband in the danger and excitement of overseas missions; she thus rejects her domestic role, but under the protection of religious conviction.[10] Augusta Evans's heroines also take advantage of the paradoxes inherent in apparently fixed gender role prescriptions; her Edna Earl defines women's "narrow" sphere to be "broad as the universe" based on goals that are congruent with domestic ideals, and thus justified pursues a writing career and becomes a famous literary figure. Bullard's Christine establishes a matriarchal Home that simultaneously validates women's role as a Home-maker and becomes a home base for the public promotion of women's rights. Southworth's Vivia, through the "power" she gains from Christian faith, sails around the world solving other people's problems, ignoring gender role conventions when it suits her, and forming an ideal mate for herself. The renegotiated courtship and return to marriage at the end of each of these double-proposal novels bring them in line with conventional courtship expectations while promoting reform within and without marriage. So long as the rhetoric of characters or narrators suggests that the heroines remain in some way within the letter of gender role law, these novels could redefine its spirit to suit a range of progressive purposes.

Notes

1. One could speculate that Bullard's novels had limited appeal because of these experiments, because she was not a skilled storyteller, or because they were published by small houses and so were probably not publicized and distributed as widely as many other novels were. I find the most interesting aspect of Bullard's fiction to be her intelligent insights when discussing courtships and a complex introduction of the problem of nature versus nurture in explaining human character. *Christine* shows a great improvement formally over *Now-a-Days!* but lacks the regional uniqueness of the first effort, a uniqueness that drew a compliment from one reviewer upon its publication in 1854: "Maine back-woods life, and New-England life generally, are the subjects of her sketches. She has painted always from Nature" ("New Books" 479). David S. Reynolds calls the neglect of *Christine* "heinous" and compliments Bullard for the "stylistic directness and subtle characterization" with which she makes "a passionate case for women's rights" (393).

2. The first half of the novel is an intriguing early effort at regional fiction in the tradition of later New England authors such as Sarah Orne Jewett and Mary Wilkins Freeman, although Bullard's patronizing attitude toward the "rustic" families detracts somewhat from the portrait. Reynolds notes that *Now-a-Days!* is "a precursor of local-color realism, a woman writer's consciously restrained answer to the excesses of male sensational literature" (393). Bullard, drawing on her own experiences of the "manners and customs of this, hitherto, far-off and 'unknown land,'" describes the lumber trade in the Maine backwoods in more detail than she does the social scenes later in the book (v).

3. In the story of Annie, Bullard makes explicitly feminist use of a trope of woman's fiction: "The protagonist's chief foil, the belle, is clearly articulated as a character who is liable to fall. Her temptation, attributed to the mixed appeal of flattery and material goods rather than the promptings of sexual desire, leads her to deliberately despiritualize her body" (*Woman's Fiction* xxxviii).

4. Bullard's views apparently continued to undergo change. When she took over the *Revolution*, she diversified its aims, suggesting at times that gaining the ballot in and of itself would not prove an "open sesame" to the promised land for women. She did, apparently, maintain a consistent concern with marriage; from *Now-a-Days!* through her journalistic work, she suggests or openly argues that marriage reform was paramount to improving the majority of women's lives.

5. Herndl, one of very few critics to have published an analysis of Bullard's novel, also notes that "Bullard seeks to establish an alliance between the two ideologies" of domesticity and feminism (65); "Bullard clearly knows that her audience is probably not already committed to suffragism and is inclined toward domesticity. She works at not alienating those women who do not want to lecture or work outside the home, while urging them to be more sympathetic with those who do" (67). Herndl analyzes Bullard's use of illness as a plot device designed to "suture" feminism and domesticity; I consider how the double-proposal works in similar ways with these at times competing and at times complementary discourses.

6. *The Hidden Hand,* perhaps Southworth's most popular work, was serialized three times before being published as a book.

7. Southworth never specifies the painful "truths" for which Wakefield sacrifices his popularity; her character is willing to face social ostracism, but we never know for what cause. In her postwar novels, she allows her radical characters to argue openly for social reform and criticizes those she feels are responsible for social ills. In *Vivia,* all remains vague.

8. Southworth describes politics as a meaningless cacophony of party quarreling, newspapers full of editorial exaggerations, and ostentatious stump speeches, implying that it is an escape from the important business of life, rather than its focus.

9. The hasty winding up of Austin and Theodora's courtship probably resulted from the pressure Southworth's editor was putting on her to finish the story, which had already run well beyond its proposed length (see Coultrap-McQuin 67).

10. R. Pierce Beaver interprets the role of American Protestant women in world missions as "the first feminist movement in North America," suggesting that through their commitment to the church, women who entered missions and those at home who supported missions were pioneers in organizing women for a cause and in demonstrating women's strength.

FOUR

Britomarte, the Man-Hater:
Courtship during the Civil War

E. D. E. N. Southworth's post–Civil War serial *Britomarte, the Man-Hater,* published in two volumes as *Fair Play; or, The Test of the Lone Isle* (1868) and *How He Won Her* (1869), includes the typical features of Southworth's best-selling novels: action-adventure plots alternate and intersect with sentimental-domestic plots, courageous and unconventional heroines contrast with traditional true women, and realistic descriptions and events are interwoven with highly improbable sensational episodes. That much of the second volume of the narrative is set during the Civil War might appear to be incidental to Southworth's entertaining story; she suggests as much herself: "I shall not burden this light and simple story with the politics of civil war. I shall only allude to it where it immediately concerns the people of whom I am writing" (*Fair Play* 354). But where the war "immediately concerns the people" of whom Southworth writes, it also immediately concerns the people *for* whom she writes. In addition to promoting her own pro-Union politics, the Britomarte serial investigates how the Civil War acted upon those aspects of American life that had interested Southworth in her antebellum novels: the lack of security for women within the home, the restrictive nature of gender roles, and the consequent and profound importance of marrying wisely.

Southworth's Civil War novel, though presented as another entertaining narrative, participated in the crucial cultural work undertaken by Americans as they attempted to understand, explain, define, and control the momentous impact of the war. The war created havoc or at least disruption in almost every area of life, and conventional nineteenth-century distinctions between the genders were no exception. The notion of "separate spheres" and generalizations about the distinct attributes of women (ruled by the heart) and of men (ruled by the head) never did reflect reality even for the privileged white classes, but as the Civil War disrupted homes and forced women to take on new roles, it became difficult to protect even the linguistic fiction that men and women inhabited different spheres or that they could be defined by different characteristics. In her narrative Southworth explores the effect on four heroines when the Civil War shatters the fragile, and artificial, barriers that had been rhetorically constructed between the public and the private world, the political and the domestic sphere. No one could pretend any longer that the domestic space could be protected from the rough male world. Categories treated as naturally separate in antebellum language collapsed under the pressures of war. Love and courtship could not be kept distinct from political loyalties. In fact, women themselves were no longer always distinguishable from men. The task of Southworth in her pair of novels was, in part, to use double-proposal plots to examine the disruptions war forced onto the characters' lives, to chart new paths for women in the territory opened by the destruction of old barriers, and to negotiate marriages that would heal personal and national wounds, helping to reconstruct a domestic and public order in which women could retain some of the responsibilities and privileges that they had proven they deserved during the war.

Southworth's postwar serial capitalizes upon war-born changes in women's lives to demonstrate that women are stronger and more complex than conventional ideology allowed. She set her story largely in Washington, which as a border city and the seat of federal government was a strategic location for a tale about how the Civil War disrupted domestic life in both northern and southern families. Four heroines—Alberta Goldsmith, Erminie Rosenthal, Elfie Fielding, and Britomarte Conyers—open the narrative dressed alike in white graduation gowns, planning futures that are subsequently disrupted by the war in a variety of ways, demonstrating how thoroughly the Civil War may have redirected and redefined women's roles and women's understanding of those roles. Three of Southworth's four heroines are given double-proposal plots, and conventional gender ideology would have suggested that since women are ruled by the heart, their political commitments would be subject to their emotional ones. Not so for these heroines. In both courtship renegotiations and individual developments, the political and the personal are intertwined. By linking narrative structure with historical events, Southworth suggests that while women do indeed love passionately, they may be at least as passionate about their political convictions.

To make this point without violating the conventions of popular women's novels, Southworth historicized her adventure tale while disavowing interest in writing about the war: "It would be presumptuous in a mere story-writer to dwell upon these magnificent themes, so much beyond her power of treatment. This story does not pretend to be a history of the campaign or of any portion of it; it is only a simple narrative" (*How He Won Her* 468). Despite such disclaimers, Southworth interlaces her "simple narrative" with references to particular battles, significant dates, and historical figures, invoking enough conventional history to remind a reader that the story is set in quite real, and quite recent, times. She alludes gingerly, for example, to the assassination of Lincoln, enhancing her novel with the "seriousness" of history even as she excuses herself for mentioning it: "Let us reverently pass over that awful calamity of April the fourteenth, which followed so swiftly upon the winged feet of Victory, quenching all her lights of joy and of triumph in darkness and in blood. The Nation's holy sorrow is too sacred a subject to be treated here" (*How He Won Her* 480). And when Southworth describes a Confederate prison "as I saw it in May, 1865," she vouches for her own historical veracity. She even invites her readers to call upon their own memories: "Everyone knows how hopefully the campaign of the Spring of 1864 opened. In almost every engagement the Union arms triumphed" (366).

But Southworth is selective in invoking history and does not encourage her readers to think about the pressing problem of race. In the wake of emancipation, she fails to imagine a role for freedmen even though in one of her antebellum novels, *Mark Sutherland* (1853), serialized as *India; or, The Pearl of Pearl River*, she had celebrated a character who chose to sacrifice his wealth and free his slaves. Southworth joins many of her contemporaries in imagining the Civil War to be about the disunion and reunion of a white America. Nina Silber finds that white northerners, sympathizing with the defeated planter class, "eventually cast southern blacks outside their reunion framework altogether" (6), while Kathleen Diffley observed that black characters in Civil War stories usually die on the battlefield protecting whites or continue as servants in white households (53). Diffley's second category describes the one black character who appears regularly in *Britomarte*. Southworth devotes just one-half of one page to acknowledging emancipation and the black contribution to the Union war effort: Britomarte is freed from a Richmond prison by black Union soldiers who are being joyously welcomed "by the colored population on the sidewalk" (*How He Won Her* 476). Southworth is more than ready to gloss over issues of race to promote the particular interests of white women and, more generally, the progress of white reconciliation.

Thus Southworth's central subject is the impact of the Civil War on gender roles as the genteel white classes had conventionally defined them. The war intervenes in the heroines' courtship plots and provides narrative and historical space in which women could take, in fact had no choice but to take, aggressive roles. Her novels reveal the same patterns of expanded opportunity for women during the war and varying degrees of retrenchment after the war that have been discovered and examined in recent years by social historians. A woman's war job was to "keep the home fires burning," but in the absence of men, she also had to supply the fuel. In the border states and in the South, she moreover often found herself watching the home itself burn down unless she could defend it. Planter class women frequently took control of plantations, managing overseers and slaves and directing agricultural and financial operations. Occupations were opened to women in the North and South as men were absorbed by the armies and labor was needed to supply soldiers with the necessities of war and civilians with the necessities of life. Many women who did not work for wages extended traditional domestic skills into the public realm. Many of them organized large volunteer groups, demonstrating impressive managing skills. Others broke a strong taboo by nursing wounded soldiers in public hospitals. By choice or by necessity, thousands of women breached convention to serve their men, their country, or their own desire for expanded liberty. Whether individuals embraced gender transformation or had it thrust upon them, the war forced reconsideration of conventional gender roles in both the North and the South.[1] Southworth's *Man-Hater* narrative provides us with one contemporary exploration of the very trends that have only recently been researched by historians.

For one of her four heroines the breach of convention results in tragedy. Alberta Goldsmith, the heiress of a wealthy planter, rejects her family to marry Corsoni, an itinerant Italian. She does not, however, reject her southern upbringing. On the contrary, she inspires her husband to fight for the rebel cause, and both are killed by one bullet when a Union force attacks their guerrilla band. Southworth's depiction of Alberta Goldsmith's fate is a cautionary fable about the tragic end of the "model young lady of her set" (*Fair Play* 31), a southern belle who is raised only to ornament family circles and therefore does not internalize the moral standards that motivate the other three heroines. As the narrator puts it, "So far from having any affinity or mission on this earth, she had scarcely a sentiment or an opinion of her own" (31). A woman who is such a blank slate is vulnerable, at the mercy of her passions and unable to reason on serious moral or political issues. With the outbreak of the war, Alberta commits herself to her husband and her Confederacy. Southworth's "model" southern belle comes to a tragic end, but not because she abandons traditional feminine passivity. Rather, she dies because she acts for a mistaken cause.

Consider the contrast of Erminie's double-proposal story, in which Southworth uses the circumstances of war to argue that the ideal "true woman" of the North may have strength untested by her usual domestic employments and to suggest that the country would benefit from a revised understanding of true womanhood. Erminie has a contented home life. Although her mother is dead, her father is a benevolent patriarch and her brother a loving protector. When she leaves school, she falls in love with Colonel Eastworth, a "distinguished son of South Carolina" (57) whose good looks, heroic military background, and "superiority in age" attract her because "reverence was so large an element" in her love (72); they are quickly betrothed, but her father asks them to wait two years because Erminie is too young to marry. Had the Civil War not intervened, she would have been peacefully transferred from loving patriarchal father to loving patriarchal husband. But instead, Southworth gives Erminie a courtship and marriage that is emblematic of the division and reunion between North and South.

The war disrupts the courtship and challenges Erminie to prove she is more than a simple domestic creature. Eastworth is blinded by ambition and by secessionist propaganda, becoming embroiled in a (failed) plot to prevent Lincoln from taking office. When discovered, he escapes to serve as a general in the Confederate army. He takes advantage of his residence in the Rosenthals' home to carry on clandestine activities. Neither Erminie nor her father, both committed Unionists who assume Eastworth is on their side, notices anything amiss; Erminie does not even catch on when Eastworth becomes upset over her rendition of "The Star-Spangled Banner" (371–73). The Rosenthal household, like much of the North, perhaps, failed to take secessionist talk seriously, and Erminie, "who was no more of a politician than her father, and had no more misgivings about the safety of the national union than she had about the certainty of her own union with the husband of her choice, went gaily about her household business" (369). Erminie is still bounded by her domestic space, but the narrator foreshadows the conflict that will disrupt both national and private unions.

Domestic ideal though she is, Erminie is no more fully defined by her conventional gender role than was Alberta, the model (and misguided) southern belle. In Erminie, Southworth offers an embodiment of the traditional "true woman," yet the heroine has strengths and convictions not accounted for by typical true woman ideology. When she discovers that Eastworth is a rebel, she refuses to elope with him to the South as he expects her to do. Eastworth assumes that Erminie can easily transfer her allegiances, personal and political, from father to husband because she is a domestic creature; he tells her, "Daughter-like, you take your opinions from your father, and, parrot-like, repeat the words he uses, without attaching much meaning to them" (450). He is wrong. He attempts to "plead the cause of Secession with all the arguments by which astute leaders influence the opinions of people. . . . But they made no impression on the mind of Erminie Rosenthal" (452–53). The simplicity of her faith, instead of making her pliable, makes her strong: "I see this all too clearly to deceive myself. I have loved this Union so much! . . . And would you aim a death-blow at her? . . . I would give my life—almost my soul—to save you from this vortex!" (452). Eastworth departs for the South while Erminie remains in Washington to volunteer as a nurse. Erminie's interproposal plot parallels the story of many historical women, as she extends her role as nurturer beyond the bounds of home, testing and extending her own endurance. Erminie refers to the hospital as "a great school for the spirit" (*How He Won Her* 41–42). When Eastworth returns at the end of the war, defeated, humbled, and mutilated, Erminie has grown from a naive girl into a strong woman, and she plans to continue her active role to help heal her country.

The parallel between Erminie's "union" and the country's "Union" is sustained throughout her plot. Reconciliation is possible because General Eastworth recants his Confederate convictions. Erminie welcomes Eastworth back, to his amazement: "What a welcome, and how unworthy I am to receive it! Do angels always welcome returning sinners so, Erminie?" (495). He protests that he is "old and gray and broken and mutilated," having lost his right arm "in a bad cause"; furthermore, he is "poor and penniless. . . . My once spotless name is stained with reproach" (496). All this makes no difference to Erminie, and "these two were reconciled, and this was but the forerunner of a deeper and broader reconciliation yet to come" (496). Southworth obviously hopes that the North, like Erminie, will welcome the South back into the Union without rancor. Once married, Eastworth and Erminie go to Virginia, planning to work to "restore order and industry in their own section of country, and to promote peace and good-will between the North and the South" (511). In narrating the story of Erminie's war experiences, Southworth redefines the concept of "true woman," suggesting that the many domestic women who proved themselves during the war should be understood as having a substantial postwar role to play in healing both their families and their country. This fictional representative of a cultural icon has been strengthened by asserting herself as a political as well as a domestic creature. Southworth appears to have understood a phenomenon explained by LeeAnn Whites, who maintains that women's war work "served to reveal the way in which their own domestic labors literally created, or at least underpinned, the public position of their men" (136–37). Erminie's story suggests that the country will benefit by allowing women to continue to extend their domestic labors beyond the home.

This argument itself is not new. Southworth is writing in the tradition of domestic authors who envisioned the home as a positive and active influence on the public realm. Harriet Beecher Stowe's *Uncle Tom's Cabin* is perhaps the most famous example of a novel in which domestic influence is exerted for political ends. The writers in the woman's fiction tradition identified by Nina Baym were, along similar lines, "thinking about a social reorganization wherein their special concept of home was projected out into the world" (*Woman's Fiction* 48). Baym adds that the "decade of the 1850s was the high point of their fiction because the motives of self-development and social reform could run together so smoothly" (49). The Civil War provided the opportunity for women to prove that domesticity had the strength antebellum novelists had claimed for it. When Eastworth first proposes to Erminie, he arrogantly assumes that she is exclusively a domestic creature, and although appreciative of how adeptly she arranges rooms and plans meals, he fails to recognize the depth and strength of her convictions and the clarity of her sense of political as well as domestic duty. He understood the domestic role to be entirely subordinate to the political interests of the head of household, whereas Erminie had a more inclusive vision. When she welcomes him back, her love unchanged in spite of his humiliation, he recognizes her moral superiority and sees the strength and clear-mindedness that goes with it. Through the double proposal, Southworth invokes historical parallels and literary precursors to negotiate a marriage that will strengthen the woman's role and humble the man so that he recognizes and must rely on that strength.

The progressive impetus of Southworth's courtship plot becomes clearer when her story is contrasted with other post–Civil War writing that imagined national reunion through private unions. Kathleen Diffley found that approximately one-fourth of romance stories of the period "aligned courtship rituals with sectional politics," but that such tales usually featured a northern suitor and a southern heroine to imply that the conquered South must submit to the government of the North (62–63). Nina Silber discovered the gendered reunion metaphor to be pervasive in both fiction and nonfiction. She argues that the "image of marriage between northern men and southern women stood at the foundation of the late-nineteenth-century culture of conciliation and became a symbol which defined and justified the northern view of the power relations in the reunified nation" (6–7). In their reunion stories Southworth's contemporaries typically presented the South as conquered and submissive, and therefore feminine, and the North as triumphant and dominant, and therefore masculine. Erminie and Eastworth's union inverts this power relationship, as the male represents the defeated South who must be forgiven, while the female stands for the strong, true, and victorious North, waiting patiently for her wayward partner to repent and acknowledge her moral superiority.

Thus, while Southworth's narrative implies on one level that men will benefit from women's extended role, she also reveals her awareness that increased power for women may be tied to decreased power for men. In the defeated South, surviving men were often physically mutilated as well as economically and ideologically stripped. Eastworth, with arm amputated and secessionist politics recanted, suggests the fate of planter class men, who were forced to dismantle the slave system upon which they had founded their claims of racial and gender superiority. According to the historian George Rable, when southern men failed to successfully defend themselves and their homes, they were perceived as "no longer men," while at the same time, women gained strength because, through their contributions to the war, they "no longer saw themselves as passive victims" (137). Southworth apparently comprehended how the war had opened possibilities for extended women's roles and more egalitarian marriages, and under the protection of a conventional courtship closure, she inverts the typical reunion courtship and marries the chastened Eastworth to the strengthened Erminie. Southworth thus manipulates literary conventions and Reconstruction politics to recast gender roles.

In Elfie Fielding's courtship plot Southworth examines the relationship of a second politically divided couple who never reconcile their political commitments, although they are briefly reconciled in marriage. Both Elfie and her suitor, Albert Goldsmith, are Southerners, but Elfie remains loyal to the Union while Albert conspires with Eastworth before joining the band of Confederate guerrillas led by Alberta Goldsmith's husband, Corsoni. Elfie is forced to flee to Washington as a refugee because she displays the Union flag and shoots a man who tries to take it down: "The first public act of my life resulted in getting our house burned over our heads!" (404). She later discovers the rebel plot brewing in the Rosenthal house when Albert, assuming that she is on the Confederate side, unwittingly discusses it with her. Elfie breaks her engagement, denouncing secession in terms that articulate her understanding of a continuity between political and domestic relations: "If a state has the right to secede from the Union, a county has the same right to secede from a state; and a township to secede from a county; and a farm from a township; and the barn from the farm; and the husband from the wife, and the child from the father!—and there you have disintegration and anarchy!" (*Fair Play* 429). Albert wants to marry Elfie immediately and take her South, but she refuses: "She loved him and hated him at the same moment; her heart was breaking, and she wished for death. But she never dreamed of flinching from her duty!" (428). Elfie links her private decision to terminate her courtship with political rhetoric: "If I were fool enough to marry you this week, why, next week, or next month you might secede from *me!*" (431). She reports Eastworth's plot to the government, although in so doing she endangers the man she loves, and then attempts to get herself drafted by the Union using her androgynous middle name, "Sydney"; her father refuses to let her go to war, but he does buy a substitute for her.

Albert, like Eastworth, refuses to believe that a woman's political loyalties could be stronger than her private affections. He kidnaps Elfie and, in spite of her violent opposition (she nearly tears his ears off with her bare hands), forces her through a marriage ceremony while promising not to consummate that marriage without her consent: "You shall be as sacred to me as my sister" until "you will forgive me and love me" (*How He Won Her* 272). Elfie is rescued by Union forces and returns to Washington, where she helps Erminie in the hospitals. Albert, like Eastworth, is badly wounded and loses a limb (in his case a leg). Elfie, overcome by grief and love, dons her hated wedding ring and acknowledges her marriage so that she may nurse him. Each recognizes the other's right to a different opinion; Albert tells Elfie, "Diametrically opposed as we are, we are each of us true to our firmest convictions of duty. . . . And so far each of us is right" (348). But because Albert dies, he and Elfie are never faced with the problem of reconciling their marriage with their irreconcilable political divisions.

No doubt Northerners, like Elfie, find the fallen and disarmed (or dislegged) rebel easier to love than a rebel in arms: "When I saw *him* at the head of his band; strong, rampant, insolent; in arms against the government; doing his arrogant will with everybody, and with myself among the rest, I *hated* him. . . . And now, when I see him stretched, broken, helpless, and writhing in agony in that bed, as if it was a rack, I feel as if my cruel prayers had been granted, and I had brought him to it!" (*How He Won Her* 332–33). But

only converted rebels and those true to the Union are left to promote reconciliation; Southworth cannot envision a union between characters whose
public commitments are not compatible. Elfie can express her love for Albert only after he admits her right to hold to her own convictions and after
he can no longer exert "his arrogant will" over her. In this courtship, again
featuring a couple whose sectional allegiances invert the more common motif,
the North (coded female) survives while the unrepentant South (coded male)
dies. In addition to pointing out that Confederate ideology is doomed,
Southworth conflates history and narrative to suggest that, especially given
the death of so many men, the reunified nation must rely on its strengthened women for survival.

While Alberta, Erminie, and Elfie all illustrate ways in which women
could be politicized and energized by the war, the fourth heroine, the "Man-
hater" Britomarte Conyers, is the most aggressively political and action-ori-
ented of them all. Her prolonged courtship with Justin Rosenthal (Erminie's brother) is resolved only after the Civil War has offered the heroine the
opportunity to display the incredible courage and bravery of which she is
capable. Britomarte rebels "against the fate that made her woman and the
law that limited her liberty to woman's sphere" and vows never to marry and
therefore to subject herself to laws and customs that circumscribe her freedom (*Fair Play* 29). She draws unabashedly feminist conclusions about "not
only the rights of married women to the control of their own property and
custody of their own children, but the rights of all women to a competition
with men in all the paths of industry and a share with them in all the chances
of success" (53). Justin finds in her words "much of right, strongly asserted"
("strong" probably carrying the pejorative connotation associated with
"strong-minded women") and quickly falls in love with her. Britomarte, to
her dismay, returns his passion, but "she combatted that love with all the
strength of her strong will" (111). Britomarte and Justin survive a shipwreck,
build a home on a deserted island ("chaperoned" by the Irish servant Judith),
fight pirates, and then return home to act in the theater of the Civil War.

Fair Play contains passionate and well-reasoned arguments about wom-
en's wrongs and their need for political protection. Britomarte lectures Justin and Erminie's father, the gentle but firm patriarch Dr. Rosenthal, when
he claims to have had "no hand in making these laws or encouraging these
customs"; the heroine points out, "You live under these laws without raising
pen or voice to modify them. You profit by these customs without ever re-
membering that you do so" (125). Her concerns for women go beyond her
class, and at least tentatively beyond her race, and she draws on personal

observation and statistics to prove her case. She deplores the unequal working conditions and pay for working-class women that exist because "your
diabolical laws and customs have not only barred against woman in almost
every field of labor, but have reduced her to the lowest pittance of wages in
those few fields in which you permit her to work" (122); she asks that her lis-
tener "take into consideration the humanity of freeing the poor white slave
women of the cities" in addition to "the slaves of the plantations" (124). She
further notes that among the "semi-professional classes . . . the male teacher gets from ten to twelve hundred dollars a year, the female, for teaching
the same branches and doing the same amount of work, gets but two hundred and fifty or three hundred" (122–23). Britomarte vows to live a life of
protest rather than submit to the unfair play of laws and customs: "In the
first place, so long as the barbarous law in changing a woman to a wife makes
her a nonentity, I will not marry. . . . In the second place, so long as your
barbarous customs close half of woman's legitimate field of labor, and open
the other half only to admit her to work at degrading rates of wages, I will
not work for any wages whatever. . . . In the third place so long as man continues to wrong woman, I will never accept assistance from any man whom-
soever" (125). Britomarte moderates her hatred of men gradually, talking less
of women's rights as circumstances give her more opportunities to act.

The transition between the two volumes of the serial, as the action moves
from fantasy island to historicized war, suggests what Southworth, as a writer
interested in women's lives, found so valuable in the changes brought about
by the Civil War. To put antebellum heroines in positions where they could
display their strengths, she created fantastic situations. Her best-known
heroine, Capitola Black of *The Hidden Hand,* dressed as a boy to survive the
streets of New York, fought a duel in defense of her own honor, rescued a
maiden from a forced marriage, and captured a dreaded outlaw. And while
Capitola's transgressive adventures clearly comment upon contemporary
gender roles and restrictions, they of necessity carry an air of the fabulous
that is underscored by the wild, even gothic, settings in which they take place
and by the quest romance language Southworth uses to describe them. When
the men in that novel leave to fight in the Mexican War, the narrator reluc-
tantly leaves Cap at home, commenting, "Our little domestic heroine, our
brave little Cap . . . when women have their rights, shall be a lieutenant-
colonel herself. Shall she not, gentlemen?" (348).[2] The Civil War offered
Southworth the opportunity denied in the earlier conflict. Using the cross-
dressing and role-playing strategies that made Capitola successful, and working herself for a time when "women have their rights," Britomarte does in-

deed fight in battles and rise in rank (to captain) in a man's army. The fantastic adventures of Southworth's earlier fiction continue, but are now historically situated.

Britomarte says that the war allowed men to prove their heroism and therefore earn her regard, but it also offered opportunities for women. While many women remained in their home communities to tend the house and participate in local volunteer efforts, others, both northern and southern, went to war even if the war was not coming to them. Most often, they worked as nurses or other support personnel for soldiers, but also, more frequently than has been suspected, they became soldiers themselves. Historians have documented that many women served dressed as men in Union and Confederate armies (both as enlisted soldiers and as officers) and that many women who served as nurses, daughters of the regiment, or vivandieres came under fire. Catherine Clinton notes that "over four hundred women were discovered posing as soldiers" (85), and Richard Hall suggests that women perhaps made a much greater contribution than that because (like Southworth's Britomarte) they kept their secret during and after the war whenever possible; one Civil War veteran was not discovered to be female until 1911 (20–26).[3] Elfie announces, "Nothing but our crinoline, if that is to stand for our sex, keeps thousands of us out of the army!" (*How He Won Her* 338). Hundreds did breach convention, abandon their crinoline, and enter the army, as Elfie attempts to do, and as Britomarte succeeds in doing, demonstrating "patriotism, courage, fortitude, and self-devotion" as valiantly as any male soldier (*How He Won Her* 509).

Whereas Erminie's work in the hospitals and Elfie's heroic defense of her own home, effort to be drafted, and willingness to betray her lover to the federal authorities attest to women's heroism and patriotism, Britomarte's actions outdo them both. While her adventures are more harrowing and dramatic than were Capitola's, many parts of Britomarte's story might have been drawn from historical accounts. Amy Clarke joined the Confederate Army with her husband and suffered two wounds before being taken prisoner, redressed in women's clothes, and returned to her home (Faust, *Mothers of Invention* 203). And Emma Edmonds entered the Union Army as a man, later assuming various disguises to penetrate Confederate lines on spying missions (Sizer 117). Britomarte's adventures recall the experiences of both these women. Dressed as a man, she enlists in Justin's regiment and becomes his aide; she later dons other disguises as an undercover agent for the Union. She participates heroically in armed conflict, at times leading charges into the teeth of enemy fire, and she spies for information that leads to the capture of the rebel guerrilla band. The heroine is finally caught and imprisoned; she was "more than a suspected spy in the hands of the enemy, and as such, she was only saved from the usual fate of a spy by that consideration for her sex which restrained her captors from putting a woman to death for anything less than a capital crime proved upon her . . . by direct testimony" (469–70).

Southworth justifies Britomarte's "unwomanly" behavior in the war by tying it to her great love for Justin, deflecting criticism that might be directed at how Britomarte cross-dresses, lives with men in army camps, fights in battles, and spies on enemies: "Justin, my beloved, I abjured my womanhood, disguised myself and followed you to battle; I have been by your side on twenty well fought fields; I have dared what woman never dared before, that I might be ever with you!" (440); in other words, Britomarte is more, not less, womanly for having "transformed and disfigured" herself (441). Southworth's rhetoric has shifted; whereas she once called her readers to admire the "brilliant Amazon" because of her strength and talents, she now adds to that heroine's character the trait of supreme selfless love. The "manly" strengths Britomarte demonstrates throughout the novels are derived from, rather than existing in spite of, her "womanly" traits. The story of Britomarte and Justin represents the possibilities for expanded roles for women and for progressive marriage within this new order, even an order in which unjust marriage laws are still in effect.

Yet Southworth is not excessively optimistic about the increased power women might be able to take in marriage or about the increased respect they might be able to command as a result of their heroic activities during the war. She must have been aware of the desperate efforts at retrenchment undertaken by men who returned from war longing to reassert their dominance over the domestic sphere. The reassertion was particularly crucial in the South, as Whites explains: "Confederate men looked to the domestic arena as their one remaining location of legitimate domination just as the same war that had defeated them on all other terrains had increased, however painfully, the autonomy of their women" (136). And Elizabeth D. Leonard finds that in the North, women had to struggle to maintain the advances they made during the war, for early postwar historians were creating "a carefully constructed postwar image of Yankee womanhood designed to circumscribe the social and political consequences of wartime stresses on the gender system" (182). To a degree, the conclusion of Southworth's novel seems to follow the same design, to participate in the common historical pattern wherein, following the disruption to domestic life caused by war, women and men return with relief to household relations reflecting conservative prewar ideologies of gender.[4] Following their wedding, Justin asks Britomarte, "How about Woman's Rights now, sweet wife?" to which she responds with a protest that sounds like a younger Britomarte, but with a disclaimer: "While I live . . . I will advocate the rights of woman—*in general.* But for my individual self, the only right I plead for is woman's dearest right—to be loved to my heart's content all the days of my life!" (512). Britomarte compromises her political convictions by accepting happiness for herself in marriage to her beloved fellow soldier. Elfie does not recant her unionist convictions, but she does accept her rebel suitor as a husband so that she can fulfill her wifely role as nurse and deathbed attendant. And Erminie envisions her future domestic role as promoting the healing of national wounds, but does, after all, marry her reformed Confederate soldier. The *Britomarte* narratives may work in part to restrain postwar anxiety about women's increasing power by intimating that women had always been political as well as domestic creatures and that despite this truth, women were ready to fulfill their old duties as well as to claim some new ones. Perhaps the title change between serial publication and two-volume novel signifies most strongly the conservative shift. The serial title, *Britomarte, the Man-Hater,* focuses on the single heroine as women's rights activist, while the novel titles, *Fair Play* and *How He Won Her,* stress the courtship and foreshadow the marriage ending.[5]

But for two thick volumes Southworth celebrates Britomarte's strength and independence, and the images of Britomarte the Man-hater, the soldier, and the spy far outweigh the brief final pages during which, in the afterglow of wartime glory, she accepts marriage. And in history as in these novels, returning to prewar conditions or ideas is not so easy. Many women appreciated the increased liberty and strength they gained during the war and were reluctant to return to a sphere as circumscribed as it had been before the war. Others, deprived of male support, were forced to fend for themselves and their children whether they desired independence or not. Still others, particularly in the South, having discovered they could not rely on men to defend and support them, retained a degree of autonomy in self-defense. And many of the men left by the war were weakened, physically or economically, and therefore were forced to rely on the work of their women. Thus the widened horizons of possibilities for women combined with the demands of rebuilding the Union could not be controlled by revisionary postwar rhetoric; popular works such as Southworth's would make sure that reactionary postwar voices did not go unchallenged. A "simple story" like Southworth's had all the potential influence wielded by popular literature cast in historical context: "This is the power of popular culture: to offer large numbers of people explanations of why things are the way things are—and what, if anything, can be done about it. Infuse this power with history—explanations of how things came to be the way they are—and you have a potent agent for influencing the thinking, and thus the actions, of millions of people" (Cullen 13). Despite her protestations to the contrary, Southworth's voice spoke through her narrative to a popular audience about the meaning of the war. Out of the confusion the Civil War infused into conventional concepts of gender roles, Southworth's novels redefined traditional feminine virtues by recasting women's sphere as both political and domestic and by advocating marriages that are built on this broadened definition of women's role. As Britomarte's final words remind the reader, women "in general" need and have earned increased political and legal rights. Their heroic behavior during the Civil War should help to convince doubters that women are fit to participate in public spheres of action, and that, in fact, the survival and healing of the nation depend on the growing strength of its women.

Notes

1. Nina Silber concludes that "the Civil War had wreaked havoc on the stability and rigidity of the Victorian code of gender. . . . Women everywhere had assumed new responsibilities and new roles which ran counter to accepted notions of the feminine sphere" (28). Elizabeth D. Leonard, in *Yankee Women: Gender Battles in the Civil War*, reveals in detail how three northern women capitalized on the needs and opportunities brought to women by the war, while LeeAnn Whites, in *The Civil War as a Crisis in Gender*, explores how the privileged white community of Augusta, Georgia, confronted threats to gender roles and redefined them to protect as best they could the southern notions of gender roles and white identity that were thrown into disarray by the Civil War. Leonard writes that the Civil War "rapidly made untenable the strict adherence of northern, middle-class Americans, at least, to this very particular, and in many minds apparently fixed and perfectly harmonious web of ideals about the social roles and relative power of men and women and about their proper interaction" (xxii). Whites finds that "gender roles as well as gender relations played a critical role in the initial outbreak of the war, as well as in its course, its conduct, and its eventual outcome in the 'reconstruction' of the South. For individual men and women, this moment of gender transformation in the social order at large created a crisis in the very way that they perceived their appropriate gender roles" (3). Drew Gilpin Faust argues that while southern women did develop new identi-

ties because of their accomplishments during the war, their experiences should not be construed as positive: "This new sense of self was based not in the experience of success but in desperation, in the fundamental need simply to survive" (*Mothers of Invention* 243).

2. *The Hidden Hand* has received a significant amount of critical attention, no doubt in large part because the Rutgers edition has made it widely available. As work by Alfred Habegger, Joanne Dobson, Lynette Carpenter, Amy E. Hudock, and Katharine Nicholson Ings shows us, *The Hidden Hand* rewards multiple readings from varied perspectives. The Britomarte serial surely deserves similar study.

3. Hall surveys women's roles as vivandieres, daughters of the regiment, and nurses; Lyde Cullen Sizer and Hall discuss the role of women spies in the Civil War. Marilyn Mayer Culpepper collects and analyzes extensive primary materials that reveal how women acted in and were acted upon by the Civil War.

4. Karen Lystra's study of nineteenth-century courtship correspondence suggests that private correspondence registered the same kinds of war-related disruption in gender relations that historians have documented and that Southworth explored: "Although men's and women's outward role behavior may not have changed greatly, evidence indicates there was more tension over sex roles from the Civil War to the end of the century than in the antebellum period. Certainly the Civil War itself may be a factor in what appears to be a new level of sex-role insecurity in postbellum male-female relationships" (147).

5. A reviewer for *The Nation* suggests an opportunistic justification for the title change, arguing that the novel's title was changed from "'Britomarte, the Man-Hater'. . . or something equally felicitous and suggestive" to *Fair Play* to capitalize on the popularity and superior reputation (among the critical elite) of the novelist Charles Reade, who had published a novel entitled *Foul Play* about a pair of lovers stranded on an island ("Recent Publications" 55).

FIVE

Elizabeth Stuart Phelps:
Professional Women and Traditional Wedlock

A declared reformer and advocate for women's rights, Elizabeth Stuart Phelps ranks with Laura J. Curtis Bullard as the most openly radical of the writers considered in this study. In particular, she believed that women deserved better education and access to a wider range of employment opportunities. Critics have praised her for the overt feminism of *The Story of Avis* (1877) and *Doctor Zay* (1882), both of which demonstrate feminist principles that she also expressed in a series of essays.[1] In the two novels Phelps combines character development with double proposals to depict heroines whose initial desire to forego marriage in favor of careers gives way to a reluctant choice to marry and pursue their careers with promised spousal support. *Avis* is further notable for Phelps's persuasive and sensitive depiction of the mundane daily struggles and inevitable family crises that occupy the protagonist's time and erode her energies after she marries. Phelps is the only author in this study who followed a renegotiated marriage "beyond the ending" (in Rachel Blau DuPlessis's phrase) to reveal the difficulties a couple faces when they undertake an egalitarian marriage in an unequal society.

Nevertheless, viewed from a contemporary perspective, Phelps is as much a backward- as a forward-looking writer. In her novels she enlarges the scope of women's career possibilities and explores the challenges of two-career marriages in a "modern" way, but also relies upon courtship codes that reproduce restrictive assumptions about male and female differences. As a New Englander who grew up in a Calvinist household under the influence of a stern but loving minister-father (her mother, whose best-selling *The Sunny Side* [1851] was a novel about the joys and pains of being a minister's wife, died when Phelps was eight years old), Phelps may be seen as attempting to negotiate between old and new loyalties. She held strong religious principles (a fact interpreted by contemporary critics as *ipso facto* conservative) but her theology challenged traditional religious dogma.[2] For Phelps, moral and religious conviction were not only consistent with but largely justified her advocacy of women's rights.

In her autobiographical *Chapters from a Life* (1896), Phelps reflects on the social context of her life and work: "The last thirty years in America have pulsated with moral struggle. No phase of society has escaped it. It has ranged from social experiment to religious cataclysm, and to national upheaval" (265). And she hesitantly ponders her personal rebellion in the context of national change: "It is almost impossible to understand, now, what it meant when I was twenty-five, for a young lady reared as I was, on Andover Hill, to announce that she should forthwith approve and further the enfranchisement and elevation of her own sex. Seen beside the really great martyrdoms and dedications of the 'causes' which throb through our modern life, this seems an episode only large enough to irritate a smile" (250). The title character from *Doctor Zay* (1882) expresses the relation between the progressive individual and her society in less modest terms: "There are new questions constantly arising . . . for a woman in my position. One ceases to be an individual. One acts for the whole,—for the sex, for a cause, for a future" (122). The dialogue generated by Phelps's double-proposal fiction with other authors and with history reveals and explores the tensions arising between the two views summarized above: that personal revolution might appear trivial when juxtaposed with great historical movements, but then again, that an individual, in challenging norms and living a progressive life, might "act for the whole" and help reform society.

Phelps was well established as a writer before she published her two double-proposal novels. Her first major success came with *The Gates Ajar* (1869), a best-selling view of the afterlife written to comfort the many thousands of American women grieving over family members lost in the Civil War. She was known for several popular series of children's stories and published short fiction as well as novels steadily throughout her career. Included in her nonfiction writing are articles advocating women's rights and antivivisection legislation, a memoir of her father's life, and a popular interpretation of the life of Jesus. Phelps married Herbert Ward in 1888, undertaking for herself a two-career marriage with, at best, mixed success. In spite of ill health and domestic strain, she wrote steadily after her marriage, both on her own and in collaboration with her husband, until her death in 1911.[3]

The evident tension in Phelps's double-proposal novels goes deeper than the career versus marriage plot, which is the focus of the characters as well as of many critics. Contradictions exist within her characterizations of heroines, reflecting the troubled dialectic of change and conservatism she shared with her culture. Phelps entertains a nostalgic fascination with essentialized concepts of gender that she declines to set aside even when she is most precisely detailing the social pressures and material limitations her culture places on women.[4] Her heroines pursue their careers and claim a strong role in marriage, but Phelps still occasionally presents them as passive objects of display, from the narrator's as well as from the suitor's point of view. To be sure, Phelps does not subscribe to the same essential notions of gender that were assigned to women by the conservative social arbiters from whom Barbara Welter drew her outline of the "Cult of True Womanhood." But Phelps believes women are essentially, even mystically, different from men, and she also believes that women deserve the right to self-determination. Her praise of strong women, however, is sometimes strained when the narrator participates in just the sort of objectification of their bodies that the heroines occasionally rebel against. At times, both Avis Dobell and Atalanta Zaidee Lloyd (the full name of Dr. Zay) appear trapped by a narrative that holds them, static, for our admiration and then praises their efforts at maintaining autonomy and forging careers.

In her double proposals Phelps questions the optimism of earlier double-proposal works and challenges the ease with which those texts reformed suitors. She poses a question generally avoided in earlier texts: How can a woman balance career with marriage? *Avis* enters a dialogue most prominently with *Aurora Leigh*, but also responds to *Jane Eyre, Christine,* and perhaps *Vivia.* In each intertextual link, Phelps takes the tentative answers offered through other double proposals and challenges them. For earlier writers, reforming one man seemed to promise a reformed marriage; Phelps is conscious that change is not so easily achieved. She acknowledges that marriage is difficult and that a marriage challenging social norms will be particularly stressful. The painful self-denial required of an independent woman who in real life accommodates herself even to a renegotiated marriage is obscured or deflected by the conclusions of *St. Elmo* and *How He Won Her* but is explored in *Avis,* which charts the daily pressures that require the wife to defer her career so she can serve her husband and children. *Doctor Zay* does not follow the couple past the wedding; still, its documented effect on readers has been to produce doubt that the renegotiated marriage will be happy because the risks incurred by a heroine who marries a man morally weaker than herself (as also happens in *Christine, Vivia,* and perhaps *Beulah*) are not glossed over. Phelps maintains that the expectations of a husband socialized to a culture built on conventional gender roles will inevitably resemble those of other husbands even if his proposal rhetoric promises a renegotiated, egalitarian, two-career marriage. Simply because a man promises to let a woman continue her career after marriage and to support her in her professional life does not mean he can or will fulfill these promises. Furthermore, a man so weakened and wounded that he is forced to depend on a woman will not necessarily make a better husband; he may be a worse one. For Phelps, a woman cannot "create" a man to "suit her" as a "suitor" simply by painting his portrait or nursing him out of illness or injury. Her cultural critique of the double-proposal literary tradition takes two related tacks: first, (re)-creating the new man will take more than isolated circumstances, more than a lover's inspired protest that he desires to participate in an egalitarian marriage; and, second, even where good intentions prevail in both partners, living out a renegotiated marriage in a backwards and unsympathetic world will be difficult to impossible.[5]

That Phelps aimed for social change by challenging readers' expectations about courtship and marriage was apparent to her earliest reviewers, several of whom attest to how her novels disturb the reading process. In reviewing *The Story of Avis* in 1878, a writer for *The Nation* argues that "under the guise of fiction the book is really a protest against marriage" and that Phelps has been influenced by George Eliot "with regard to detestations of modern society." The reviewer also notes that Avis's "married life was not of a sort to cheer the sentimental reader" and that "the days have gone by, apparently, when young people will get romantic ideas of life from novels" ("Recent Novels" 202). A reviewer of Phelps's *Friends* for *The Nation* in 1881 also attests, albeit sarcastically, to the challenge of reading Phelps, arguing that, as with *Avis,* "the mental process of the average intelligent person, upon taking it up, will doubtless be an endeavor, more or less conscious, to account for its idiosyncrasies" ("Recent Novels" 258). An 1882 review of *Doctor Zay* in the *Independent* illustrates just such a mental endeavor on the part of a reader. This reviewer variously processes the contradictory pulls of the novel toward career and toward marriage as "inconsistent sentimentalism," "unconscious irony," and even "satire," concluding that the character is clearer about the problem than is the author: "However bravely Miss Phelps may struggle for a way out of the dilemma, the heroine herself never fails for a moment to perceive that she must choose whether to be a woman and a wife or a doctor without sex" ("Literature" 10). And the book is acknowledged as an effort toward social change that is based in the reality of some women's lives: "Doctor Zay . . . is rather the type of a womanhood which Miss Phelps wishes to introduce into the world than of one which is already there; though ambitious women will recognize a basis of truth in the struggle between her womanly impulses and the professional aspirations which call them to a life where the limitations of sex are not recognized" ("Literature" 10).

As these reviews suggest, Phelps understands that reforming marriage poses the problem of creating change (in the individual or the family) in a larger culture that is struggling toward reform at a pace far behind the utopian expectations of its more progressive members. For Phelps herself, as recounted in *Chapters from a Life,* the relationship between personal and cultural change was brought into focus when her reading of *Aurora Leigh* was juxtaposed with the outbreak of the Civil War. She read *Aurora Leigh* during the summer of 1860, when she turned sixteen: "I owe to [Barrett Browning], distinctly, the first visible aspiration (ambition is too low a word) to do some honest hard work of my own in the World Beautiful, and for it" (65–66); the onset of the Civil War followed some nine months later. *Aurora Leigh* provided personal inspiration to contribute to "the World Beautiful," while the Civil War brought home the impact of national politics even to relatively remote New England: "Then comes a morning when the professors cannot read the papers for the news they bring. . . . For the black day of the defeat at Bull Run has darkened the summer sky" (73). Barrett Browning's ambitious model seemed to have combined with the drama and anguish of war to inspire Phelps to write. She recalls that the first story she wrote, not counting her juvenile forays, was a war story, "the beginning of anything like genuine work for me" (74–75). The war also occasioned *The Gates Ajar,* which both established Phelps's reputation and proved to her that an individual woman could influence her culture: "Into that great world of woe my little book stole forth, trembling. . . . I do not think I thought so much about the suffering of men . . . but the women,—the helpless, outnumbering, unconsulted women" (*Chapters* 97). Barrett Browning challenges women to pursue their dreams of self-fulfillment, and especially their artistic aspirations, while the Civil War, decimating the male population and revolutionizing the structure of the country, demanded that women, "whom war trampled down, without a choice or protest," sacrifice for and serve a government they had, as Phelps recognized, no voice in choosing (*Chapters* 98). Susan Coultrap-McQuin suggests that Phelps was drawing on the confidence inspired by the success of *The Gates Ajar* when she "confronted her conservative family with the declaration that she would henceforth work for women's rights" (174).

She had found her means to connect personal with social change, to extend the "purely selfish, personal way" in which she had first recoiled from "the old ideas of womanhood" into the broader cultural milieu (*Chapters* 99).

In Phelps's fiction as well as in her memoirs, *Aurora Leigh* and the Civil War become motifs that represent two powerful imperatives for change, both of which share the pattern of disruption and reconciliation found in double-proposal fiction. *The Story of Avis* juxtaposes *Aurora Leigh* with the Civil War much as *Chapters from a Life* does. When Avis returns to the United States from studying art abroad, she finds her country sliding into war. Although she is determined to pursue her personal goals, the war interferes: "'I shall get to work to-morrow,' said Avis. . . . But to-morrow [her friend] Coy came over to take her to the chapel, where the women of Harmouth sat with hushed voices, rolling bandages and picking lint. The butchery of Bull Run had fallen upon the mangled land" (78).

Aurora Leigh and the Civil War are so crucial to *Avis*'s plot that Phelps confuses Avis's age to make her artistic awakening correspond with the publication of *Aurora Leigh* in 1857 (which Avis reads when she is sixteen) and her courtship battles at age twenty-six correspond with the Civil War's "summer of battles" in 1861.[6] Avis thus was either "born" in 1835 (which would correspond with the Civil War dating) or in 1841, according to the *Aurora Leigh* dating, so she is three or nine years "older" than her author.[7]

Avis suffers from the conflicting demands of her artistic vocation and her country's struggles. She wants "nothing" of the outside world of men, "the great unholy world, in which seers struggled and sinned for their visions. Let them go fighting and erring on. God spoke in another way to women," but then she asks herself, "Who could make a picture till the war was over?" Torn by the internal conflict, she shuts out the sound of boys singing war songs, takes a liqueur, and lapses into a stream of visions from which she emerges knowing what and why she will paint: "The sphinx, the great sphinx, restored. . . . The mystery of womanhood stood before her, and said, 'Speak for me'" (83). Avis's decision to promote the cause of women through her art (which parallels Phelps's decision to write *The Gates Ajar* for women) illustrates one way a northern woman, distanced from the war but preoccupied with the drive for reform, could claim a role in the "moral struggle" with which America "pulsated."

The Civil War, recast into the novel *Avis*, represents the violent male world in which Avis must be a woman and an artist, but war also operates as a doubled metaphor in her personal life, representing both the battle between Avis and Philip Ostrander and Avis's internal conflict when struggling against her attraction to him. Phelps portrays courtship as a "battle between the sexes" in which the heroine can either "defend her cause" (and continue to be a career-oriented single woman) or "surrender" (and submit herself to a risky marriage). In the first proposal scene, the heroine successfully defends herself against the encroaching suitor. Then, in a final proposal scene that otherwise reproduces motifs from double-proposal predecessors, Phelps portrays the woman as weakening. Before the renegotiated proposal, Avis has been worn down by her internal battle, so that her pity for Ostrander's war wound moves her to capitulate to him when he reappears in the deceptive guise of a reformed and physically weakened suitor.

Over and over again in *The Story of Avis*, Phelps uses the verb *to win* to describe courtship. The narrator announces that "within the soul of every unwon woman abides eternal youth" (16). Philip Ostrander finds that "his ardor deepened under her denial. He had always thought he should learn to hate a woman who had been too easily won" (72). And after their engagement, Philip perceives Avis as a "strong, sweet woman, wooed, but not yet won" (120); then after the wedding: "Deeps beyond the lowest deeps in her nature were yet unwon. His manhood gathered itself to be worthy of their mastery" (138). And then after their separation: "His wife was not a woman to be won lightly for the second time" (220). Within such a model of courtship, the protagonist is always on the defensive, virtually denied volition except in a resistance that is doubly dangerous because she is fighting against herself as well as against her suitor. If, for the Phelps heroine, success lies in defending her own territory, then to be won is to lose and marriage signals a defeat.

In Phelps's telling, not the suitor's aggression but the heroine's inner turmoil eventually leads to her capitulation. Avis finds herself trapped by the internal struggle that Phelps described in *Chapters from a Life* in relation to her mother: "She lived one of those rich and piteous lives such as only gifted women know; torn by the civil war of the dual nature which can be given to women only" (12). When Avis finds herself responding to Philip, she discovers this dangerous dual nature. She no longer has a single-minded devotion to art, and she is dismayed at her emotional reaction to Philip's arrogant assertion that "we love each other" (63): "What was the weakness in her nature that had made this experience possible? and what the tumult there which made it memorable, stamped it upon her like the mould of a great sorrow, or a wild joy?" (65). On the one hand, Avis believes that "success—for a woman—means absolute surrender, in whatever direction. Whether she paints a picture, or loves a man, there is no division of labor possible in her economy" (69). Yet Avis finds herself wanting both to paint a picture and to love a man. Whereas Avis had rejected the Civil War as a man's war, insisting that "God spoke in another way to women," it yet becomes the metaphor by which Phelps describes women's internal struggle and their battle with the men who would "win" them. Despite efforts to shut out "the great unholy world" of men, "civil war" tears at Avis from within and without.

Avis exposes herself to eventual defeat when she agrees to "gratify Mr. Ostrander" (as her father puts it) by painting his portrait (51). Avis the artist is enchanted with Philip before Avis the woman succumbs. Working on Philip's portrait, she "found much beauty—and more, the better she knew it—in Philip Ostrander's face" (54). She opens herself to friendship with him, to her own immediate dismay: "She had allowed this man a momentary privilege, sacred and mystical to her as her maidenly dim vision of the rights of plighted love" (58). While painting a portrait of Philip that flatters him, as her friend Coy notices (59), Avis in effect begins to seduce herself. But although Philip's beautiful face and beautiful voice at length do attract the woman as well as the artist, Avis rejects his first proposal.

The first proposal scene between Avis and Philip is a battle that leaves Avis physically and emotionally exhausted; while she resists the proposal, she loses some of her self-possession. When she feels that "a battle was impending . . . the whole force of her, soul and body seemed to garrison itself" (66). Under the influence of Philip's persuasion, she finds herself "swaying and uncertain" but at length he realizes that "the tide of an emotion stronger than he had ever witnessed in her had turned and was setting out from him" (70). At the close of the scene, Avis, "prone as a fallen Caryatide [sic]" in the grass, "flung out one bent elbow as if she had been warding off a blow" to tell Philip: "For your soul's sake and mine, you are the man I *will* not love" (73). Phelps is not the first double-proposal author to suggest that the "will" does not control "love," and the internal weakening that begins in Avis during the first proposal reveals that the artist is vulnerable to the desires of the woman.

Several events conspire to weaken Avis's resolution before Philip proposes again. Avis's friend Coy accepts a proposal from John Rose, and Avis reveals how she idealizes romantic love and betrothal. To Avis, Coy's "young, trans-figured face" appears to belong to "a holy object that she might not touch." Furthermore, Avis "had almost a consciousness of indelicacy, as if she had usurped one of John Rose's new and sacred rights" (88). Then Avis hurts her hand rowing and is unable to work. In her forced inactivity, she discovers that "there seemed to be great spaces in her nature, into which she neither cared nor dared to look, and which the events of the summer had imperceptibly enlarged, like the boundaries of a conquering country" (96). Thus she is already losing her internal civil war when Philip, who had enlisted in the Union Army after Avis rejected him, returns to Harmouth wounded from battle. He knows that "had he come to her again in the power of his manhood, he might again have gone as he came. It was his physical ruin and helplessness which appealed to the strength in her" (99–100). Because his weakness attracts her, and because she has herself been weakened, Avis's internal struggle intensifies. She tells the confused Philip that loving him is, for her, "like death. . . . It is civil war" (106).

Avis tries to resolve her personal civil war by promising herself to be both artist and wife; she accepts Philip by telling him, "I have decided that I cannot resign my profession as an artist" (110). She is not, however, comfortable with her decision: "Her betrothal fitted upon her impatiently, like the first articles in a treaty of capitulation only looking askance as yet towards a dreaded surrender in which a passionately defended lost cause was to go down" (111). The "treaty" signed between Avis and Philip, and between Avis's two warring natures, reads like a promising renegotiated marriage in the tradition of double-proposal fiction. Philip insists, "I do not want your work, or your individuality. I refuse to accept any such sacrifice from the woman I love." While the narrator warns of the superficiality of his commitment— "Ostrander uttered this daring sentiment as ardently as if he had ever thought of it before, and as sincerely as if it had been the watchword of his life"— Avis wants to believe him: "I have wondered sometimes if there were such a man in the world. . . . I knew it would be all over with me when I found him" (107–8). But in *The Story of Avis* the second proposal has only the appearance of renegotiation. While Philip's weakened state reminds a reader of the chastened, wounded, and blinded Edward Rochester or Romney Leigh, it turns out that Philip's blindness is moral rather than physical.[8] The egalitarian marriage rhetoric he offers with such apparent sincerity cannot guarantee a new marriage union any more than diplomacy could recreate the national union; battle, struggle, suffering, sacrifice are unavoidably part of domestic reconstruction as well as national revolution.

The problem of the self-destructive dual female nature posed by Phelps is exacerbated because her heroine idealizes romantic love and marriage, and while her idealism partakes of visions of egalitarian marriage, she remains trapped by cultural assumptions concerning the husband's rights over the wife. Avis, newly betrothed, envisions the joy of marriage: "Down through the years she suddenly saw herself transfigured by happiness. She saw her whole nature deepening, its lightest grace or deepest gift illuminated, herself idealized, by love" (121). Avis's expectations depend on her belief that Philip is "so tender, and so noble above his fellows, so true that he could be proud of the woman he loved," in other words, that he is a new man. But she still subscribes to cultural ideals of womanly submission in marriage. She reflects on how Philip's "generous humility had exalted him . . . to the king-ship of her" and longs "to make herself worthy of so royal a love. She began to be glad with a proud pleasure that it was in the nature of things that she should sacrifice more for Philip than he for her" (122).

Avis is crippled not only by these fantasies of unegalitarian love but also by the narrator's objectifying descriptions of her. Indeed, Phelps seems to participate in the same cultural process against which the heroine struggles, so that the very language of the novel is locked in civil war. Sentences often reveal how Phelps is trapped between a conservative allegiance to the ideal of feminine self-sacrifice and a progressive desire for more female assertive-ness: "The self-distrust which had shrunk at the first rebuff of ardor was [Avis's] preservation now. She abandoned herself to the grating drudgeries involved in mastering the *technique* of art with a passion of which it were not discerning not to say that it added to the fire of the artist something of fem-inine self-abnegation" (37). Indeed, how to combine the artist with the fem-inine? Here, it takes a particularly painful double negative.

In addition, the novel frequently treats Avis as an art object to be admired; at times the narrator gazes at Avis, while at others the gaze is attributed to characters. Avis sometimes appears to invite the gaze, at others to resist it. In the opening of the novel Phelps explains at awkward length why Avis places herself in front of a carmine-colored curtain: "She had a fierce kin-ship in her for that color. . . . She did not expect it to be understood; she did not care that it should be; perhaps she imperfectly understood it herself: she only knew that it made her happy to be near it. . . . Besides, she knew per-fectly well that the curtain became her" (7). Avis chooses a "shadowed cor-ner" of the parlor, yet consciously sets herself off to be admired. The narra-tor later describes Avis by the seashore as a "full lithe length there, a perfect panel against the sky and sea," and Philip enters the scene to order Avis not to move. Avis is annoyed at herself for submitting: "Avis, perhaps because she had just obeyed him in standing still to be looked at, had turned a little coldly" (98–99). The narrator "freezes" Avis into position before Philip does, and Avis's coldness would seem to be directed at the narrator and the reader as well as at Philip and herself. The language that traps Avis indexes the novel's conflicted position and reveals Phelps's unwillingness or inability to give up the mystique of the feminine.

Phelps's characterization and narrative treatment of Avis reveal the essentialized concepts of gender to which she subscribes. She believes women share an inherent capacity for deep and self-sacrificing love and that they are somehow made of a spiritually "finer" fiber than men. Romantic, self-forgetting love pours forth from the woman when she has been "won"; this love transfigures Coy and entrances both Avis and the narrator. Avis shares with Coy the capacity for love, but she has an equal capacity to devote herself to her vocation. Phelps does not recognize the "loving" aspect of the traditional feminine as a social construct but as "nature." Phelps shares Avis's belief that "[God] has set two natures in me, warring against each other. He has made me a law unto myself" (107).

While the courtship plot in *Avis* reproduces woman as object to be won and the narrative voice at times objectifies the heroine and at others endorses her subjectivity, the development plot constructs a "new" woman who successfully enters traditionally male-dominated professions with ambition and confidence. Both Avis Dobell and Dr. Zay envision their work as life-long, all-absorbing careers. Both are committed professionals as no earlier American double-proposal heroine had claimed to be.[9] They reject first proposals not because the suitor is flawed (though he is) or because they are opposed to marriage but because they believe profession and marriage each demand complete self-devotion. Avis tells Philip, "Marriage . . . is a profession to a woman. And I have my work" (71). Dr. Zay sends Waldo Yorke away twice: first when she believes he has mistaken his dependency on her for love and second when she does not believe he could be happy with a professional wife: "You have been so unfortunate as to become interested in a new kind of woman. . . . You would come home, some evening, when I should not be there (but I should feel worse not to be there than you would to miss me). You would need me when I was called somewhere urgently . . . and then it would seem to you that you were neglected, that you were wronged" (244).

In creating an ambitious and talented artist in Avis and a successful and committed doctor in Dr. Zay, Phelps enters late nineteenth-century cultural and fictional dialogues about professional women as a clearly progressive voice. But when she casts her career heroines into double proposals and raises the issue of how professional women could marry, she betrays the conflicts and limitations within her reformist views. Phelps first takes up the theme of the woman as artist, introduced in earlier double-proposal fiction like *Jane Eyre* and *Vivia*.[10] Avis's artistic visions recall the paintings Rochester chose from Jane Eyre's portfolio as her most impressive. Jane Eyre painted for personal pleasure and as part of her teaching duties, but Avis seems to recall

Jane's visions as she attempts to imagine how a woman could create professional art to represent women's experiences. Among the scenes rejected by Avis during her visionary episode is one of a "titanic wave . . . [that] held both the passion and the intellect of the sea. Above its crest there was flung one human hand, and a strip of pearl-white sky" (82); one of Jane Eyre's watercolors is a picture of "a swollen sea" where a shipwreck has just occurred and "a drowned corpse glanced through the green water; a fair arm was the only limb clearly visible" (157). Jane Eyre also painted a "woman's shape to the bust," which was a "vision of the Evening Star" and a veiled "colossal head." Rejecting the vision of drowning along with other scenes of misery and heartbreak, Avis at length chooses for her first (and last, as it turned out) masterpiece the colossal Sphinx through which she hoped to speak for the "mystery of womanhood" (83).

Avis (re)creates the Sphinx, painting it as it might have looked before worn down by centuries: "The crude Nubian features she had rechiselled, the mutilated outline she had restored; the soul of it she had created." She assumes a "mystery of womanhood" that needs representation because it cannot speak for itself: "The lion's feet of her no eye can see, the eagle's wings of her are bound by the hands of unrelenting years; only her mighty face remains to answer what the ages have demanded, and shall forever ask of her" (143). The Sphinx is equated with womanhood in general and with Avis in particular. Avis is herself described as a "great, dumb, protesting goddess, whom some light hand had just dragged from the bosom of the earth to the glare of day" (64). The painting thus represents some of the most painful tensions in the novel: woman as object, yet created by the woman artist; woman as an ancient mystery, yet subject to the "light hand" of a weak suitor and the "glare" of trivial daily cares.[11]

The Sphinx painting itself is made possible when Avis rejects Philip's first proposal; she conceives and begins the painting during the 1861 "summer of battles." Had she accepted Philip, her career would have been cut so short that even this single masterpiece would likely not have been created. On the other hand, she finishes the Sphinx after her marriage, and the picture is described as "the child of their union" (143). The Sphinx is created through the civil wars of the novel yet is also the only great painting Avis ever produces because those battles exhaust her. The Sphinx, in both the metaphorical and the narrative structure of the novel, demonstrates the paradox confronting the woman who would be both artist and wife. When she produces the painting, Avis is trying to reconcile her warring natures by giving the Sphinx a voice. She herself, however, is silenced after the success of this one great painting.

Through her art, Avis attempts to create change, both at a cultural level (the Sphinx is her attempt to represent and glorify voiceless "womanhood" for her contemporaries) and in her personal life. Avis paints the portrait of her lover as did Theodora of Southworth's *Vivia* (1857). Like Theodora, Avis idealizes that lover and later marries him. Southworth promises us that Theodora and Austin's marriage will be happy in spite of Austin's faults; Phelps shows us that Avis and Philip's marriage will be deeply troubled. Theodora overcomes a bad marriage and hard physical labor to paint again, better than before. But Avis has been so worn down by her marriage that she can no longer paint well after Philip dies. She reports to her father, "My pictures come back upon my hands. . . . They tell me my style is gone." Her hand is stiff and clumsy from the strains of nursing her son Van during a fatal illness, yet "the stiffness runs deeper than the fingers" (244). Southworth blithely combines the artist with the "true woman" in Theodora's self-deprecating and self-sacrificing character; Phelps explores the painful conflicts created within Avis by the desire to be both womanly and professional. Phelps is not persuaded that a woman artist can remake her suitor by painting a flattering portrait of him; Avis cannot change Philip's character by idealizing him.

While Phelps demonstrates how conflicted the impulse to reform could be within an author committed both to essential concepts of gender roles and to reform of women's position, Edward Payson Roe's *Barriers Burned Away* (1872)—which may have influenced Phelps in her writing of *Avis* a few years later—provides a contrasting example of unconflicted retrenchment in the face of feminist reform. Roe was a clergyman-turned-writer who wrote at least fifteen novels over a very successful seventeen-year career.[12] *Barriers,* his first novel, took off "steadily and then phenomenally," eventually selling a million copies (Carey 36).[13]

Roe inverts the gender roles of the typical double-proposal novel, portraying a long-suffering and noble suitor (an exemplary type of the self-made American man) who is rejected by a wealthy, spoiled woman whom he loves in spite of his awareness of her considerable faults (which include coquetry, cruelty, vanity, pride, skepticism, and ambition). Christine Ludolph has talent as a painter but can infuse no true emotion into her work because she lacks true feeling. Christine decides to encourage Dennis Fleet's pursuit so that she can paint his face when it is full of emotion. The first proposal scene, then, finds Dennis passionately proposing while Christine busily paints his expressive face. In his anger at her cruelty and coldness, he mars the painting and lectures her: "You have deceived in that which is most sacred, and with sacrilegious hands have trifled with that which every true man regards as holy" (281). Subsequent events, including the Chicago Fire, which threatens their lives and destroys the Art Building that displays the Ludolphs' wealth, "burn away" the barriers created by class, spiritual, and personal differences. The ending of the novel finds the heroine contrite, pious, and reformed; she is a German baroness but chooses to describe herself as "a simple American girl" (470). The narrator tells us that she "has lost sight of the transient laurel wreath which she sought to grasp at such cost to herself and others, in view of the 'crown of glory that fadeth not away'" (471). She accepts Dennis's renewed proposal with "a little cry of ecstasy, like the note of joy that a weary bird might utter as it flew to its mate" (471).

In contrast to this rendition of woman as bird, man as mate/keeper, Phelps uses extensive bird imagery in *The Story of Avis* to represent the plight of the heroine, participating in a metaphorical tradition in women's writing that Ellen Moers has traced in, among other texts, *Jane Eyre* and *Aurora Leigh*. Moers suggests that birds may not be merely "a species of the littleness metaphor" (as Roe's Christine-bird clearly is); rather, women may choose bird metaphors because birds may be tortured as boys can torture girls, because they "can be ministered to by girl-victims" and because they "are beautiful and exotic creatures, symbols of half-promised, half-forbidden sensual delights." Finally, because "birds are soft and round and sensuous, because they palpitate and flutter when held in the hands, and especially because they sing, birds are universal emblems of love" (245). Phelps invokes all of these possibilities in her bird metaphors. Avis identifies with the birds who destroy themselves flying into the lighthouse during storms. She tries to save one such bird but it dies wrapped inside Philip Ostrander's overcoat (46–49). When she accepts Philip, she moves toward him "blindly, like the bird to the light-house . . . and put both hands, the palms pressed together as if they had been manacled, into his" (110). Christine moves toward sure safety, whereas Avis flies into danger. Christine has willingly and happily given up her personal ambitions to serve her husband, but Avis, though also idolizing her husband, will yet attempt to retain personal goals. Roe's portrait of the artist woman reveals how an author could reinscribe conservative gender values over an ambitious heroine and use the double-proposal plot to suggest that the heroine, rather than the hero, needed humbling and reforming. Roe dismisses the problem of the woman as would-be artist by conflating her with such well-known female character types as the coquette and the cold, rich debutante and then subsumes her into a conventional marriage through a double-proposal plot. In *Barriers Burned Away* Roe implies that if ambitious women like Christine would give up the "transient laurel wreath," they could be happy rather than miserable. But Phelps will not concede this point: "[Avis] did not know how to express distinctly, even to her own consciousness, her conviction that she might have painted better pictures—not worse—for loving Philip and the children; that this was what God meant for her, for all of them, once, long ago" (244). Phelps insists that the eventual realization of egalitarian, two-career marriages is itself divine will for the good of individuals and the world.[14]

For Roe, the solution to the problematic, ambitious woman was a conversion experience that would draw out the true and loving woman within her, at which point any desires she had contrary to traditional domestic goals would magically melt away. In contrast, Avis's artistic talent remains "a rebellious prisoner" (234). But Roe was not the only novelist to try to contain the new, ambitious woman within familiar stereotypes, to deny that change was underway. William Dean Howells undertook a similar project with *Dr. Breen's Practice* (1881), in which he depicts a heroine who abandons her misguided pursuit of a medical career as soon as she falls in love. Howells's voice was the most conservative in a group of novels about women doctors published within a few years of each other. When *Dr. Breen's Practice* was published, a reviewer for *The Nation* commented, "The plot is founded on an idea which has, so far as we know, not been utilized in fiction before" ("Recent Novels" 18). But clearly the historical moment for considering the issue of women doctors and marriage had arrived. Phelps had already begun *Doctor Zay* (1882) when *Dr. Breen* came out, but agreed, at Howell's request, to wait to publish the first installment until *Dr. Breen* had finished its run. Two years later Sarah Orne Jewett published *The Country Doctor* (1884), in which the protagonist resists a persistent suitor and remains single. Jewett thus uses multiple proposals to reject marriage altogether, as Phelps herself had done in *The Silent Partner*. Authors, readers, and reviewers perceived these novels as being in dialogue with one another. As a preface to *Doctor Zay*'s first installment, the *Atlantic* printed a letter from Howells to Phelps, in which he assures readers that Phelps did not borrow ideas from him. He suggests that readers "interested in the problems touched" would appreciate the coincidence of plot and subject matter ("Note" 518). Phelps believed the contrast between her Dr. Zay and Howells's Dr. Breen "may be all the better for my doctor." Phelps wrote Howells that she "did not feel that Dr. Breen is a fair example of professional women; indeed, I know she is not for I know the class thoroughly from long personal observation under unusual opportunities" (qtd. in Masteller 135). When Jewett's novel followed *Doctor Zay* two years later, reviewers noted the coincidence of subject matter; a critic for *The Nation* commented, "The fact that such writers as Mr. Howells, Miss Phelps and Miss Jewett should within four years so carefully study what is practically the same subject, makes it worth while to compare their stories closely." This reviewer contrasts the authors' treatments of the professional heroine and of the conflict between career and love ("Recent Novels" 96). Authors and readers understood the novels to be engaging the linked issues of women's advancement in the professions and the problems for the conventional family created by that advancement.

Phelps had reason to believe that the late nineteenth century was significantly more friendly to aspiring women than the midcentury had been; her own success, and her observation of other professional women, provided her with evidence that this was so. Heroines had often been writers, they had occasionally been artists in other media, but they had not been physicians. Thus, the heroine as doctor represented the vanguard of women advancing, and advancing successfully, into the professional realm.

The historical changes to which the novels responded are summarized in Michael Sartisky's essay on the late nineteenth-century medical profession, printed as an afterword to the Feminist Press edition of *Doctor Zay*. Sartisky sets the three woman doctor novels in the context of the "culture of professionalism" increasingly absorbing a middle class that "found itself compelled to consolidate its social position and turned to professionalization to make itself indispensable to the new social and economic order" (264). Before medicine was professionalized, women "had the freedom to act as medical practitioners, especially as midwives, so long as such activities were defined as domestic functions" (267). As medical schools, licensing laws, and professional associations tried to consolidate the position of doctors, women were excluded more firmly from the medical profession. For a time, however, "the stronger the resistance on the part of the regular physicians to women or to the alternative sects [including homeopathy, Dr. Zay's method], the more they thrived; this was especially true in Boston" (273). In the 1880s, then, women may well have appeared to be successfully staking out a significant portion of the medical profession, but in the decades to follow, women's medical colleges would begin to close down rather than flourish, and fewer women doctors would practice. In retrospect, Sartisky concludes, "The period in the late nineteenth century which witnessed the growing involvement of women in the practice of medicine was a temporary social phenomenon which was able to exist because of the immature state of the institutionalization of the medical profession" (278). For Howells, Phelps, and

Jewett, then, women doctors in the Northeast appeared to be the vanguard of women's advancement, winning a battle to become respected professionals. Thus they became an excellent subject for the exploration of whether a professional woman could or should marry.

If Howells confidently depicts his heroine doctor abandoning career for marriage and Jewett as confidently decides the heroine should reject marriage for career, Phelps struggles to reconcile a doctor as confident and talented as Jewett's to an imperious and, at least initially, conservative suitor. In *Doctor Zay,* chronologically the last of the nineteenth-century double-proposal novels I have located, Phelps attempts again to imagine a couple approaching an egalitarian marriage through double-proposal negotiation. Perhaps because she felt so confident that women would continue to advance steadily, without the periodic setbacks that were to occur, she took on the domestic structure that more than a century later still challenges the American middle class: the two-career marriage.

Not content to praise the single life for professional women and leave marriage for women of a more domestic nature, Phelps explored how a woman might be able to enjoy the benefits of both married life and career pursuit, and she used the plot of the double proposal to suggest the problems confronting a career woman who wanted to marry. The earliest double-proposal fiction often placed renegotiated marriages at a distance from societies unprepared to accept them: Jane and Rochester isolate themselves at Ferndean; Linda and Robert Graham venture overseas as missionaries; Aurora and Romney Leigh borrow language from Revelation to project their marriage in apocryphal imagery. But as the century progressed and double-proposal writers became avowedly feminist, novelists began to depict renegotiated marriages as remaining within a society to help improve it. In Bullard's *Christine,* Christine Elliott and Philip Armstrong reside in New York furthering the good work of Christine's Home. In Southworth's *How He Won Her,* Erminie Rosenthal and General Eastworth move to the South to help the defeated section recover after the Civil War. Such marriages with such missions partake of the utopian, with characters looking forward to a better day already foreshadowed by their marriages.

Phelps suggests that the utopian marriage cannot be realized until men cease to expect that their wives will submit to and serve them. She elaborated this vision for marriage explicitly in 1874 in a "dream" wedding with rewritten vows. In this new marriage service, each partner speaks the same vows and neither promises to obey: "You, therefore, promise to . . . consider any claim of one to legislate for the other, as foreign to the spirit of a righteous marriage and to the letter of your vows. You believe that the sweet restraints and large liberty of mutual love shall serve you in the settlement of all difference of opinions, and that your happiness will be increased by your recognition each of the other's freedom of personal judgment, and action" ("A Dream within a Dream" 110). The day of truly egalitarian marriages invoked in "A Dream within a Dream" will arrive only when men can overcome the "imperiousness" that generations of fathers have bred into them. Whereas Phelps represents the feminine nature as God-given, as fundamentally and essentially different from the masculine nature, the male characteristics she identifies as standing in the way of egalitarian marriage are not necessarily immutable, but rather are culturally constructed, passed down from father to son. As Dr. Zay tells her suitor, "A happy marriage with such a woman demands a new type of man," and, for men, expectations of what a wife should be and do "is an inherited instinct. Generations of your fathers have bred it in you" (244). Waldo Yorke has a start on becoming a new man because his mother controlled his early education: "My mother . . . believes in all that sort of thing about women. I never thought of it till this minute. It used to mortify me when I was a boy; then it only bored me. I shall kiss her for it when I get home!" (245). As this passage suggests, male instinct is not so easily educated away in Phelps's novels as it was in earlier double-proposal novels; the process may be underway, but just as women will not arrive at their full potential for several generations (*Avis* 246), men too will only slowly evolve.

The suitor's male qualities of egotism, selfishness, and imperiousness are not easily erased by egalitarian rhetoric. Philip Ostrander, trying to overcome Avis's resistance during the first proposal scene, suggests that God intends them to demonstrate a new kind of marriage: "Suppose a man and woman had been made and led and drawn to one another, just to show that the tolerance of individuality, even the enthusiasm of superiority, could be a perfectly mutual thing," to which Avis responds, "There may be such women in the world. . . . I have never seen such a man. Only lovers think it to be possible" (70). When Avis herself becomes a lover, she too begins to think it possible. Waldo Yorke, promising to support Dr. Zay's career instead of demanding she give it up, exclaims, "Why, what kind of a fellow should I be, if I could approach a woman like you, and propose to drink down her power and preciousness into my one little thirsty life,—absorb her, annihilate her,—and offer her nothing but myself in exchange for a freedom so fine, an influence so important, as yours" (239). Dr. Zay, while not yet ready to accept Yorke, is impressed: "I have never thought but that you would desire the woman you loved to be like other women, to give up everything," yet she concludes, "You and I are dreaming a dream. It has a waking, and that is marriage" (240). She is convinced that Yorke would eventually "chafe under this transitional position," the position of trying to become "a new type of man" (244).

It is something, as Dr. Zay says, just to hear a man talk of accepting a two-career marriage. But renegotiated rhetoric is just a first, and tentative, step forward, and Phelps is unpersuaded by the optimism of earlier double-proposal writers that a wounded and humbled man who learns to speak in egalitarian language is ready to live an egalitarian marriage. In *Avis*, Phelps considers and rejects the earlier double-proposal hypothesis that wounding a man will make him more appreciative of the heroine and more apt to allow the heroine autonomy within marriage. As Carol Farley Kessler points out, "Phelps reveals more clearly [than Barrett Browning] the cost to a woman of even an unhealthy husband, if he is socialized to imperious (patriarchal) ways. . . . Maimed men could acquire a new mode of control in requiring women's care" (Introduction xviii). In *Doctor Zay* Phelps inverts the wounded suitor convention; Dr. Zay rejects Waldo Yorke when he is physically weak and she is enviably healthy but accepts him later when he has recovered his health and she has been sick.

Philip Ostrander is perhaps Phelps's direct answer to an earlier double-proposal hero also from Maine, Philip Armstrong of Laura J. Curtis Bullard's *Christine* (1856). Both are male flirts with a history of inconstancy, but intensely in love with the heroines, whom they recognize as their spiritual superiors; they struggle to overcome their faults in spite of good intentions. Both wound the heroines by taking advantage of innocent young country women for their own selfish pleasures (Grace Minor commits suicide when Philip Armstrong rejects her; Susan Wanamaker Jessup marries a man she does not love who alternately beats and abandons her). Christine and Avis share artistic sensibilities and an intense distaste for housework. Both finally agree to marry their suitors after the men become invalids. Both Philips confess quite early in the novels that they are morally inferior to the heroines and both are right. But a crucial difference between *Christine*'s and *Avis*'s double-proposal plots is that Christine has had years to pursue her feminist goals and establish herself as a public figure before she marries, while Avis makes the mistake of marrying while yet on the verge of a promising career. Again, Christine discovered her Philip's true character before marriage, but only slowly, after the wedding, does Avis become aware of her husband's faults. Phelps suggests that a relationship will not be equal just because a man is conscious of his moral inferiority and becomes physically weaker than a woman. Avis discovers this painful lesson as she struggles through marriage with a physically and morally weaker man: "She bowed to the great and awful law of married story, by which, so surely as life and love shall one day wear themselves to death and calm, we may know that it shall befall the stronger to wear the yoke of the weaker soul" (178). To "wear the yoke" of the weaker soul, Phelps insists, is no improvement over being dominated by a stronger one. But as this marriage progresses, both characters achieve a secondary success. Avis comes to love her husband not as she idealized him nor as he idealized himself but "as God made him," while Philip, through a second disabling (tuberculosis), more successfully learns, as Kessler puts it, "to accept a limited dependence and to yield dominant ways" (Introduction xviii). Change is slow and painful and requires sacrifice. The new union cannot be easily brought about by promises of renegotiated marriage. Phelps makes her critique of the reformed suitors in earlier literature explicit: "[Avis] would have been uneasy if Philip had undergone a transfiguration like a hero in a novel, in which his weaknesses were sublimated, and his faults idealized beyond recognition" (234).

While Phelps describes the new woman as not yet fully realized in history (*Avis* 246), the flaws in the men are a larger problem in her novels, and she is particularly interested in how a new man might be created. In *Doctor Zay*, the only of the women's novels in this study to be written from the suitor's perspective, Phelps undertakes this project explicitly. With the exception of Timothy Morris, critics generally read *Doctor Zay* as the story of its title character's probably ill-fated plan to combine career and marriage. But almost the entire book is written from Waldo Yorke's point of view; he is, technically, the protagonist of the novel, and his challenge is to learn how to court Dr. Zay: "How was a man going to approach this new and confusing type of woman? The old codes were all astray" (186). As Morris argues, "the novel works through its reflector-character's erotic desires, teaching that character, and readers both male and female, to understand and value a female professional" (143). Through double-proposal plotting, Phelps constructs a story about the conversion of a conventional man from unquestioning acceptance of traditional, chauvinistic values to aspirations of becoming a "new man" who could marry a "new woman" and try to succeed in a two-career marriage.

Doctor Zay, though revealing some of the same tensions between conservative and progressive impulses that I have identified in *Avis,* is less mortgaged to idealized notions of the feminine. Phelps continues to employ battle metaphors in the courtship scenes of *Doctor Zay,* but they are less pervasive than they are in *Avis.* When the relationship between physician and patient begins to shift to courtship between heroine and hero, Waldo Yorke recognizes Dr. Zay's defiance: "It was like the challenge before a battle" (153), and later, "her eyes, like sleepless sentinels, forced him off" (208). Dr. Zay, a generation younger than Avis, also idealizes the married state but she does not use the language of "kingship" and "sacrifice" to which Avis succumbed. She tells Waldo that she has known of only three marriages that came up to her lofty ideal: "A perfect marriage is like a pure heart: those who have it are fit to see God. Any other is profanity to me; it is a desecration to think of. . . . It would kill me to miss it" (241). And later, when she at length accepts Yorke, she warns him, "If we fail, we shall be the most miserable people that ever mistook a little attraction for a great love" (258). Finally, Dr. Zay, like Avis, is an object of admiration, although she is rarely held static by the narrator as she is in this early scene: "The figure of the dainty driver in the phaeton, erect, slender, and blue, sat motionless as a caryatid out of employment. The eyes of the traveler in the buggy vigilantly pursued it" (22). Instead, in *Doctor Zay,* the male gaze is almost entirely attributable to the suitor. The first evening Waldo pays Dr. Zay a social call, "the undisguised admiration in his eyes roamed over her with daring leisure" (156).

But while Phelps still maintains her allegiance to codes of femininity that permit her to treat her heroine as an object to be admired and pursued, Dr. Zay is more successful at establishing her career and defying the gaze of her suitor than was Avis Dobell. She has a successful practice when the novel opens whereas Avis was still proving herself as an artist when Philip begins to court her. One of the tableaux viewed by Waldo Yorke works to undermine, rather than reinforce, his assumptions about women and the comfort of the male gaze:

> She lighted her German student lamp on the office table, and, pulling a formidable professional book towards her, without a moment's irresolution, plunged into its contents with the headlong dash which only an absorbing intellectual passion gives. She leaned her head upon her hand, with her controlled profile towards him, while she read. . . . The young man had seen for himself what all the little feminine protest in the world could never have made patent to his imagination: a woman absorbed in her business, to whom a man must be the accident, not the substance, of thought. (128)

In *Dr. Zay,* Phelps's attention shifts from portraying the anguish of a heroine caught by the inner struggle of a dual nature to "making patent" to the suitor the reality of the professional woman. Toward this end, Phelps deploys the wounded suitor convention differently than she did in *Avis;* this time, being wounded teaches the hero, through gender role inversion, what a woman's life is like. Moreover, he becomes physically stronger as the court-ship progresses and is at the peak of health when Dr. Zay accepts his pro-posal. Yorke's relationship with Dr. Zay begins when he is injured in a car-riage accident in rural Maine and she treats his wounds; his attitude toward her is described as "loyal helplessness" and he speaks in a "vague, submissive tone" (65). In the first half of the novel he continually attempts to inscribe Dr. Zay into a matrix of femininity he can be comfortable with; she as con-tinually manages, without "de-feminizing" herself, to confound his attempts. His invalid experience teaches him to sympathize with women—"How *dare* men ridicule or neglect sick women?"—and their positions are often de-scribed as inverting gender roles (84). Dr. Zay's mannerisms seem "a more natural expression of irritation among men than women" (95), and she "pos-sessed a power which was far more masculine than feminine, of absorption in the immediate task" (133). Yorke, increasingly resenting his submissive position as he regains health, tells Dr. Zay, "It's not easy when you've done so much for him, for a man to look on, like a woman, this way" (112); he lat-er comments, "I am cherishing a host of feminine virtues," and concludes, "I shall make rather a superior woman by the time I get well" (134).

But while Yorke's forced inactivity and dependence bring him to sym-pathize with women generally, respect Dr. Zay in particular, and reconsider his chauvinistic attitude toward "doctresses" (63), she is unimpressed when it also brings him to a declaration of love, which she diagnoses crisply: "You are not in love. . . . You are only nervous" (190). He accuses her of being "unwomanly," but she is firm, insisting that he is "confusing his gratitude and his idleness and his suffering with other feelings so much greater" (199). She tells him he requires "absolute separation from all this pathological sentiment, and the exciting cause of it" (211).[15] But at length Yorke admits he respects her position: "You are the only woman I ever saw who was able to save a man from himself!" (213). He returns home to Boston and his mother to finish healing.

When Yorke returns, Dr. Zay greets him with the exclamation, "You are well!" (227). Their courtship resumes on the new footing of equal physical health, and she no longer claims he confuses gratitude and dependence with love. In the battle that follows, Yorke tries being "imperious," demanding, and aggressive, but "she defied him, soul and body" (228–29). Then, he speaks to her "in a tone from which the last cadence of self assertion had died" and "in a manly timidity that well became him" (229–30). She confesses she loves him, but begs him to leave, protesting, "I have lost my self-possession. . . . I have lost—myself" (231). Yorke "felt more a sense of awe than of transport, at the sight of her royal overthrow" (230).

Phelps's language is ambiguous; she still relies on battle imagery, and although the verb *to win* has disappeared, Dr. Zay is described as "overthrown" and "lost." Yorke's language and actions are also ambiguous, and he seems a hybrid of the traditional masculine attributes of imperiousness and aggression and "new man" characteristics; the phrase *manly timidity* aptly registers the apparent paradox. He proposes to her in persuasive renegotiated-proposal language: "I offer you the devotion of a man who has belief in the great objects of your life; in whom you have created that belief" (239). Dr. Zay is impressed, yet this scene ends in yet another rejection, and Yorke returns to Boston wifeless once again.

In *Doctor Zay* Phelps employs the interproposal space differently from the way she does in *Avis*. In the earlier novel the artist heroine begins her one masterpiece in that space and the hero is wounded in battle, but the couple does not advance in their understanding of one another; that growth occurs after marriage instead. In the later novel the doctor heroine begins to recognize that her youthful health will not last indefinitely, and the hero spends a winter pursuing his profession as a lawyer, whereas before he met Dr. Zay he had spent almost all his time in leisure activities. Thus, the heroine learns that work will not necessarily answer all her needs, while the hero learns not to shirk his work simply because he has no brilliant prospects. He tells Dr. Zay that he has "sat in my office and prayed for clients. . . . Greatness is not thrust upon me. But I've *sat* there" (234), and she approves of his efforts. The renegotiations between Dr. Zay and Waldo Yorke are more convincing than those between Avis and Philip. While Waldo doubtless retains some troubling masculine characteristics, he has demonstrated a willingness to be guided by Dr. Zay, and he has convinced both of them that his love is not merely the by-product of a patient-caretaker relationship.

The final catalyst for Dr. Zay's capitulation to marriage is not her suitor's illness (as it was for Avis), nor yet his regained health and new progressive attitudes, but her own bouts with sickness and subsequent fatigue. When Yorke returns for the second time, she has suffered from diphtheria and exhaustion and in spite of her magnificent health and stamina is weak from illness and overwork.[16] Yorke "overtakes" her (the analogy with the mythical Atalanta is made explicit) in a moment when she is completely exhausted, and she is finally persuaded: "She was worn out, poor girl. He did not disturb her silence, which he felt stealing upon himself deliriously, as if it were the first fumes from the incense of her surrender" (254). But yet her behavior is not entirely described in terms of surrender, and Dr. Zay is more assertive with Waldo than Avis was with Philip. Throughout the final proposal scene, which takes place in her buggy, they shift the reins back and forth, no doubt foreshadowing the nature of their marriage: "I believe—in—*you*," Dr. Zay comments, "But I don't believe in your driving. . . . Give me the reins! If you don't mind—please" (257). She "vaguely resents" the assertiveness with which he follows her to her rooms and warns him, "It is a problem that we have undertaken,—so hard, so long! No light feeling can solve it; no caprice or selfishness can live before it" (258). Dr. Zay clearly understands how difficult a two-career marriage will be, whereas Avis had to discover this truth after her wedding.

Phelps wrote a novel that ends with a promised marriage, but left readers in serious uncertainty as to the happy outcome of that marriage. Because she was successful in presenting the two-career marriage as a "long and hard" path for a couple to walk, readers immediately responded with doubt to the proposed union between Yorke and Dr. Zay. Such doubt may have also been the result of Phelps's reputation (in particular as established by *Avis*), the influence of the verisimilitude school of realism promoted by Howells and others in the late nineteenth century, and perhaps the years of work done by exploratory novelists including those writing in the double-proposal tradition. The courtship form had become quite pliable by the 1880s, and the idea that marriage could be a negotiable, optional outcome (as double-proposal novels as well as other experimental novels had been implying for the previous thirty or more years) had become an idea that could be central to a novel and the discourse surrounding it when published.

From the moment of its publication, Phelps's ambiguous novel created dialogue over the problem of courtship and the two-career marriage, a dialogue that moves fluidly from literary to cultural debate. A critic for the *Literary World*, yoking courtship plotting with cultural mandates, speculates that Phelps would have preferred the characters to remain unmarried, but that "they became too much for her. . . . Love is stronger than authorship." Dividing potential readers according to age, the reviewer continues, "To young readers, at least, the ending of the tale will appear satisfactory. With older ones the question will perhaps arise whether, after all, Doctor Zay's reasoning on the marriage question were not wiser than her final decision" ("Doctor Zay" 371). Many original readers of *Doctor Zay* did indeed focus on the probable success or failure of the marriage. Kessler summarizes a review from *Critic* that concluded the novel ended too abruptly, "thus not solving the problem of the marriage in process," in comparison to *Avis*, "where painting could more easily be integrated into marriage than medicine" (*Elizabeth Stuart Phelps* 126). A reviewer for the *Independent* does not believe in the possibility of the marriage at all: "The story ends with marriage impending and ends wisely, for it could not be continued with Dr. Zay in the normal relations of wife" ("Literature" 10). Henrietta H. Bassett, writing for the *Woman's Journal,* does not object to the two-career marriage, but wishes that Phelps "had provided Zay a stronger man more worthy of her choice and conquest than Yorke" (278), but Lucy Larcom "would rather Zay had not married" (qtd. in Kessler, *Elizabeth Stuart Phelps* 126–27).

Twentieth-century critics continue the conversation, suggesting the persistence of the dialogic power of the novel and of our cultural concern with two-career marriages. Kessler argues that when Dr. Zay is "overcome" by Yorke it is "less a statement of [her] preference than of [her] being finally ground down" (*Elizabeth Stuart Phelps* 74). Lori Duin Kelly, however, believes that Yorke has successfully become a "new man and thus a fit companion for the new type of womanhood. . . . It is to be a marriage of equal partners" (78). Valerie Fulton similarly argues that the changes in each character enable them "for the first time . . . to meet on equal terms" (249), while Jean Carwile Masteller finds the ending "ambiguous," suggesting that "their union may be only the beginning of Dr. Zay's defeat" (144–45). Susan Ward merely notes that Phelps "sidesteps the problem of portraying the happy marriage of two professionals" (217). Sartisky labels the ending "about as ambivalent an embrace of matrimony as one can find," arguing that "Phelps's resorting to this romantic convention in contradiction of the weight of evidence of Yorke's limitations serves to generate serious reservations on the part of the reader and thus undermines the convention itself" (293, 319n77).

I would argue that the convention most strongly undermined in *Dr. Zay* and in *The Story of Avis* is not the convention of the marriage ending but the convention of the strong ideal suitor. Certainly the weak suitors bothered early reviewers. The critic for the *Independent* confesses being "at loss what to make of the characterless sort of man who carries off Dr. Zay" ("Literature" 10), while the reviewer for *The Nation* finds Ostrander "but a poor creature," so flawed as to be "unnatural," having "all the faults, this side of wife-beating and vice, of a married man" ("Recent Novels" 202). One reviewer asked this question outright, again blending critique of the novel with social commentary: "Are there some men, who, while still strong and manly, would be quite content as the years go on to share with the public in a large and generous way the time and society of the one whom they had chosen of all others to be their own peculiar treasure and household divinity? We have our doubts about Yorke being that kind of a man" ("Doctor Zay" 371). And in her review Henrietta H. Bassett focuses entirely on Yorke's inadequacy, finding his behavior to be "as snobbish and traditional as Adam's homemaking" and arguing that if Yorke had in fact been the "new type" he "would have sifted his claim more rigidly to so microcosmic a woman" (278). But Phelps's social critique may be pinpointed just here: these weak suitors are the only male characters in the novels to even consider entering two-career marriages. No other male character, in either novel, is held up as a potentially better candidate for "the new man," as an alternative suitor for the heroine. Phelps's double-proposal novels suggest that only men who had characteristics the culture might define as "weak" would consider trying to become "new men."

Perhaps a young man on the verge of a career might be willing to be "equal" to a talented wife already embarked on a profession, but only if he does not demonstrate the autocratic behaviors characteristic of men completely entrenched in patriarchal privilege. Avis's father marries a talented wife but cannot countenance the suggestion that she might have wanted to do anything but be his wife. In the younger generation, John Rose is far more morally stable than Philip Ostrander, but he also expects to control his wife. The potential new man must be pliable, changeable; yet it is Philip's pliability and inconstancy that damage both his career and his marriage. The new man must be able to accept the capacities of the new woman, and that characteristic must be taught from an early age; because of his mother's influence, Waldo Yorke is capable of recognizing Dr. Zay's talent, but then his dependency on his strong mother may also have contributed to his lazy attitude toward his own career. That both Avis and Dr. Zay are slightly older than their suitors is not coincidental. Phelps believed an age advantage could help women negotiate egalitarian relationships. A few years after she published *Doctor Zay* and four years before her marriage, "Phelps discussed with understanding approval the marriage to younger men of Germaine de Stael, Margaret Fuller, Charlotte Brontë, and George Eliot. These women seemed thereby to have managed egalitarian relationships" (Kessler, *Elizabeth Stuart Phelps* 79).[17] Phelps's fictional world suggests how she interprets her historical moment. She pragmatically concludes that if a new man is to be created within an unreformed society, he must be young and flexible and his career prospects should probably be inferior to those of his wife.

The Story of Avis, unlike any other double-proposal novel I have located (including Phelps's own *Doctor Zay*), follows the couple past the wedding to examine how the renegotiated marriage works out. Multiple factors conspire to make it first difficult and finally impossible for Avis to continue her career successfully. Philip's personal weaknesses are a large part of the problem, for he selfishly concentrates entirely on his own fledgling career as a professor (which he fails to fulfill) and assumes that Avis will meet all domestic responsibilities in addition to painting. Debts he incurred before their marriage complicate their finances. Then Avis becomes a mother, and Phelps introduces yet another allegiance into Avis's character. Avis, the narrator notes, "was lacking in what is called the maternal passion as distinct from the maternal devotion." She had drawn her ideas of parenting "chiefly from novels and romances, in which parentage is represented as a blindly deifying privilege, which it were an irreverence to associate with teething, the midnight colic, or an insufficient income" (150–51). Crises small and large keep Avis from work, and Phelps explicitly links Avis's experience, exceptional a character as she is, with that of women as a group:

> Women understand—only women altogether—what a dreary will-o-the-wisp is this old, common, I had almost said common-place, experience, "When the fall sewing is done," "When the baby can walk," "When house-cleaning is over," "When the company has gone," "When we have got through with the whooping-cough," "When I am a little stronger," then I will write the poem, or learn the language, or study the great charity, or master the symphony; then I will act, dare, dream, become. (149)

Avis eventually becomes dangerously ill, Philip flirts with another woman, their older child, Van, dies, and Philip contracts tuberculosis.

Avis and Philip's marriage fails, and thus Phelps comments on the shortcomings of double-proposal plotting. The renegotiated proposal is revealed as insufficient to solve the problem of realizing an egalitarian marriage in an unequal society: Avis expects too much of herself and has idealized her husband; Philip is unable or unwilling to make the sacrifices necessary to enable Avis to paint; children introduce new responsibilities and further divide Avis's energies. Phelps shows that the double proposal is an imperfect fictional device for dealing with women's real-life questions. Lovers, she says, believe anything to be possible; they cannot anticipate the challenges of marriage itself.

But while Phelps questions the efficacy of double courtships, she does not abandon the concept of renegotiating relationships. Within the second half of the novel, in which she develops the "married story" (178), a second narrative of disruption and reconciliation takes place. The double proposal is replaced by a double marriage, and Phelps contrasts the heroine's two marriages to the same man. Avis and Philip separate but reconcile when they travel to Florida because of his bad health. At this point he "wins" her for the second time, and she finds deep satisfaction because she "could love her husband just as God had made him" (234). She finds their new relationship "more a prophecy than a fulfilment [sic] of hope" (234), and one remembers the Sphinx, also more a prophecy of what might be than itself a fulfillment. Phelps does not "write beyond the ending" of the second version of the union of Philip and Avis, does not attempt to explore whether the prophecy can now be fulfilled; Philip dies and Avis returns to Harmouth to join her baby daughter, Wait, and make a life for the two of them. The possibility for change is delayed for another generation at least.

That the struggle for what Stanley Cavell has called "the reciprocity or equality of consciousness between a woman and a man" appears to come up short of its utopian goals in Phelps's fiction has several explanations (17). First, she is unable to escape from conservative ideals of women's sacrificing nature and of hierarchical marriage. In addition, she is acutely aware of the difficulties and restrictions presented by the pragmatic aspects of developing an egalitarian relationship in an unequal society. Finally, she associates male strength with male domination and appears to believe that only untried and flexible, and therefore potentially weak, men would consider undertaking egalitarian, two-career marriages. In the conclusion of *Avis* Phelps evokes a utopian vision of the marriage of a new woman and a new man, but her rhetoric contains impossible contradiction and tension:

> We have been told that it takes three generations to make a gentleman: we may believe that it will take as much, or more, to make A WOMAN. A being of radiant physique; the heiress of ancestral health on the maternal side; a creature forever more of nerve than of muscle, and therefore trained to the energy of the muscle and the repose of the nerve; physically educated by mothers of her own fibre and by physicians of her own sex,—such a woman alone is fitted to acquire the drilled brain, the calmed imagination, and sustained aim, which constitute intellectual command. (246)

Such a woman deserves a man "whose daily soul is large enough to guard her, even though it were at the cost of sharing it, from the tyranny of small corrosive care which gnaws and gangrenes hers,—such a man alone can either comprehend or apprehend the love of such a woman" (246). Phelps offers no estimate of how long it will take to create such a man. However, she promises the new man more than ever of what men have always wanted—a woman's surrender and reverence. Once this ideal man has "won" the woman, "reverence and surrender radically begin their life in her" (247). Determined to have it both ways, Phelps can only fit her new man and woman into an elevated, romanticized, and profoundly conservative marriage model.

Phelps's double-proposal novels embody the tense dialectic between change and retrenchment that characterized the late nineteenth century as the culture struggled to accommodate or confront the new woman who had apparently made significant inroads in traditionally male-dominated public arenas. Could this new woman be integrated into marriage and thus fully participate in both her traditional and revolutionary roles? At the end of her story Avis sits "as the country, wasted by civil war, pauses to look off upon the little neutral state" (249), hoping her daughter, Wait, might discover the "Holy Grail" and realize her full potential as a woman. Dr. Zay, of the same generation as young Wait Ostrander, confronts the threshold of marriage with bravery and trepidation: "It is a problem that we have undertaken,— so hard, so long!" (258). Possibly Dr. Zay is a step closer than Avis to becoming "competent to the terrible task of adjusting the sacred individuality of her life to her supreme capacity of love and the supreme burden and perils which it imposes upon her" (*Avis* 246). But Phelps does not seem to realize that she herself lays a "supreme burden" on her heroines by insisting on the mystique of women's "supreme capacity of love," a seductive ideal she is unwilling or unable to give up in service of women's advancement. One early reviewer, writing about Dr. Zay, recognizes just this conflict: "If her large prospectus was not to be narrowed by marriage, still the old ideals of marriage came in play between them. She questioned her claim to his concert tickets and stray litigations, and without thinking of her own, wants to make him a divine happiness" (Bassett 278).

Phelps is in this sense one of the most conservative writers in this study, for at times it appears she would reinscribe, with deeper strokes than ever before, idealized visions of women's nature and therefore of women's roles; but on the other hand, perhaps she only takes a tendency always present in double-proposal fiction to a logical extreme. In earlier chapters in this study I point out how writers hold on to conservative notions with one hand while trying to reform women's roles with the other. Caroline Hentz staunchly defended the antebellum Southern hierarchy while insisting that privileged women ought to be given more autonomy within it. Augusta Evans roundly denounced the women's rights movement while depicting a heroine who intellectually bested any man with whom she came in contact. E. D. E. N. Southworth's ambitious and individualistic heroines were always counterbalanced by other characters who were idealized "true women." Such rhetorical push-me pull-you stances appear, from a contemporary perspective, to harbor irreconcilable differences, and we can speculate that authors sometimes deployed a conservative flank to distract the attention of gatekeeper audiences from their more radical counterattacks. But we can also speculate that the tensions inevitably found in double-proposal novels, and in other experimental novels as well, also reproduce tensions within the authors and, ultimately, within the culture itself. Each move toward marriage reform contains previous marriage models as well as challenges to them; each active, self-determining heroine maintains a tight grip on some traditional feminine ideal. Phelps, writing at the end of the nineteenth-century double-proposal tradition, may well bring these counterforces to their most extreme level of tension. Her heroines are the most determinedly careerist of any in this study; consequently, perhaps, rather than in spite of it, her ideals of women's nature and marriage union partake of the most deeply entrenched traditional paradigms.

Notes

1. Susan Coultrap-McQuin summarizes Phelps's feminist convictions as follows: "[She] argued in support of woman suffrage, coeducation, varied employment opportunities, equality in marriage, and dress reform" (174). Carol Farley Kessler and Lori Duin Kelly also discuss Phelps's articles, written for the *Independent* and *Woman's Journal.*

2. Phelps may have been attacked more violently for her religious than for her secular dissension. *The Gates Ajar,* a novel that offered a comforting picture of the afterlife as a beneficent "daily life" much like that on earth, except one in which wrongs would be righted, created a furor among orthodox reviewers. Mary Angela Bennett notes that "the teachings of the book were pretty generally attacked as unscriptural by reviewers, and there is no gainsaying their charges" (50). Readers responded to Phelps as though she were a spiritual teacher; Kelly argues that Phelps became a "lay minister" of sorts and thus "carved out a niche for herself in a profession which, in her time, was all but closed to women" (26). Phelps herself recalled the reception of *The Gates Ajar* in these terms: "Religious papers waged war across that girl's notions of the life to come, as if she had been an evil spirit let loose upon accepted theology for the destruction of the world" (*Chapters from a Life* 118).

3. Her biographers on the whole depict the marriage as a failure; occasional letters and the anonymously published *Confessions of a Wife* (1902) suggest it was indeed difficult to be an older, ailing, successful author married to a young, healthy,

struggling writer. Bennett comments, "Not to dwell too long on an unpleasant subject, the truth of the matter is that the marriage was not a success" (92). Kessler notes that "[Phelps's] probable need for companionship had thus led her into a marriage of uncertain reward" (*Elizabeth Stuart Phelps* 82), while Kelly unhesitatingly labels the marriage "failed" (17).

4. My analysis of *The Story of Avis* focuses on the artist's development and on the courtship plotting, but Jack H. Wilson, also responding to the conservative undercurrent in Phelps's novel, has persuasively identified a third narrative strand, a bildungsroman of Avis's ethical and spiritual development into a loving woman: "The growth of Avis into a fuller feminine nature has been the objective of the bildungsroman text. As it has unfolded, Avis' commitments to her art and to her intellectual and emotional independence have been progressively exchanged for a number of traits that served to define the essence of woman in the nineteenth century" (69).

5. When Phelps's heroines Dr. Zay and Avis Dobell attempt to combine career and marriage, they take on a challenge that earlier heroines created by Phelps rejected as impossible. In *The Silent Partner* (1871), Phelps portrays a pair of ambitious heroines, one from the privileged class and one from the working class, both of whom reject proposals from men they believe they could have loved in order to pursue loftier goals. The upper-class heroine, Perley Kelso, uses her influence to relieve the suffering and poverty of the laboring classes, and the working-class Sip Garth becomes a street preacher, rejecting established churches to take her message straight to her people. Perley tells her suitor, "I have no time to think of love and marriage. . . . If I married you, sir, I should invest in life, and you would conduct it. I suspect that I have a preference for a business of my own" (260–62). Sip refuses to marry because she will "never bring a child into the world to work in the mills"; as she is grieving over the lost possibility of marriage, she recognizes her calling to "'set up for a preacher,'" which makes her "a very happy woman" (287, 291). On the final page of the novel Phelps describes Perley's face as one that "begged for nothing. It was opulent and warm. Life brimmed over at it" (302).

6. Avis was "perhaps sixteen" when she took "her little blue-and-gold girls' copy of 'Aurora Leigh' to read in the wide June weather" (30–31). At nineteen, Avis is sent to Europe to stay a year, but remains to study "for nearly six years of hard work and hard homesickness" (38). The summer following, when Philip pursues Avis, is dated as the summer of "Fair Oaks, The Seven Days, Cedar Mountain, Bull Run, Harper's Ferry, Antietam" (76), in other words, 1861. Avis then must be twenty-six years old when the novel opens in April 1861; in other words, she could not have been sixteen in 1857 in order to read *Aurora Leigh* when it was published and pursue a career for six years before accepting Philip.

7. The text also invokes the year 1857 when the narrator comments to her readers, "Avis had now plunged into a life which extremely few women in America, twenty years ago [*Avis* was published in 1877], found it either possible or desirable to lead" (36).

8. Philip is continually described as appearing "dull and blind," and in the first proposal scene, Avis is "dazzled" and "half-blinded" herself (67, 69). Philip's metaphorical "blindness" clearly signals his inability to recognize the significance of Avis's artistic gifts and his general moral blindness (Avis discovers later that Philip jilted his first fiancée and neglected his aging, widowed mother); Avis's blindness derives from her response to Philip, for the more she is attracted to him, the less she can see his weaknesses.

9. Even Edna Earl of *St. Elmo,* the most successful of American double-proposal heroines, does not justify her writing as a life-long career commitment, but as a God-ordained extension of her womanly role. Christine Elliott is committed to a cause, rather than to a career. On the British side of the double-proposal tradition, Aurora Leigh, of course, is the model for the professional heroine who also marries.

10. The story of the artist's development is rare in women's novels compared with novels by men. Linda Huf, noting consistent differences between male and female *Künstlerromans,* points out some reasons a woman might hesitate to write a portrait of the artist heroine. With its special concern with development of genius as well as justifying a woman's pursuit of art and providing for her material needs to support her in that pursuit, books such as *The Story of Avis* must overcome significant prejudices against women's pursuit of self-fulfillment (it is "selfish") and of artistic immortality (women lack the genius to be artists).

11. Phelps provides sharp realistic details of the daily pressures that undermine Avis's attempts to work on her masterpiece after marriage: "It was not much, perhaps, to set herself now to conquer this little occasion; not much to descend from the sphinx to the drainpipe at one fell swoop; not much to watch the potatoes while Julia went to market, to answer the door-bell while the jelly was straining, to dress for dinner after her guests were in the parlor, to resolve to engage a table-girl tomorrow because Julia tripped with the gravy" (140).

12. Glenn O. Carey reports that Roe "became one of America's best-selling novelists, the undisputed leader in total book sales from 1872 to 1888, with unusually large sales continuing at least to 1910" (1). In his novels Roe extends his clergyman's role and advocates "the lifelong value of accepting the principles of Christ, and of having faith in God and His concern for those who follow His concepts" (69). Roe wrote at least one other double-proposal novel, *What Can She Do?* (1873). In that work Roe advocates that women learn trades so that they can support themselves if need be. The courtship plot tells a renegotiating story very like that in *Barriers Burned Away;* an upper-class heroine, forced to earn her own living when her father dies bankrupt and in disgrace, learns to accept and then love a peasant neighbor who helps her in her efforts at gardening. Perhaps one clue to Roe's popularity is how he combined a woman's fiction plot (the heroine fends for herself when her family lets her down) with a conservative double-proposal message (the heroine, in overcoming the class-bound arrogance that motivates the initial refusal, leaves behind her materialistic values and in so doing becomes more "womanly").

13. Reviewers, at least in the secular press, did not share readers' enthusiasm. Roe was promptly categorized as a religious author with minimal literary talent. A critic for *Appleton's*, noting that *Barriers Burned Away* "attracted much attention" when it first appeared as a serial in a New York paper entitled *Evangelist*, comments that "the work is well calculated to please the religious reader" ("Editor's Table" 93). A reviewer for *The Nation* wrote in 1873, "In spite of all that is unnatural and artificial in this story, it is easy to see how it may be popular among those who dread the ordinary work of fiction. The author has profited little, however, by the labors of his predecessors, and we have found him exceptionally tedious and uninteresting" ("Recent Novels" 219).

14. Phelps would have observed that some of her talented female contemporaries seemed to be achieving the goal. Kessler observes that in Phelps's generation, a few women artists did "escape stereotypic outcomes" and apparently maintain egalitarian marriages (*The Story of Avis* 265n3).

15. Morris aptly notes that Dr. Zay's original refusal "subtly deconstructs an ideology of marriage proposals: that the choice is all the woman's. When a woman actually takes control of the encounter and critiques the man's offer, instead of offering a 'yes' or a demure 'no' that will be read as a 'yes,' she triggers incomprehension and verbal violence from the man" (146). While Morris is writing only of *Doctor Zay*, his analysis could apply to most of the double-proposal suitors discussed in this study. The deconstruction of marriage proposal ideology had been underway for decades before Phelps wrote her narrative.

16. Perhaps Phelps is here critiquing the position represented later by Jewett that remaining single is the best choice for women who want to retain control over their lives. A woman who is sick and lacks immediate family is in a miserable situation. Biographers have linked Phelps's own decision to marry partly to her bouts with illness and loneliness. She came to know Herbert Ward better because he spent "long hours reading to the old family friend [Phelps] who was then in very poor health" (Kelly 17). Kessler argues that "to maintain her unmarried status in a society valuing the married, Phelps would have needed friends or relatives emotionally closer to her than was the case by the mid-1880s" and lists the friends and family members Phelps was losing to death and illness (79).

17. Phelps's husband was seventeen years younger than she was, a fact exploited by the press with malicious delight when she married. Kelly discusses the "maternal and solicitous" nature of Phelps's early interaction with Herbert Ward, while Bennett reports that Phelps's anxiety concerning how the newspapers would treat her marriage was well-founded (89).

Twentieth-Century Plots

WRITING in 1866 about a recent novel, a British reviewer frets over the possibility that popular fiction might have the power to contribute to social change. The following passage echoes, or presages rather, Hans Robert Jauss's contention that literature can bring "newly articulated experiences to the level of consciousness":

> But books which do not represent society as it is, or ever was, may yet have a powerful influence on manners. They may indicate what things are going to be, and foreshadow the changes time is on the eve of working. The novel which portrays manners and modes of action preposterous to our observation may, if it is powerfully written, bring about its verification by hitting the fancy of a class open to new impressions, and impatient of present restraints. An undisciplined fancy may imagine things for which it has small warrant and no general example, yet only anticipate: planting seeds which shall bear fruit in another generation, and suggesting to untutored fancies possibilities before undreamt of. ("A Religious Novel" 276)

To what degree have the seeds planted by the "undisciplined fancies" of progressive nineteenth-century writers borne fruit in the twentieth-century United States? While conservative models of marriage are of course still pervasive and women continue to struggle for fair treatment in the workplace, the political and social position of women, the process of courtship, and the conventions and laws governing marriage have indeed evolved in the directions envisioned by earlier writers, including those who wrote in the double-proposal tradition. Many couples form their partnerships on egalitarian grounds of just the sort that Avis Dobell envisioned; plenty of those partnerships dissolve under pressures very like what Avis endured, but others survive and flourish. When I first began lecturing my friends on the fascination of double-proposal stories, one commented with amusement and a bit of wonder that she herself had lived such a plot. She refused a proposal from her high school sweetheart and freed herself to continue her education unencumbered by personal obligations; she explored possibilities for careers in music, in teaching, and in writing, and she spent her summers in pursuit of new experiences, squeezing roe from salmon in Alaska or working as a nanny in Connecticut. Four years later the relationship was renewed and she married her former boyfriend. She was sure that for her and her partner, as for the fictional couples I studied, marriage was more solid, personal growth better established, the future more secure emotionally as well as practically because they had separated for an interim. Marriage was better than it would have been had they become engaged five years earlier.

But yet fantasies of Mr. Right, romantic love, and happily-ever-after marriages maintain their grip on our imaginations and their often pernicious influence on our lives. Even when contemplating the thoroughness with which "serious" twentieth-century authors have transformed or exploded conventional courtship plotting, any stroll through a bookstore reveals dozens of mass-produced romance fictions by "nonserious" writers that feed the same old fantasies. But wherever the courtship plot thrives, we should expect to see the double proposal, modified to new cultural conditions but still generating dialogue through its inherent comparison of two versions of one couple's relationship. A group of energetically engaged readers of romance novels celebrated the strength of the heroine of a double-proposal novel published in 1971, Elsie Lee's *The Diplomatic Lover.* Janice Radway reports: "They proudly exclaimed that [the heroine] Nanny 'spoke six languages,' was 'a really good artist,' and 'did not want to marry him even though she was pregnant' because she believed he was an 'elegant tomcat' and would not be faithful to her" (80). The three readers interviewed by Radway are delighted with the heroine's independence, but Radway argues that the author undermines that independence by marrying the heroine to the hero after all: "These untraditional skills and unconventional attitudes are obviously not seen as fulfilling or quite proper by Lee herself because they are legitimated and rendered acceptable at the novel's conclusion when the hero convinces Nanny of his love, refuses to live without her, and promises to take care of her in the future" (80). The readers, however, see the ending not as legitimation or as capitulation but as "ultimate triumph" because the protagonist "maintains her integrity on her own terms by exacting a formal commitment from the hero and simultaneously provides for her own future in the only way acceptable to her culture" (81). In other words, she has renegotiated her marriage within the narrative structure of a double proposal and a counter-plot.

The dialogue generated by *The Diplomatic Lover* between the involved readers and the detached critic corresponds to the conversations provoked a century ago by popular double-proposal novels. Radway stands in the place of social arbiters of that time, although her ideological perspective is diametrically opposed to theirs. Whereas the intellectual elite of the nineteenth century were sometimes disturbed by the strength heroines manifested in negotiating their marriages through double proposals, Radway is troubled by the weakness they demonstrate in succumbing to marriage after all. Then as now, intellectuals worried about the pernicious effect popular novels might have on the "untutored fancies" of undiscerning readers. But now as then, readers categorized as "undiscerning" are probably just discerning something different from what we think they are.

Another recent explanation of the appeal of romance novels for both tutored and untutored fancies is Suzanne Juhasz's *Reading from the Heart*, which combines personal narrative with skilled textual analysis. Juhasz, writing for people who love to read rather than only for other scholars, studies her emotional responses to novels in order to understand them intellectually. Two of the texts she reads feature double proposals: *Pride and Prejudice* and *Jane Eyre*. Juhasz's discussion testifies to the enduring power of old double-proposal stories to inspire conversation. When Elizabeth Bennett rejects Darcy's first proposal, Juhasz reports that she is dismayed and fearful that "Elizabeth has just said no, in the most irrefutable way, to the man who truly loves her," even though she recognizes that "neither person is ready for marriage at this point" (40). When the second proposal is accepted, Juhasz recognizes both emotionally and intellectually that the couple now shares "true love," which for Austen is "mutual, unconditional, and nurturing" (49). As for *Jane Eyre*, Juhasz's reactions changed over time, so that her discussion of that novel becomes a dialogue between her old and her new reactions. As a younger reader, she felt the same dismay when Jane first separated from Rochester that she experienced when Elizabeth rejected Darcy: "I would do almost anything to avoid parting and separation" (146). But her reaction to the ending did not give her the satisfaction she felt at the conclusion of *Pride and Prejudice*: "I am left adrift by this happy ending. I always have been, even when I, too, loved Mr. Rochester and wanted only for this marriage to occur" (154). Analysis enables Juhasz to explain her discomfort and the change in her reading of the novel, for she finds that the serious flaws in the relationship are not resolved in the conclusion; she would not want "a marriage like theirs," in which Jane has to mother Rochester. Juhasz explains her readings using D. W. Winnicott's psychoanalytic theories of infant development and baby-mother bonding; she determines "how a heroine would need to grow in the textual environment of her novel and what it would mean for her to arrive at self-identity for her happy ending" (253). In the case of the double-proposal novels, the contrast between the faulty first proposal and the nurturing conditions of the second proposal reveal what growth is necessary and help to explain what conditions enable the heroine to achieve self-identity.

So the double-proposal plot lives on, in incarnations of romance fiction such as *The Diplomatic Lover,* in university press reprints of American novels such as *St. Elmo, Beulah,* and *The Story of Avis,* and in the perpetual popularity, in print, on film, and even on stage, for readers, scholars, viewers, and reviewers of original double-proposal texts, particularly *Persuasion, Pride and Prejudice,* and *Jane Eyre.* Each of those stories was filmed for television or cinema during the 1990s, and *Jane Eyre* was even rendered as a musical on a Toronto stage in 1996. Whatever the context of the publication or the production, and whatever other appeals they surely have, these stories become the source of dialogue about changing cultural understandings of love, women's roles, and marriage.

In addition to reprintings, revivals, reworkings, and perhaps relivings of the doubled courtship plot, a more modern version of the doubled pattern has evolved. Stanley Cavell identifies a film genre comparable to the double proposal that he terms the "comedy of remarriage," a plot structure characteristic of major romantic comedies of the 1930s and 1940s. For example, in *The Awful Truth* (1937), Irene Dunne and Cary Grant, who are in the process of getting a divorce, take turns trying to break up each other's new romance and are reconciled just before their divorce decree is finalized. And in *His Girl Friday* (1940) Rosalind Russell and Cary Grant, divorced at the start of the film, rekindle their romance in the process of investigating a murder for their newspaper. The "drive of [the plot of remarriage]," Cavell tells us, "is not to get the central pair together, but to get them *back* together, together *again*" (2). He argues that this genre is crucially different from other treatments of marriage and divorce because it creates a "conversation . . . of a sort that leads to acknowledgement; to the reconciliation of a genuine forgiveness; a reconciliation so profound as to require the metamorphosis of death and revival, the achievement of a new perspective on existence" (19).

The increased flexibility of marriage itself in the twentieth century—the relative ease of procuring separation or divorce—enables marriage rather than courtship to become the site of negotiation, and in its new version the plot retains its tendency to engage with the dynamics of social change. Of course, the beginnings and endings of traditions and trends in literature always resist being fixed. Caroline Hentz, the earliest of the American double-proposal authors, wrote a double-marriage plot herself in her final novel, *Ernest Linwood*. Linwood is a violently possessive husband who is "cured" only after separation and reconciliation. And the second half of *The Story of Avis* also presents a double-marriage plot, though without the optimistic ending characteristic of the films Cavell discusses. In *Writing a Woman's Life* (1989), Carolyn G. Heilbrun attests to the relevance of Cavell's *Pursuits of Happiness*, labeling it "perhaps the best marriage manual ever published" (93). According to Heilbrun, Cavell offers powerful insights that might enable us to free ourselves somewhat from the romance and marriage paradigms that restrict our understanding of women's lives: "That first, thunderous, compelling attraction must not lead to marriage because it cannot lead to remarriage; it is therefore not marriage at all, but passion, the relationship of lovers" (94). She suggests that "we must look, with Cavell's guidance, at that marriage in middle age that is remarriage; we must look for its conversations, for its qualities of friendship, above all, for its equality and the equality of the man's and woman's quests" (95). Heilbrun's advice echoes the recommendations of double-proposal narratives as well as their double-marriage successors. The basic pattern of union, disunion, and reunion has deep-rooted and far-reaching resonance.

The analyses offered by Juhasz and Cavell suggest that the appeal of such plots may be traced to patterns of human consciousness. Whereas Juhasz invokes a psychoanalytic model to read the data of her own reader responses, Cavell's paradigm pulls together genre analysis, the historical context of the films, and the work of a range of philosophers, including Hegel, Heidegger, Kierkegaard, Kant, and Emerson. Cavell concludes that the double-marriage films "may be understood as parables of a phase of the development of consciousness at which the struggle is for the reciprocity or equality of consciousness between a woman and a man." For Cavell, this "phase of development" is historically situated, and the films are "primary data for what I would like to call the inner agenda of a culture" (17). Perhaps, just as the *Blackwood's Edinburgh Magazine* reviewer feared, this "inner agenda" grew in part from the unrestrained imaginations of earlier writers. As Cavell says about the comedies of remarriage, such stories "harbor a vision which they know cannot be fully domesticated, inhabited, in the world we know. They are romances. Showing us our fantasies, they express the inner agenda of a nation that conceives Utopian longings and commitments for itself" (18). Perhaps these longings and commitments will continue to bear fruit in succeeding generations.

No wonder that the double proposal continues to be rendered again and again in the twentieth century. Our culture continues to produce and consume double-proposal stories, with or without the blessing of social arbiters or literary critics. Narratives that correspond so closely to our psychological needs and our social possibilities, that give us a focus for conversation and a tool for negotiating cultural norms are sure to retain their power to inspire. "Every shadowy creation that takes other imaginations," wrote the nervously prophetic *Blackwood's Edinburgh Magazine* reviewer, "is likely to consolidate itself in course of time" ("A Religious Novel" 276).

WORKS CITED

[Abbot, Miss A. W.] "Female Authors." *North American Review* 72 (Jan. 1851): 151–77.

Adams, Maurianne. "*Jane Eyre:* Woman's Estate." *The Authority of Experience: Essays in Feminist Criticism.* Ed. Arlyn Diamond and Lee R. Edwards. Amherst: University of Massachusetts Press, 1977. 137–59.

Armstrong, Nancy. *Desire and Domestic Fiction: A Political History of the Novel.* New York: Oxford University Press, 1987.

Bakhtin, M. M. "Discourse in the Novel." *The Dialogic Imagination.* Ed. Michael Holquist. Trans. Caryl Emerson and Michael Holquist. Austin: University of Texas Press, 1981. 259–422.

Bakker, Jan. "Twists of Sentiment in Antebellum Southern Romance." *Southern Studies* 26 (Fall 1993): 3–13.

Bardes, Barbara, and Suzanne Gossett. *Declarations of Independence: Women and Political Power in Nineteenth-Century American Fiction.* New Brunswick: Rutgers University Press, 1990.

Barnes, Elizabeth L. "Mirroring the Mother Text: Histories of Seduction in the American Domestic Novel." *Anxious Power: Reading, Writing, and Ambivalence in Narrative by Women.* Ed. Carol J. Singley and Susan Elizabeth Sweeney. Albany: State University of New York Press, 1993. 157–72.

Barrett Browning, Elizabeth. *Aurora Leigh, a Poem.* Chicago: Academy Chicago, 1979.

Barry, Kathleen. *Susan B. Anthony: A Biography of a Singular Feminist.* New York: New York University Press, 1988.

Bassett, Henrietta H. "Dr. Zay's Husband." *Woman's Journal* 13 (Sept. 2, 1882): 278.

Bauermeister, Erica R. "*The Lamplighter, The Wide, Wide World,* and *Hope Leslie:* Reconsidering the Recipes for Nineteenth-Century American Women's Novels." *Legacy* 8.1 (1991): 17–28.

Baym, Nina. "The Myth of the Myth of Southern Womanhood." *Feminism and American Literary History.* New Brunswick: Rutgers University Press, 1992. 183–96.

————. *Novels, Readers, and Reviewers: Responses to Fiction in Antebellum America.* Ithaca: Cornell University Press, 1984.

————. *Woman's Fiction: A Guide to Novels by and about Women in America, 1820–1870.* 2d ed. Urbana: University of Illinois Press, 1993.

Beaver, R. Pierce. *American Protestant Women in World Mission: A History of the First Feminist Movement in North America.* Rev. ed. Grand Rapids, Mich.: William B. Eerdmans, 1980.

Bennett, Mary Angela. *Elizabeth Stuart Phelps.* Philadelphia: University of Pennsylvania Press, 1939.

"Belles Lettres." Rev. of *Aurora Leigh. Westminster Review* 67 (Jan. 1857): 306–26.

"Belles Lettres." Rev. of *Grace Lee. Westminster Review* 63 (Apr. 1855): 588–604.

"Book Notices." Rev. of *The Planter's Northern Bride. DeBow's Review* 16 (1854): 443–44.

"Book Notices." Rev. of *St. Elmo. Southern Review* 1 (Apr. 1867): 493–97.

Boone, Joseph. *Tradition Counter Tradition.* Chicago: University of Chicago Press, 1987.

Boyle, Regis Louise. *Mrs. E. D. E. N. Southworth, Novelist.* Washington, D.C.: Catholic University of America Press, 1939.

Brontë, Charlotte. *Jane Eyre.* 1847. Ed. Q. D. Leavis. Harmondsworth, England: Penguin, 1966.

Brown, Herbert Ross. *The Sentimental Novel in America, 1789–1860.* Durham: Duke University Press, 1940.

Brownstein, Rachel M. *Becoming a Heroine: Reading about Women in Novels.* Harmondsworth, England: Penguin, 1982.

Bullard, Laura J. Curtis. *Christine; or, Woman's Trials and Triumphs.* New York: DeWitt and Davenport, 1856.

————. "Elizabeth Cady Stanton." *Our Famous Women: An Authorized Record of the Lives and Deeds of Distinguished American Women of Our Times.* Kansas City: S. F. Junkin, 1887. 602–23.

————. *Now-a-Days!* New York: T. L. Magagnos, 1854.

Carey, Glenn O. *Edward Payson Roe.* Boston: Twayne, 1985.

Carpenter, Lynette. "Double Talk: The Power and Glory of Paradox in E. D. E. N. Southworth's *The Hidden Hand." Legacy* 10.1 (1993): 17–30.

Cavell, Stanley. *Pursuits of Happiness: The Hollywood Comedy of Remarriage.* Cambridge, Mass.: Harvard University Press, 1981.

Child, Lydia Maria. *Selected Letters, 1817–1880.* Ed. Milton Meltzer and Patricia G. Holland. Amherst: University of Massachusetts Press, 1982.

Clinton, Catherine. *The Other Civil War: American Women in the Nineteenth Century.* New York: Hill and Wang, 1984.

————. *The Plantation Mistress: Women's World in the Old South.* New York: Pantheon Books, 1982.

[Collins, Wilkie.] "Petition to Novel-Writers." *Littell's Living Age* 52 (Jan. 17, 1857): 180–85.

Cooper, Helen. *Elizabeth Barrett Browning, Woman and Artist.* Chapel Hill: University of North Carolina Press, 1988.

Cott, Nancy F. "Passionlessness: An Interpretation of Victorian Sexual Ideology,

1790–1850." Ed. Nancy F. Cott and Elizabeth H. Pleck. *A Heritage of Her Own: Toward a New Social History of American Women.* New York: Simon and Schuster, 1970. 162–81.

Coultrap-McQuin, Susan. *Doing Literary Business: American Women Writers in the Nineteenth Century.* Chapel Hill: University of North Carolina Press, 1990.

Cowie, Alexander. *The Rise of the American Novel.* New York: American Book, 1948.

"Critical Notices." Rev. of *Eoline. Southern Quarterly Review* 22 (July 1852): 280.

"Critical Notices." Rev. of *Marcus Warland. Southern Quarterly Review* 22 (July 1852): 257.

"Critical Notices." Rev. of *The Planter's Northern Bride. Southern Quarterly Review* 26 (July 1854): 255.

"Critical Notices." Rev. of *Rena. Southern Quarterly Review* 20 (July 1851): 264.

Cullen, Jim. *The Civil War in Popular Culture: A Reusable Past.* Washington, D.C.: Smithsonian Institution Press, 1995.

Culler, Jonathan. *The Pursuit of Signs: Semiotics, Literature, Deconstruction.* Ithaca: Cornell University Press, 1981.

Culpepper, Marilyn Mayer. *Trials and Triumphs: Women of the American Civil War.* East Lansing: Michigan State University Press, 1991.

Davidson, Cathy N., ed. *Reading in America: Literature and Social History.* Baltimore: Johns Hopkins University Press, 1989.

———. *Revolution and the Word: The Rise of the Novel in America.* New York: Oxford University Press, 1986.

Degler, Carl. *At Odds: Women and the Family in America from the Revolution to the Present.* Oxford: Oxford University Press, 1980.

D'Emilio, John, and Estelle B. Freedman. *Intimate Matters: A History of Sexuality in America.* New York: Harper and Row, 1988.

Derby, J[ames] C[ephas]. *Fifty Years among Authors, Books, and Publishers.* New York: G. W. Carlton, 1884.

Diffley, Kathleen. *Where My Heart Is Turning Ever: Civil War Stories and Constitutional Reform, 1861–1876.* Athens: University of Georgia Press, 1992.

"Disenthralment of Southern Literature." *DeBow's Review* 31 (Oct.–Nov.1861): 347–61.

Dobson, Joanne. "The American Renaissance Reenvisioned." *The (Other) American Traditions: Nineteenth-Century Women Writers.* Ed. Joyce W. Warren. New Brunswick: Rutgers University Press, 1993. 164–82.

———. "The Hidden Hand: Subversion of Cultural Ideology in Three Mid-Nineteenth-Century American Women's Novels." *American Quarterly* 38.2 (Summer 1986): 223–42.

"Doctor Zay." Rev. *Literary World* 13.22 (Nov. 4, 1884): 371.

DuBois, Ellen Carol. *Feminism and Suffrage: The Emergence of an Independent Women's Movement in America, 1848–1869.* Ithaca: Cornell University Press, 1978.

duCille, Ann. *The Coupling Convention: Sex, Text, and Tradition in Black Women's Fiction.* New York: Oxford University Press, 1993.

DuPlessis, Rachel Blau. *Writing beyond the Ending: Narrative Strategies of Twentieth-Century Women Writers.* Bloomington: Indiana University Press, 1985.

"The Duty of Southern Authors." *Southern Literary Messenger* 23 (Oct. 1856): 241–47.

Eagleton, Terry. *Marxism and Literary Criticism*. Berkeley: University of California Press, 1976.

"Editorial Miscellany." Rev. of *Beulah*. *DeBow's Review* 27.4 (Oct. 1859): 490–94.

"Editorial Notes—American Literature." Rev. of *Ruth Hall*. *Putnam's Monthly* 5 (Feb. 1855): 212–20.

"Editor's Easy Chair." Rev. of *Ruth Hall*. *Harper's New Monthly Magazine* 10 (Mar. 1855): 549–58.

"Editor's Table." *Southern Literary Messenger* 17 (Aug. 1851): 517–19.

"Editor's Table." Rev. of *Barriers Burned Away*. *Appleton's Journal* 9.199 (1873): 93.

"Elizabeth Barrett Browning." *Southern Literary Messenger* 30 (Feb. 1860): 146–53.

Evans, Augusta Jane. *Beulah*. Ed. Elizabeth Fox-Genovese. Baton Rouge: Louisiana State University Press, 1992.

———. *St. Elmo*. Tuscaloosa: University of Alabama Press, 1992.

Faust, Drew Gilpin. Introduction *Macaria; or, Altars of Sacrifice* by Augusta Jane Evans. Baton Rouge: Louisiana State University Press, 1993. viii–xxix.

———. *Mothers of Invention: Women of the Slaveholding South in the American Civil War*. Chapel Hill: University of North Carolina Press, 1996.

Fetterley, Judith. "Commentary: Nineteenth-Century American Women Writers and the Politics of Recovery." *American Literary History* 6.3 (Fall 1994): 600–611.

Fidler, William Perry. *Augusta Evans Wilson, 1835–1909: A Biography*. Tuscaloosa: University of Alabama Press, 1951.

Fiedler, Leslie A. *Love and Death in the American Novel*. New York: Dell, 1960.

Fleenor, Juliann E., ed. *The Female Gothic*. Montreal: Eden Press, 1983.

Forrest, Mary. *Women of the South Distinguished in Literature*. New York: Charles B. Richardson, 1866.

Fox-Genovese, Elizabeth. Introduction to *Beulah* by Augusta Jane Evans. Baton Rouge: Louisiana State University Press, 1992. xi–xxxvi.

———. *Within the Plantation Household: Black and White Women of the Old South*. Chapel Hill: University of North Carolina Press, 1988.

Friedman, Jean E. *The Enclosed Garden: Women and Community in the Evangelical South, 1830–1900*. Chapel Hill: University of North Carolina Press, 1985.

Fulton, Valerie. "Rewriting the Necessary Woman: Marriage and Professionalism in James, Jewett, and Phelps." *Henry James Review* 15.3 (Fall 1994): 242–56.

Genovese, Eugene D. *The Slaveholders' Dilemma: Freedom and Progress in Southern Conservative Thought, 1820–1860*. Columbia: University of South Carolina Press, 1992.

Gilbert, Sandra, and Susan Gubar. *The Madwoman in the Attic: The Woman Writer and the Nineteenth-Century Literary Imagination*. New Haven: Yale University Press, 1979.

Goshgarian, G. M. *To Kiss the Chastening Rod: Domestic Fiction and Sexual Ideology in the American Renaissance*. Ithaca: Cornell University Press, 1992.

"Grace Lee." Rev. *North American Review* 81.168 (July 1855): 263–67.

Green, Anna Maria. *The Journal of a Milledgeville Girl, 1861–1867*. Ed. James C. Bonner. Athens: University of Georgia Press, 1964.

Green, Katherine Sobba. *The Courtship Novel, 1740–1820: A Feminized Genre*. Louisville: University Press of Kentucky, 1991.

Habegger, Alfred. *Gender, Fantasy, and Realism in American Literature.* New York: Columbia University Press, 1982.

———. "A Well Hidden Hand." *Novel: A Forum on Fiction* 14.3 (Spring 1981): 197–212.

Hall, Donald E. *Fixing Patriarchy: Feminism and Mid-Victorian Male Novelists.* Washington Square: New York University Press, 1996.

Hall, Richard. *Patriots in Disguise: Women Warriors of the Civil War.* New York: Paragon House, 1993.

Harris, Susan K. "'But Is It Any *Good?*': Evaluating Nineteenth-Century American Women's Fiction." *American Literature* 63.1 (Mar. 1991): 43–61.

———. *Nineteenth-Century American Women's Novels: Interpretive Strategies.* Cambridge: Cambridge University Press, 1990.

Hart, James D. *The Popular Book: A History of America's Literary Taste.* New York: Oxford University Press, 1950.

Hart, John S. *Female Prose Writers of America with Portraits, Biographical Notices, and Specimens of Their Writings.* 5th ed. Philadelphia: EH Butler, 1870.

Hawthorne, Nathaniel. *Letters of Hawthorne to William D. Ticknor: 1851–1864.* Newark: Carteret Book Club, 1910.

Heilbrun, Carolyn G. *Writing a Woman's Life.* London: Women's Press, 1989.

Hentz, Caroline Lee. *Eoline; or, Magnolia Vale.* Philadelphia: T. B. Peterson, 1852.

———. *Linda; or, The Young Pilot of the Belle Creole: A Tale of Southern Life.* Philadelphia: T. B. Peterson, 1850.

———. *Robert Graham: A Sequel to "Linda."* Philadelphia: T. B. Peterson, 1855.

Herndl, Diane Price. "The Dilemmas of a Feminine Dialogic." *Feminism, Bakhtin, and the Dialogic.* Ed. Dale M. Bauer and S. Jaret McKinstry. Albany: State University of New York Press, 1991. 7–24.

———. *Invalid Women: Figuring Feminine Illness in American Fiction and Culture, 1840–1940.* Chapel Hill: University of North Carolina Press, 1993.

Holstein, Suzy Clarkson. "'Offering Up Her Life': Confederate Women on the Altars of Sacrifice." *Southern Studies* 2.2 (Summer 1991): 113–30.

Howells, William Dean. *Dr. Breen's Practice.* Boston: Houghton-Mifflin, 1881.

———. "Note." Preface to *Doctor Zay* by Elizabeth Stuart Phelps. *Atlantic Monthly* 49 (Apr. 1882): 518.

Hudock, Amy E. "Challenging the Definition of Heroism in E. D. E. N. Southworth's *The Hidden Hand.*" *American Transcendental Quarterly* 9.1 (Mar. 1995): 5–20.

Huf, Linda. *A Portrait of the Artist as a Young Woman: The Writer as Heroine in American Literature.* New York: Frederick Ungar, 1983.

Hunt, Robert. "A Domesticated Slavery: Political Economy in Caroline Hentz's Fiction." *Southern Quarterly* 34.4 (Summer 1996): 25–35.

Ings, Katharine Nicholson. "Blackness and the Literary Imagination: Uncovering *The Hidden Hand.*" *Passing and the Fictions of Identity.* Ed. Elaine K. Ginsberg. Durham: Duke University Press, 1996. 131–50.

"An Inquiry into the Present State of Southern Literature." *Southern Literary Messenger* 23 (Nov. 1856): 387–91.

"Jane Eyre: An Autobiography." Rev. of *Jane Eyre. Littell's Living Age* 17 (June 10, 1848): 481–87.

Jauss, Hans Robert. *Toward an Aesthetic of Reception.* Trans. Timothy Bahti. Minneapolis: University of Minnesota Press, 1982.

Jewett, Sarah Orne. *A Country Doctor.* Boston: Houghton-Mifflin, 1884.

Jones, Anne Goodwyn. *Tomorrow Is Another Day: The Woman Writer in the South, 1859–1936.* Baton Rouge: Louisiana State University Press, 1981.

Juhasz, Suzanne. *Reading from the Heart: Women, Literature, and the Search for True Love.* New York: Viking, 1994.

June, Jennie. *Jennie Juneiana: Talks on Women's Topics.* Boston: Lee and Shepard, 1864.

Kaplan, Cora. Introduction to *Aurora Leigh and Other Poems* by Elizabeth Barrett Browning. London: Woman's Press, 1978. 5–36.

Kelley, Mary. *Private Woman, Public Stage: Literary Domesticity in Nineteenth-Century America.* New York: Oxford University Press, 1984.

Kelly, Lori Duin. *The Life and Works of Elizabeth Stuart Phelps, Victorian Feminist Writer.* Troy: Whitson, 1983.

Kennard, Jean E. *Victims of Convention.* Hamden: Archon, 1978.

Kessler, Carol Farley. *Elizabeth Stuart Phelps.* Boston: Twayne, 1982.

———. Introduction to *The Story of Avis* by Elizabeth Stuart Phelps. New Brunswick: Rutgers University Press, 1985. xiii–xxxii.

Kessler-Harris, Alice. *Women Have Always Worked: A Historical Overview.* Old Westbury, N.Y.: Feminist Press, 1981.

Leach, William. *True Love and Perfect Union: The Feminist Reform of Sex and Society.* New York: Basic Books, 1980.

Leonard, Elizabeth D. *Yankee Women: Gender Battles in the Civil War.* New York: Norton, 1994.

Lettis, Richard. *Dickens on Literature: A Continuing Study of His Aesthetic.* New York: AMS Press, 1990.

"Literary Notices." Rev. of *Ruth Hall.* *Godey's Lady's Book and Magazine* 50–51 (Feb. 1855): 176–77.

"Literary Notices." Rev. of *Ruth Hall.* *Knickerbocker* 45 (Jan. 1855): 84–86.

"Literary Notices." Rev. of *Ruth Hall.* *National Era* 9.431 (Apr. 5, 1855): 54–55.

"Literary Notices." Rev. of *Vivia; or, The Secret of Power.* *The Chicago Magazine: The West as It Is.* Chicago: J. Gager, 1857. 268.

"Literature." Rev. of *Doctor Zay.* *Independent* 34 (Nov. 16, 1882): 10.

Lystra, Karen. *Searching the Heart: Women, Men, and Romantic Love in Nineteenth-Century America.* New York: Oxford University Press, 1989.

Machor, James L. "Fiction and Informed Reading in Early Nineteenth-Century America." *Nineteenth-Century Literature* 47.3 (Dec. 1992): 320–48.

———. "Historical Hermeneutics and Antebellum Fiction: Gender, Response Theory, and Interpretive Contexts." *Readers in History: Nineteenth-Century American Literature and the Contexts of Response.* Ed. James L. Machor. Baltimore: Johns Hopkins University Press, 1993. 54–84.

Masel-Walters, Lynne. "Their Rights and Nothing More: A History of *The Revolution,* 1868–70." *Journalism Quarterly* 53 (Summer 1977): 242–51.

Masteller, Jean Carwile. "The Women Doctors of Howells, Phelps, and Jewett: The Conflict of Marriage and Career." *Critical Essays on Sarah Orne Jewett.* Ed. Gwen L. Nagel. Boston: G. K. Hall, 1984. 135–47.

McMillen, Sally G. *Southern Women Black and White in the Old South.* Arlington Heights, Ill.: Harlan Davidson, 1992.

Mermin, Dorothy. *Elizabeth Barrett Browning: The Origins of a New Poetry.* Chicago: University of Chicago Press, 1989.

Miller, Nancy. *The Heroine's Text: Readings in the French and English Novel, 1722–1782.* New York: Columbia University Press, 1980.

"Miss Evans—St. Elmo." Rev. of *St. Elmo. DeBow's Review* 3.3 (Mar. 1867): 268–73.

"Modern Novelists—Great and Small." *Littell's Living Age* 45 (June 16, 1855): 643–54.

Moers, Ellen. *Literary Women.* Garden City, N.Y.: Doubleday, 1976.

Morris, Timothy. "Professional Ethics and Professional Erotics in Elizabeth Stuart Phelps's *Doctor Zay.*" *Studies in American Fiction* 21.2 (Autumn 1993): 141–52.

Moss, Elizabeth. *Domestic Novelists in the Old South: Defenders of Southern Culture.* Baton Rouge: Louisiana State University Press, 1992.

[Moulton, William U.] *The Life and Beauties of Fanny Fern.* New York: H. Long and Brother, 1855.

"Mrs. Browning's Aurora Leigh." Rev. *Littell's Living Age* 52 (Feb. 14, 1857): 427–30.

Mussell, Kay J. "'But Why Do They Read Those Things?': The Female Audience and the Gothic Novel." *The Female Gothic.* Ed. Juliann E. Fleenor. Montreal: Eden Press, 1983. 57–68.

Newberry, Julia. *Julia Newberry's Diary.* New York: Norton, 1933.

"New Books." Rev. of *Now-a-Days! Littell's Living Age* 43.549 (Dec. 2, 1854): 479–80.

Newell, Robert Henry. *The Orpheus C. Kerr Papers, Volume 1.* New York: Blakeman and Mason, 1863.

"New York Literary Correspondence." Rev. of *Beulah. Ladies' Repository* 20.2 (1860): 125–27.

"New York Literary Correspondence." Rev. of *Women of the South Distinguished in Literature. Ladies' Repository* 21.1 (1861): 58–61.

Nichols, Nina da Vinci. "Place and Eros in Radcliffe, Lewis, and Brontë." *The Female Gothic.* Ed. Juliann E. Fleenor. Montreal: Eden Press, 1983. 187–206.

"Notices of New Works." Rev. of *Berenice. Southern Literary Messenger* 22 (June 1856): 477–80.

"Notices of New Works." Rev. of *Emily Herbert; or, The Happy Home. Southern Literary Messenger* 20 (1854): 770–72.

"Notices of New Works." Rev. of *Robert Graham. Southern Literary Messenger* 21 (May 1855): 328.

"A One-Sided Correspondence." *Overland Monthly and Out West Magazine* 5 (1885): 402–14.

Papashvily, Helen Waite. *All the Happy Endings: A Study of the Domestic Novel in America, the Women Who Wrote It, the Women Who Read It, in the Nineteenth Century.* New York: Harper and Brothers, 1956.

Parker, Ada R. *Letters of Ada R. Parker.* Boston: Crosby and Nichols, 1863.

Pattee, Fred Lewis. *The Feminine Fifties.* New York: Appleton-Century, 1940.

Phelps, Elizabeth Stuart. *Chapters from a Life.* Boston: Houghton, Mifflin, 1896.

———. *Doctor Zay.* New York: Feminist Press, 1987.

————. "A Dream within a Dream." *Daring to Dream: Utopian Stories by United States Women, 1836–1919.* Ed. Carol Farley Kessler. Boston: Pandora, 1984.

————. *The Silent Partner.* Ridgewood, N.J.: Gregg Press, 1967.

————. *The Story of Avis.* Ed. Carol Farley Kessler. New Brunswick: Rutgers University Press, 1985.

Pratt, Annis. *Archetypal Patterns in Women's Fiction.* Bloomington: Indiana University Press, 1981.

Proctor, Adelaide Anne. "A Woman's Answer." *The Family Library of Poetry and Song.* Ed. William Cullen Bryant. New York: Fords, Howard, and Hulbert, 1880.

Rable, George. "'Missing in Action': Women of the Confederacy." *Divided Houses: Gender and the Civil War.* Ed. Catherine Clinton and Nina Silber. New York: Oxford University Press, 1992. 134–46.

Radway, Janice. *Reading the Romance: Women, Patriarchy, and Popular Literature.* Chapel Hill: University of North Carolina Press, 1984.

"Recent Novels." Rev. of *Barriers Burned Away. The Nation* 16 (Mar. 1873): 219.

"Recent Novels." Rev. of *A Country Doctor. The Nation* 39.996 (July 1884): 96–97.

"Recent Novels." Rev. of *Dr. Breen's Practice. The Nation* 34.862 (Jan. 1882): 18.

"Recent Novels." Rev. of *Friends. The Nation* 33.848 (Sept. 1881): 257–59.

"Recent Novels." Rev. of *The Story of Avis. The Nation* 26.664 (Mar. 1878): 202–3.

"Recent Publications." Rev. of *Fair Play; or, The Test of the Lone Isle. The Nation* 8.187 (Jan. 1869): 55.

"A Religious Novel." Rev. of *The Old Helmet. Blackwood's Edinburgh Magazine* 99 (Mar. 1866): 275–86.

Rev. of *Beulah. Southern Literary Messenger* 31 (Oct. 1860): 241–48.

Rev. of *Ruth Hall. Southern Quarterly Review* 27 (Apr. 1855): 438–50.

Reynolds, David S. *Beneath the American Renaissance: The Subversive Imagination in the Age of Emerson and Melville.* New York: Alfred A. Knopf, 1988.

Rittenhouse, Isabella Maud. *Maud.* Ed. Richard Lee Strout. New York: Macmillan, 1939.

Roe, Edward P[ayson]. *Barriers Burned Away.* 1872. Upper Saddle River, N.J.: Literature House, 1970.

————. *What Can She Do?* New York: Dodd and Mead, 1873.

Romero, Lora. *Home Fronts: Domesticity and Its Critics in the Antebellum United States.* Durham: Duke University Press, 1997.

Ronald, Ann. "Terror-Gothic: Nightmare and Dream." *The Female Gothic.* Ed. Juliann E. Fleenor. Montreal: Eden Press, 1983. 176–86.

Rothman, Ellen K. *Hands and Hearts: A History of Courtship in America.* New York: Basic Books, 1984.

Russ, Joanna. "'Somebody's Trying to Kill Me and I Think It's My Husband': The Modern Gothic." *The Female Gothic.* Ed. Juliann Fleenor. Montreal: Eden Press, 1983. 31–56.

Sartisky, Michael. Afterword to *Doctor Zay* by Elizabeth Stuart Phelps. New York: Feminist Press, 1987. 259–321.

Scott, Anne Firor. *The Southern Lady: From Pedestal to Politics, 1830–1930.* Chicago: University of Chicago Press, 1970.

Seidman, Steven. *Romantic Longings: Love in America, 1830–1980.* New York: Routledge, 1991.

Silber, Nina. *The Romance of Reunion: Northerners and the South, 1865–1900.* Chapel Hill: University of North Carolina Press, 1993.

Sizer, Lyde Cullen. "Acting Her Part: Narratives of Union Women Spies." *Divided Houses: Gender and the Civil War.* Ed. Catherine Clinton and Nina Silber. New York: Oxford University Press, 1992. 114–33.

"Southern Books by Southern Authors." *The Nation* 4 (Mar. 21, 1867): 232–33.

Southworth, E. D. E. N. *Fair Play; or, The Test of the Lone Isle.* Philadelphia: T. B. Peterson, 1868.

———. *The Hidden Hand; or, Capitola the Madcap.* Ed. Joanne Dobson. New Brunswick: Rutgers University Press, 1988.

———. *How He Won Her: A Sequel to "Fair Play."* Philadelphia: T. B. Peterson, 1869.

———. *Vivia; or, The Secret of Power.* Philadelphia: T. B. Peterson, 1875.

Spacks, Patricia Meyer. *The Female Imagination.* New York: Alfred A. Knopf, 1975.

Stanesa, Jamie. "Caroline Hentz's Rereading of Southern Paternalism; or, Pastoral Naturalism in *The Planter's Northern Bride.*" *Southern Studies* 3.4 (Winter 1992): 221–52.

———. "Caroline Lee Whiting Hentz." *Legacy* 13.2 (1996): 130–41.

Stanton, Theodore, and Harriot Stanton Blatch, eds. *Elizabeth Cady Stanton as Revealed in Her Letters, Diary, and Reminiscences.* Vol. 2. New York: Harper and Brothers, 1922.

Stein, Karen. "Monsters and Madwomen: Changing Female Gothic." *The Female Gothic.* Ed. Juliann E. Fleenor. Montreal: Eden Press, 1983. 123–37.

Stoddard, Elizabeth. *The Morgesons and Other Writings, Published and Unpublished.* Ed. Lawrence Buell and Sandra A. Zagarell. Philadelphia: University of Pennsylvania Press, 1984.

Stone, Marjorie. "Genre Subversion and Gender Inversion: *The Princess* and *Aurora Leigh.*" *Victorian Poetry* 25.2 (Summer 1985): 101–27.

Stowe, Steven M. *Intimacy and Power in the Old South: Ritual in the Lives of the Planters.* Baltimore: Johns Hopkins University Press, 1987.

———. "The Not-So-Cloistered Academy: Elite Women's Education and Family Feeling in the Old South." *The Web of Southern Social Relations: Women, Family, and Education.* Ed. Walter J. Fraser Jr., R. Frank Saunders Jr., and Jon L. Wakelyn. Athens: University of Georgia Press, 1985. 90–106.

Tanner, Tony. *Adultery in the Novel: Contract and Transgression.* Baltimore: Johns Hopkins University Press, 1979.

———. Introduction to *Pride and Prejudice* by Jane Austen. 1813. Harmondsworth, England: Penguin, 1972.

Taplin, Gardner B. Introduction to *Aurora Leigh, a Poem* by Elizabeth Barrett Browning. Chicago: Academy Chicago, 1979.

Tennyson, Alfred Lord. *The Princess.* Boston: Ginn and Co., 1897.

Thaxter, Celia. *Letters of Celia Thaxter.* Boston: Houghton, Mifflin, 1895.

Todd, Janet, ed. *British Women Writers: A Critical Reference Guide.* New York: Continuum, 1989.

Tompkins, Jane. *Sensational Designs: The Cultural Work of American Fiction, 1790–1960.* New York: Oxford University Press, 1985.

Voloshin, Beverly R. "The Limits of Domesticity: The Female *Bildungsroman* in America, 1820–1870." *American Literature, Culture, and Ideology: Essays in Mem-*

ory of Henry Nash Smith. Ed. Beverly R. Voloshin. New York: Peter Lang, 1990. 93–114.

Walker, Nancy A. *The Disobedient Writer: Women and Narrative Tradition.* Austin: University of Texas Press, 1995.

Ward, Susan. "The Career Woman Fiction of Elizabeth Stuart Phelps." *Nineteenth-Century Women Writers of the English-Speaking World.* Ed. Rhoda B. Nathan. New York: Greenwood Press, 1986. 209–19.

Webb, C[harles] H. *St. Twel'mo; or, The Cuneiform Cyclopedist of Chattanooga.* New York: C. H. Webb, 1867.

Welter, Barbara. *Dimity Convictions: The American Woman in the Nineteenth Century.* Athens: Ohio University Press, 1976.

[Whipple, E. P.] "Novels of the Season." *North American Review* 67.141 (Oct. 1848): 354–69.

Whites, LeeAnn. *The Civil War as a Crisis in Gender: Augusta, Georgia, 1860–1890.* Athens: University of Georgia Press, 1995.

W[hittier], J[ohn] G[reenleaf]. "Literary Notices." Rev. of *Retribution. National Era* 3.38 (Sept. 20, 1849): 150–51.

Willard, Frances E. *Nineteen Beautiful Years; or, Sketches of a Girl's Life.* Chicago: Woman's Temperance Publication Association, 1886.

Williams, Raymond. *Marxism and Literature.* Oxford: Oxford University Press, 1977.

Wilson, Jack H. "Competing Narratives in Elizabeth Stuart Phelps' *The Story of Avis.*" *American Literary Realism* 26.1 (Fall 1993): 60–75.

Wimsatt, Mary Ann. "Caroline Hentz's Balancing Act." *The Female Tradition in Southern Literature.* Ed. Carol S. Manning. Urbana: University of Illinois Press, 1993. 161–75.

"Women and Children of America." *Blackwood's Edinburgh Magazine* 101 (Jan. 1867): 82–92.

"Women's Record at Home." *Ladies' Repository* 2.5 (1875): 460–61.

Wood, Gordon S. *The Radicalism of the American Revolution.* New York: Alfred A. Knopf, 1992.

Wyatt-Brown, Bertram. *Southern Honor: Ethics and Behavior in the Old South.* New York: Oxford University Press, 1982.

Karen Tracey earned her Ph.D. at the University of Illinois in 1994. She is currently an assistant professor of English at the University of Northern Iowa.

·

Typeset in 10.5/13 Adobe Caslon
with Adobe Caslon & ATHandle display
Designed by Paula Newcomb
Composed by Barbara Evans
at the University of Illinois Press
Manufactured by Cushing-Malloy, Inc.

University of Illinois Press
1325 South Oak Street
Champaign, IL 61820-6903
www.press.uillinois.edu